ASPECTS OF AMERICAN LIBERTY

Memoirs of the
AMERICAN PHILOSOPHICAL SOCIETY
Held at Philadelphia
For Promoting Useful Knowledge
Volume 118

ASPECTS OF

AMERICAN LIBERTY

PHILOSOPHICAL, HISTORICAL, AND POLITICAL

Addresses Presented at an Observance of
The Bicentennial Year of American Independence
By the American Philosophical Society
April 22-24, 1976

THE AMERICAN PHILOSOPHICAL SOCIETY
Independence Square · Philadelphia
1977

Library of Congress Catalog Card Number 76-50180
International Standard Book Number 0-87169-118-3
US ISSN 0065-9738

Foreword

The American Philosophical Society, oldest of our learned societies, observed the Bicentennial of American Liberty in April 1976, at its eighteenth-century Philosophical Hall on Independence Square in Philadelphia, by a symposium in which fifteen outstanding speakers discussed the historical background of the American Revolution and the creation of our republic. The President of the Society, Julian P. Boyd, opened the symposium with these poignant words:

> For the next three days, the sessions of this Annual General Meeting will be concerned with those moral and philosophical propositions which two centuries ago on this Square were proclaimed as the guiding principles of the new nation. At this opening session, we shall look back over the centuries and attempt to renew our acquaintance with those concepts of law, justice, equality, and government by consent which emerged out of many struggles against many forms of tyranny in many lands. None of these concepts was new or distinctively American. What was new was that this was a people, born of dissent, diverse in its nationalities and in its religious creeds, and out of this diversity came strength, renewal, and what the Revolutionary generation devoutly believed to be a new order in human affairs.
>
> None of those who founded the Republic grasped more immediately or more fully the risks of the new venture than the author of the Declaration of Independence. He knew as few others did that tyranny did not begin and end with George III. During that bitter, divisive, and fateful campaign of 1800, which marked for the first time in our history the peaceful transfer of power and recognized the right of an opposition to exist, Thomas Jefferson declared in a famous letter to Benjamin Rush, "I have sworn upon the altar of god eternal hostility against every form of tyranny over the mind of man." The tyrannies that disturbed him most at that moment of political oppression, when the social fabric seemed about to be torn apart, were bigotry, intolerance, ignorance, and the destruction of that social harmony without which, as he was soon to express it in the greatest of our inaugurals, "liberty, and even life itself, are but dreary things."

Thus eloquently introduced, the addresses now collected in this volume were presented to a distinguished audience by speakers chosen for the wide range of their understanding of the sources of American political freedom — a poet, a high officer of the law, a veteran public administrator, professors of classical, medieval and modern history, scholars versed in the history of religion, law, science, and statecraft.

In Philosophical Hall, as they spoke, portraits of Washington, Franklin, and Jefferson, all members of the American Philosophical Society, looked down on the twentieth-century audience, and at an evening lecture a historian of art showed us how painters and sculptors saw, in his lifetime, the central figure of the Revolution, George Washington.

In continuation of its commemoration of the events of 1776 the American Philosophical Society makes these profound, yet brilliant and eminently readable studies of our heritage of freedom available to all who would understand the thoughts and actions of those who founded our nation.

GEORGE W. CORNER
Editor

Contents

Bicentennial of What?

THERE USED TO BE a stern New England admonition that guests at table should not say grace even if asked — meaning, I suppose, even if asked by the master of the house. It was for that reason I felt obliged to decline the flattering invitation of the master of this house, your admired president and my beloved friend, Julian Boyd, to write a poem suitable to this splendid occasion and to read it here today. Poems read at the beginning of things have a way of usurping the function of a New England grace, explaining the situation to the Almighty and generally making trouble for the serious speakers who are to follow.

But that, I should honorably confess, was not my only reason. I was troubled also by the possibility of the poem. "Suitable to this splendid occasion" meant suitable to a formal meeting of the most distinguished learned society on the continent — a meeting devoted to a consideration of the most notable anniversary in the history of the Republic. And the mere thought of the consideration of that anniversary at that level, filled my mind with the echoes of a couplet:

> We have learned the answers, all the answers:
> It is the question that we do not know.

Which was all very well as a couplet but which, unfortunately, I had already written. It comes from a poem, rather rashly called *The Hamlet of A. MacLeish,* which I had published in the nineteen twenties when Einstein's ultimate equation had filled all ears but left the tongues still talking. And, though it says precisely what I feel needs most to be said about the celebration of the American Bicentennial, I see no way of going back to it without ending up on the battlements at Elsinore with a lot of youthful agonies — not to mention ghosts — which have no place in this room. So I begged off, asking if I might say my say in prose. But leaving myself also, as frequently happens when you turn to prose, with a text to explain.

1

Why did my couplet seem apt to me — seem so apt, indeed, that I could think of no other lines which would take its place? Because it seemed to me true and because truths are not interchangeable in the art of poetry: they *are* the words which speak them. It is literally true that we know the answers, all the answers, so far as the Bicentennial is concerned. We know what we are celebrating: the two hundredth anniversary of the adoption of the Declaration of Independence by the Continental Congress on the fourth day of July in seventeen hundred and seventy-six. We know — many of us by heart, what the Declaration of Independence was — its first paragraph anyway. But what that paragraph *says,* what the Declaration signifies, we neither know nor ask. Is it what its title implies — a unilateral declaration of independence from Great Britain? If so, we are celebrating an historical event which is hardly unique — Rhodesia comes most lately to mind. Or is it what its first paragraph appears to make it: the declaration of a revolution for mankind? For if it is, our celebration, as we now observe it, is superlatively inappropriate.

In the old days, when college undergraduates still read history, any college undergraduate could have told us that these are not hypothetical alternatives: that there were, from the beginning, two opinions about the Declaration and that they were held by, among others, the two great men who had most to do with its composition and its adoption by the Congress. John Adams, who supported the Declaration with all his formidable powers, inclined to the view that it was just what it called itself, a declaration of American independence. Thomas Jefferson, who wrote it, held the opposite opinion: it was a revolutionary declaration of human rights applicable to all humanity —"all men"— and to all the world. "May it be to the world," he wrote to the citizens of Washington a few days before he died, "what I believe it will be: to some parts sooner, to others later, but finally to all, the signal of arousing men to burst the chains. . . ." "The mass of mankind," he went on, "has not been born with saddles on their backs for a favored few, booted and spurred, ready to ride them by the grace of God."

Moreover these two great and famous men were not the only presidents of the Republic to choose between those two alternatives. A third, as great as either, speaking in this city at the darkest moment in our history — bearing indeed the whole weight of that history on his shoulders as he spoke — turned to the Declaration for guidance for himself and for his country and made his choice between the meanings. You know the circumstances, all of you, better than I. Mr. Lincoln had been making his way slowly eastward in February of eighteen sixty-one from Springfield to Washington to take the oath of office as president of a divided people on the verge of Civil War. He had been making little speeches in city after city as he went, saying nothing, marking time, attempting to quiet apprehensions which his irrelevancies only aggravated. He had reached Philadelphia on the twenty-first where he had been told by the detective, Pinkerton, and by Secretary Seward's son, of the conspiracy to murder him in Baltimore as he passed through the city. He had gone to Independence Hall before daylight on the twenty-second. He had found a crowd waiting. He had spoken to them.

He had often asked himself, Mr. Lincoln said, what great principle or idea it was which had held the Union so long together. "It was not," he said, as though replying directly to John Adams, "the mere matter of the separation from the mother country." It was something more —"something in the Declaration . . . [it was an extemporaneous speech and his hearers remembered his words in different forms] "something in the Declaration giving liberty not alone to the people of this country but hope to the world. . . . It was that which gave promise that in due time the weights should be lifted from the shoulders of all men."

I suppose it is evident from these fragments of recollected sentences that Mr. Lincoln was remembering Jefferson's famous letter and agreeing. But his speech, surely one of the most remarkable ever made by an American president, is moving in its own right — as moving as a great soliloquy in a tragic play. Had he not often asked himself what great principle or idea it was which had held the Union so long together — night after night, no doubt, and before dawn, waking. And how had he answered that unanswerable question he put to himself? In what great principle or idea would this new president of a collapsing nation put his trust? Anyone else, any modern president certainly, would have announced, as they all regularly do, that his trust was firmly fixed in a tremendous appropriation for defense, in new and fabulous weapons, in money . . . power. Not Mr. Lincoln. Not Mr. Lincoln even at that desperate moment. His trust was fixed in an affirmation of belief, in the Declaration — in "something in the Declaration giving liberty not alone to the people of this country but hope to the world." It was fixed, in other words, in the commitment of the

American people to the great principle or idea of human liberty —
human liberty not for themselves alone but for mankind.

It was a daring gamble of Mr. Lincoln — but so too was Mr.
Jefferson's Declaration — so was the cause which Mr. Jefferson's
Declaration had defined. Could a nation be founded in the belief
in liberty? Could belief in liberty preserve it? Two American
generations argued that issue but not ours — not the generation of
the celebrants of the two hundredth anniversary of that great event.
We assume, I suppose, that Mr. Jefferson's policy was right for
him and right for Mr. Lincoln, because it was successful. The Civil
War was won when it became openly and explicitly a war for human
liberty — a war to lift the weights from the shoulders of all men.
But whatever we think about Mr. Lincoln's view of the Declaration,
whatever we believe about the Declaration in the past, in other
men's lives, in other men's wars, we do not ask ourselves, as we
celebrate its Bicentennial, what it is today, what it is to us.

Our present president has never intimated by so much as a word
that such a question might be relevant — that it even exists. The
Congress has not debated it. The state and federal commissions
charged with Bicentennial responsibility express no opinions. Only
the generation of the young, so far as I am informed, has even
mentioned it, and the present generation of the young has certain
understandable prejudices inherited from the disillusionments of
recent years which color their comments. Tell your children —
or, if you prefer, tell my grandchildren — what Thomas Jefferson
thought of his Declaration and you will get a blank look with
overtones of embarrassment — embarrassment *for you*. Inform
them that in your opinion Mr. Jefferson's Declaration remains
the most profoundly revolutionary document ever published by a
responsible people — the only revolutionary declaration ever made
on behalf, not of a class or a creed or a special interest of one
kind or another, but of all mankind, all men, of every man — and
you will be told, with courteous amusement, that you have to be
kidding. Express your view that the nation brought into being by
that great document was, and had no choice but be, a revolutionary
nation, and you will be reminded that, but for the accidental
discovery of a piece of tape on a door latch, the president of the
United States in the Bicentennial year would have been Richard
Nixon. And so it will go until you are told at last that the American
Revolution is a figure of obsolescent speech; that the Declaration
has become a museum exhibit in the National Archives; and that,

as for the Bicentennial, it is a year-long commercial which ought to be turned off.

Well, the indignation of the young is always admirable regardless of its verbal excesses — far more admirable, certainly, than the indifference of the elders. But, unfortunately, it is the indifference of the elders we have to consider — *someone* has to consider. And not only because it is a puzzling, a paradoxical, indifference but because it is as disturbing as it is paradoxical. Does our indifference to the explicitly revolutionary purpose of the Declaration — our silence about Mr. Jefferson's interpretation of that purpose — mean that we no longer believe in that purpose — no longer believe in human liberty? Hardly. Two years ago we forced the resignation of a president we had just elected by an overwhelming majority, because we discovered that he had been engaged in a conspiracy to conceal the truth from us — which means, a conspiracy to obstruct the processes of self-government — which means a conspiracy to suppress our liberties. Rarely has the country been united as it was, and still is, in the sense of outrage which forced that resignation. There can be no doubt, I think, that we in our generation believe in our liberties, in human liberty, in Mr. Jefferson's Cause.

But if this is so, if we still believe in the cause of human liberty, why do we celebrate the anniversary of the document which defined it for us without a thought for the meaning of the definition, then or now? Why have we not heard from our representatives and our officials on this great theme? Is it because, although the Republic continues to believe in human liberty for itself, it no longer hopes for it in the world? Because it no longer thinks such a hope "realistic"? Because, aware of the apparently inexorable conquest of the earth by the most monstrous of all forms of despotism, the modern police state, the country has concluded that the Declaration of Independence is an instrument of purely historical interest and the American Revolution a fable for infants like *The Ride of Paul Revere?*

If we think that, we had better give up thinking. It is true, of course, that the police states, whatever their ideologies (the ideologies no longer matter, only the police) have succeeded in subjugating more than half humanity. They are the new "establishment," the new "existing order." But it is also true that there is not a single police state of any ideology which does not confess by its Berlin Walls, its nets of concentration camps, its prison hospitals for the "insane," its censorship of books, its silencing of mouths, its suppression of minds, that it is afraid. And that what it is most afraid of is precisely the ghost of Thomas Jefferson. Opposition from within, the police state can put down. Wars it can win for a time as Hitler won wars — for a time. But the free man, the free mind, it cannot conquer, it can only imprison, only torture, only kill.

So far, indeed, is Mr. Jefferson's Revolution from being obsolete that it is now the one truly revolutionary force in the age we live in. And not despite the police states but because of them. When the KGB is king the only possible revolution is the revolution of mankind. The revolution of Sakharov, of Solzhenytsin.

This, then, is the second puzzle, the second paradox, of the Bicentennial. If we still believe in the cause of human liberty for ourselves as the events of the last three years prove we do, and if the cause of human liberty is now the one great revolutionary cause in this inhuman world, as the police states know it is whether we know or not, then why is this greatest of our anniversaries celebrated without a word to start that music in the heart again?

Because we are afraid to affirm our purpose as a people for fear of angering those who have a different purpose? I don't think so. Because we have fixed our minds so long on the menace of the Russian purpose that we have forgotten what our own great purpose was? That is arguable. And the words which would make the argument are three: containment, McCarthyism, and Vietnam — containment abroad, McCarthyism at home, and Vietnam as the inevitable consequence of both. In 1945, when we had driven the Nazis out of Europe and the Japanese out of the Pacific in the name of human freedom and human decency, we stood at the peak, not only of our power as a nation but of our greatness as a people. We were more nearly ourselves, our true selves as the inheritors of Thomas Jefferson and Abraham Lincoln, than we had ever been before. And yet within a few years of that tremendous triumph, of the unexampled generosity of our nuclear offer to the world, of the magnificence of the Marshall Plan, we were lost in the hysterical fears and ignoble deceits of Joe McCarthy and his followers and had adopted, as our foreign policy, the notion that if we "contained" the Russian purpose, countered the Russian initiative, we would somehow or other be better off ourselves than if we pursued our historic purpose as Jefferson conceived it.

The result, as we now know, was disaster. And not only in Southeast Asia and Portugal and Africa, but throughout the world.

Containment put us in bed with every anti-Communist we could find including some of the most offensive despots then in business — despots almost as offensive as the Commissars themselves. It produced flagrantly subversive and shameful plots by American agencies against the duly elected governments of other countries. And it ended by persuading the new countries of the postwar world, the emerging nations, that the United States was to them and to their hopes what the Holy Alliance had been to us and ours two hundred years before.

But bad as all this was, the worst and most destructive effect of this breach of faith, this treason to our own past, was what it did, precisely, to ourselves. It *aged* us. When I was a young man, sixty years ago, Americans thought of their country as young — thought of the Republic as a nation still at the beginning of its history. A generation later, after the hysteria of McCarthyism and the corrosion of containment, we had become an elderly society huddled over an old man's dream — the dream of "security."

This, if I were saying grace, is what my grace would speak of, thanking God for meetings such as this where truthful and believing men like those who will address you can speak out about this tarnished time with its distortion of our history, its doubt about our future, its trust in spies, in secrets — in "security." Mr. Jefferson is present in this house, and Mr. Jefferson knew, as those who honor him know still, that there is no such thing in human life, no such thing in human history, as precisely what we call "security." He knew that what makes a people great, a nation powerful, is purpose. And what our nation celebrates this year — what it should be celebrating — is the purpose Mr. Jefferson bequeathed to us, the purpose Mr. Lincoln took for answer in his agony.

We are as great as our belief in human liberty — no greater. And our belief in human liberty is only ours when it is larger than ourselves: liberty, as Mr. Lincoln put it, "not alone to the people of this country but hope to the world." We must become again his "last, best hope of earth" to *be* the great Republic which his love once saved. We know that. We must say so even now, even toward dark, without a voice to lead us, without a leader standing to come forth. We must say it for ourselves. In this Society, this city, this Republic, we, "even we here." If we don't, no one else will say it for us.

ARCHIBALD MACLEISH
Poet; Former Librarian of Congress

Liberty in Classical Antiquity

IN THE WAR OF WORDS that preceded the secession of the Thirteen Colonies appeal was constantly made to the history and institutions of Antiquity. The operations have a wide range, from classical tags and declamation against tyranny to reasoned discourse, to arguments based on principles of universal validity.

The phenomenon will not come as a surprise. The debate was conducted by members of the educated class who shared the tastes and habits of their counterparts in western Europe. Some of them, indeed, such as James Otis, that strange and not altogether amiable character, possessed notable attainments in classical scholarship. Latin rather than Greek, it is clear. In France at the middle of the eighteenth century the study of Greek had almost faded out. The term *érudit* was used as an appellation of contempt by the fashionable *philosophes*. None the less, certain paladins of the Enlightenment did not neglect the Latin classics. Diderot produced a masterly essay on Seneca that can still be read with profit; and young Rousseau translated the first book of the *Historiae* of Cornelius Tacitus.[1]

However, as it happened, it was an aspect of Greek history that excited fervent acclaim in America: Greek colonies, precisely, with a sharp edge against England, and against Rome. James Otis was moved to declare that the Greeks were "kind, humane and just towards their colonies, but the Romans were cruel, brutal and barbarous to theirs."[2]

The antithesis is imperfect and misleading. From its foundation a Greek colony was never intended to be anything other than an independent autonomous unit. Though ties of amity and respect might subsist with the mother-city, nothing precluded fierce rivalry

---

1. The translation earned praise from Sainte-Beuve, *Premiers Lundis* (1874), p. 240.

2. Richard M. Gummere, *The American Colonial Mind and the Classical Tradition* (1963), p. 102. The present paper is deeply in the debt of that excellent book.

or armed hostilities. Otis conveniently ignored the imperial domination exercised by Athens over a variety of cities in the second half of the fifth century, which was an affront to normal Greek notions of self-government.

Again, what this man had to say about Roman colonies is far from reassuring. The *colonia* is a body of Roman citizens, a portion of the Populus Romanus enjoying unimpaired rights wherever they may have been planted, whether throughout the land of Italy, or in certain of the provinces West and East under the late Republic or in the early imperial epoch. How and why the behavior of the Roman government towards the colonies could be deemed "brutal and barbarous" passes understanding. Further, this critic left out the autonomous Italian communities in alliance with Rome.

Otis, it appears, had in mind the wide territories which the imperial Republic had conquered and annexed, and he was condemning the license with which governors of provinces pillaged and maltreated the subject peoples. Verres, the governor of the province of Sicily denounced in orations of Cicero, was the standard example, and a contemporary catchword.

If that is so, there was total confusion inhabiting the mind of James Otis — or else the advocate was artfully trading upon the ignorance of his readers. This specimen of the argument from ancient history will arouse a salutary distrust about apostles of liberty in any age — and no less about classical scholars.

The splendid and classic epoch of Greece is by common consent and a long tradition the fifth century B.C. That is to say, if for "Greece" one reads "Athens"— and if for Athens one puts emphasis on the period of ascendancy that resulted from the wars against the Persians and led to the creation of an empire. The preceding century, however, had been vital and innovatory. The cities of Hellas witnessed notable experiments in political organization — and the emergence of the concept of law. The life of the community was not to be determined any more by religion and immemorial custom, or by the personal authority of one man, or of a small group, dominant through the resources of birth and wealth. Instead, a set of rules, *nomoi,* devised by men and hence in due course subject to change, not by force but through persuasion and consent.

The pages of Herodotus offer illustration in more places than one. In the course of his invasion of Greece, Xerxes holds debate

with Demaratus, the exiled king of Sparta. The ingenuous despot
duly extols the preponderance of numbers on the Persian side,
unified in loyalty under a single command. Demaratus has a telling
answer: the Spartans are a body of free men, but they are not in
all things free — there is a master over them, namely *Nomos*.[3]

The anecdote reflects the dual but in no way discordant nature
of the liberty of the Greek *polis* at this time: freedom from external
control combined with inner order and regulation.

That the present discourse, touching briefly on certain aspects
of liberty among the Greeks, should invoke the name of Sparta
may appear an indecent paradox. Sparta stands to all time as the
the denial of individual rights, the example of regimentation —
and the ideal of reactionaries in other states. In short, the foil to
all that was excellent at Athens.

Yet Sparta, it may be contended, had not always been an abbera-
tion. For one reason or another its social order, the product of
innovation, had failed to change along the lines followed by other
communities. The Spartan system thus turned into an archaic
survival, and it became ever more rigid and repressive under various
strains and emergencies.

At Athens the advance to free institutions in its decisive stage
has been obscured by ignorance and prejudice, by myth and legend.
The figure of Solon, the parent and founder, all but eclipsed the
actions of Cleisthenes, victorious in the factional strife which ensued
soon after the fall of the tyranny in 508 B.C. It was Cleisthenes
who then remodeled and modernized the Attic state.

The terms *isonomos* and *isonomia* enjoyed a certain currency
early in the fifth century, and they have been accorded proper
attention by scholars in the recent age.[4] "Isonomia" is not itself
a form of government, but a principle and a term of approbation.
It might perhaps be paraphrased as "equality before the laws."
"Isonomia" stands in declared opposition to arbitrary power,
exercised by a person or a group. Hence its connotations may be
described as "republican" or "constitutional." We therefore come
close to the improving concept of "Liberty *and* Order."

Equality before the laws need not carry equality in all things.
Under the constitution of Cleisthenes, access to office was restricted,
nor was the popular assembly omnipotent. The Council remained,
the Areopagus, composed of ex-magistrates. Limits set to the

---

3. Herodotus VII, 104.

4. See now M. Ostwald, *Nomos and the Beginnings of the Athenian Democracy*
(1969), pp. 97-160.

power of the people may in fact be confirmed by the striking exception, the peculiar institution of ostracism (whether invented by Cleisthenes or by somebody else nearly twenty years later). When a recourse to ostracism was decided and carried out, the political leader who had earned the highest total of adverse votes was expelled for a period of ten years. Later, when the unrestricted sovereignty of the Demos was introduced, ostracism became an anachronism, which did not prevent it from being used and abused.

As will have been apparent, I have been at some pains so far to avoid speaking of democracy, a term of fatal and fluctuating ambiguity in the modern world. Among the Greeks the word *demokratia* was slow to emerge; it had a precise meaning, and it began as an appellation not always friendly and favorable.[5]

The Athenian *polis* at the time of the Persian Wars might be described as a republic, without misleading. It is that "ancestral constitution" which politicians were looking for when they attempted to curb or subvert the rule of the Demos; and theorists in a later age, had the knowledge been available, might there have discovered a system of checks and balances or a "mixed constitution."

The social and political basis of the Cleisthenic order was the middle class, precisely the *hoplites:* that is, those of the citizens who had sufficient property to acquire a suit of full armor. Theirs was the victory of Marathon. But the navy won Salamis. The ships were manned by the poorest of the citizens, warfare went on, Athens began to acquire an empire. The sailors thus emerged as a new power in the state, and their claims to honor and profit were answered in 462, when all restrictions on the sovereignty of the popular assembly were abolished.

Of the signal merits of direct rule by the whole citizen body, as of its defects and failures, this is not the place to speak. For good or ill, Athenian democracy stands as paradigmatic, though it has not attracted proper attention in every age or country. Indeed, its reputation continued in the main dubious (at least in England) until it was vindicated by the *History of Greece* written by George Grote, a banker, a politician of liberal aspirations, and one of the founders of a secular seminary (University College, London).

In the modern world democracy itself, it might be suggested, first began to grow respectable on this side of the Atlantic — but

---

5. R. Sealey, "The Origins of Demokratia," *Cal. Stud. in Class. Ant.* 6 (1974): pp. 253-295.

soon to suffer discredit through the French Revolution, from which it took some time to recover.

So far democracy. It will not be looked for in the Roman Republic. Still less will equality. In the view of the Romans it was inequitable, nay iniquitous, that equal honor should go to the highest and to the lowest in the state.

The great word is *Libertas,* generally defined in a negative fashion, through its opposite. It can have a precise and legal meaning, it is true: the status of the free man and citizen, in contrast to the slave, hence the juridical guarantees that protected the citizen against the magistrate. And *Libertas* was suitably applied to a community not subject to the arbitrary rule of a tyrant or a faction. But *Libertas* is also an emotional term in the vocabulary of political strife. The history of its vicissitudes will afford melancholy instruction.

Cicero congratulated his nation for its singular felicity: namely to possess liberty and to exercise dominion over others. It is a question, what was the *Libertas populi Romani.*

When Polybius set himself to define the Roman constitution, he discovered a blend of the three forms of government that had long been familiar to exponents of political theory: the rule of the one, the few, and the many. That is, the consuls (representing monarchic powers), the Senate, the popular assemblies.

His diagnosis is variously defective. The People voted on the great issues of war or peace, it is true, and the People elected the magistrates. But it lacked the initiative. Where in fact was policy devised and formulated, and how were candidates for office selected? The Senate, it would appear, had the preponderance in government. But that is not the true answer. Rather two elements in that body. First, the ex-consuls, with their potent *auctoritas.* Second, the *nobiles,* the descendants of consular families.

Therefore, aristocracy. The *nobilitas* regarded the state as their own possession. As one of them once exclaimed in altercation with a tribune of the plebs, what have you to do with *res publica nostra?*

In the concluding epoch of the Republic the tasks and emergencies of a world empire led to the conferment of inordinate powers on ambitious individuals, in contravention of the principles normally obtaining in oligarchies. "Liberty and the laws" therefore became the watchword of those who defended the existing order—

and the privileges of their own class. The cause of Cato and of Brutus went down in battle, and a straight line leads from the great provincial commands to the autocracy of Caesar Augustus.

The Caesars affected to base their rule on legal prerogatives. Along with the forms of the constitution, they annexed the language. Hence "Libertas Augusta" can be paraded; and in strife for the purple the usurper or the victor claims to be *vindex libertatis*.

At the same time senators confronted by despotism made appeal to *Libertas*. They had no thought of bringing back the aristocratic Republic, with free competition, ruthless and ruinous, for power and honor. Stability and Rome's dominion over the nations imposed centralized government. What men now meant by *Libertas* was the dignity and personal independence of the upper order. Political liberty had gone, irrevocably, but freedom of speech was still worth asserting.

In this concise and superficial survey, emphasis has been put on the restrictions that circumscribed political liberty in the ancient republics. The modern age was to see most of those limitations removed. In the process one of the strongest impulsions was the Declaration of Independence, affirming that "all men were created equal," that they were endowed "with certain inalienable rights."

Pronouncements of a political intent have to be interpreted with care — and with awareness of what they do not say. The omission of slavery has been a notorious occasion for perplexity or scandal. Were the eloquent and high-minded gentlemen of Virginia oblivious of the material basis of their civilization? A partial explanation avails.

The literature they read and admired took slavery for granted: the political theorists of Hellas, the Roman statesmen and orators. And the poets no less. In the *Georgics* of Virgil slaves make no contribution to the labor force.

Again, the Declaration refrains from issuing any statement in defense of property. Yet its authors accepted the "common and durable division" in society, the natural relation between ownership and civic rights or the exercise of public power. That was assumed in a familiar and classic manual of edification, the *De Officiis* of Cicero. For the master of civic wisdom, demagogues were as bad as tyrants: in criminal disregard for the rights of the propertied class they subverted order and harmony in human society.

By habit and attitudes, Englishmen of the "better sort" in the

eighteenth century offer clear resemblances to the Romans. More
than that, it is not excessive to speak of a deep affinity. It comes
out in the firm distrust of doctrine and speculation. Had the
fragments of Cicero's treatise *De re publica* been then available,
those men would have concurred with complacency in the proud
asseveration of a native achievement in law and government. Even
the wisest of the Greeks were not good enough.

As it was, the age had Bolingbroke to quote for testimony:
"Stoical morals and Platonic politics are nothing better than amuse-
ments for those who have had little experience in the affairs of the
world, and who have much leisure, *verba otiosorum senum ad
imperitos iuvenes.*"[6]

"Ingenious Colonials"— such was Franklin's label for suitable
members of this Society — ran little risk of seduction by Plato.
Historians engaged their serious attention, notably Polybius, because of the Roman Constitution, and, to a minor degree, federal
government in his native Achaea. Thucydides had less relevance.
But it will be pleasing to recall that many years later Jefferson and
Adams were exchanging impressions about Thucydides — and
about Tacitus. That was in 1812, a momentous year, and those
historians, they opined, were better than the newspapers.

Fortified by history and eloquence, the adversaries of Crown and
Parliament went in for frequent and fervent invocation of liberty.
The lawyers and orators had a conscious technique — and classical
predecessors. They were not blind to the ambiguities of political
discourse on high themes, to the deceits of ethical and emotional
terminology. From Sallust and from Tacitus they could learn, if
they needed to learn, with what fatal ease and celerity the vocabulary had been debased. Cato's oration, as composed by Sallust,
carried a powerful text.[7]

How far books may influence action is a large question in any
age. Though not immune to literature and learning, the delegates
assembled in 1787 for the purpose of constructing a constitution
were prudent and practical men. Voices were heard deprecating
the appeal to Antiquity. Hamilton was hostile, and so was Franklin.
One of the company, Randall of Massachusetts, put the matter
succinctly: "the quoting of ancient history was no more to the point
than to tell how our ancestors dug clams at Plymouth."[8]

---

6. Bolingbroke, *The Idea of a Patriot King* (1749), p. 91.
7. Sallust, *Cat.* 52, 11: "nos vera vocabula rerum amisimus."
8. Quoted by R. M. Gummere, *op. cit.,* p. 183.

Not but that Greek and Roman history added substance as well as dignity to their arduous sessions. And there were negative lessons not lost upon men with experience of affairs. Some may even have conceived doubts about the validity of the "mixed constitution." They could recall the sombre and perspicacious Tacitus. "That system," he said, "is easier to praise than produce, and, if it comes into being, it cannot last."[9] And they might be impelled to anticipate the verdict of Tocqueville.[10]

No surprise, therefore, that the delegates eschewed certain devices, ostensibly beneficial for safeguarding political stability or the liberties of the citizen. Ostracism, they saw, was a dubious protection against ambition and personal power; and they would have no time for tribunes of the plebs, an ominous name.

Mob violence at Boston was a recent warning, and Sam Adams, who organized the Sons of Liberty. Not, as some styled him, the "Cato of New England," but rather a Clodius.[11] Democracy, as the other Adams somewhere says, is "the most ignoble, unjust, and detestable form of government." The demagogue and the tyrant might combine in one person.

"We shall cheerfully acquiesce in any expedient which deprives the multitude of the dangerous, and indeed the ideal, power of giving themselves a master." That declaration could be read in a book of instant success published in London in February of the year 1776. The author of the *Decline and Fall of the Roman Empire,* close coeval to Adams and to Jefferson, had recently been elected to Parliament; and (as he later averred) he "supported, with many a sincere and silent vote, the rights though not, perhaps, the interest of the mother-country." The study of the classics may lead to contrary conclusions. Edward Gibbon was expounding "the apparent ridicule and solid advantages of hereditary monarchy."[12]

SIR RONALD SYME
Senior Fellow, Wolfson College,
Oxford

9. Tacitus, *Annals,* 4, 33.

10. A. de Tocqueville, *De la Démocracie en Amérique* 2 (ed. 17, 1888): p. 148: "le governement qu'on appelle mixte m'a toujours semblé une chimère."

11. For a firm rehabilitation, however, see Pauline Maier, "Coming to Terms with Samuel Adams," *Amer. Hist. Rev.* 81 (1976): pp. 12-37.

12. The above remarks will not be taken to convey lack of esteem for the men of the Revolution—or lack of affection for their descendants.

The Rule of Law

THERE ARE MANY INTERPRETATIONS of the phrase that is the subject of my talk, but in the city of Philadelphia I think I should begin with the famous statement of William Penn: "any government is free to the people under it, whatever be the frame, where the laws rule, and the people are a party to those laws."[1] He might have emphasized, what he only added later, that governments, like subjects, are bound by the laws,[2] but he had summed up, rather neatly, the results of some eighteen centuries of western political experience.

In the same document Penn made another perspicacious statement:

> They weakly err that think there is no other use for government than correction, which is the coarsest part of it; daily experience tells us that the care and regulation of many other affairs more soft and daily necessary make up much the greatest part of government, and which must have followed the peopling of the world, had Adam never fell."[3]

In other words, a society that has only criminal law is not apt to develop the concept of the rule of law, because criminal law is "coarse" (we would say "dirty"); because it seems deceptively simple ("guilty" or "not guilty"), and because it does not deal with matters that concern the ordinary, day-to-day affairs of the society.[4] The great majority of civilized societies never had a body

---

1. Preface to the First Frame of Government for Pennsylvania. This may be found most conveniently in *The Witness of William Penn,* ed. Frederick B. Tolles and E. Gordon Alderfer (New York, 1957), p. 111.

2. *Ibid.,* p. 112, "the frame and laws of this government . . . [are] to support power in reverence with the people, and to secure the people from the abuse of power." Article 24 of the Frame promised that neither Penn nor his heirs would infringe upon any of the liberties granted.

3. *Ibid.,* p. 110.

4. Machiavelli, *The Prince,* ch. 17, expresses this difference in an extreme, but unfortunately accurate way, when he says that it is safer to execute a rebel than to seize the property of a subject "for men forget more easily the death of their father than the loss of their patrimony."

of civil law of any importance. This is not to say that they had no standards of right conduct in dealing with such matters as contract and inheritance, but these standards (often very high standards) were binding on the individual conscience, and were not a concern of the courts. They were in the domain of "fas," not "ius" (to use the Roman distinction) of "li" and not "fa" (in Chinese terms).[5] They were enforced by social pressures; they were interpreted by the leaders of the community or by arbitration, but they did not give rise to a class of lawyers or a body of legal literature. Only where the civil law is a significant part of the work of government do we find that lawyers are an influential class and that books on law are an important part of the intellectual tradition. And it is obvious that without lawyers and authoritative treatises on law, the concept of the rule of law will not appear.

One of Penn's other phrases should be emphasized. He says that "whatever be the frame" (that is, whether the government be a monarchy, an aristocracy, or a democracy) the rule of law can prevail. It is just as well that he said this. The Greek city-states, for the most part, were aristocratic or timocratic rather than democratic, as Sir Ronald Syme has shown in his discussion of the Greek idea of liberty. But whatever their constitution, they did not develop a legal tradition that persisted in the West. The Greeks were deeply concerned with law, but since each small community had its own laws, tailored to fit the needs of that community, it was hard to develop general principles applicable to all of the Greek-ruled areas. By the time that the Greeks had developed such principles, they had been swallowed up by the Hellenistic monarchies, which, in turn, were swallowed up by Rome. Medieval aristocracies and city-states (some of the latter were at times democratic) produced no stable or impressive bodies of law. It was in the monarchies, first in the Roman Empire and then in the kingdoms of western Europe, that the concept of the rule of law appeared.

As a very rough generalization, it may be said that the need for a body of civil laws that is widely applicable, stable, and generally respected, is most likely to be felt in a state that has gained control of a wide area before it has been able to develop an adequate administrative structure. Conquest is easier than government. An army can seize territory, put down rebellions, and collect tribute, but it is not a very efficient instrument for settling the

5. See Derk Bodde, "Basic concepts of Chinese Law," *Proc. Amer. Philos. Soc.* **107** (October, 1963): pp. 375-398.

thousands of petty disputes that arise among subjects. This duty, of course, can be turned over to local leaders, but then there is always the danger that they will become too powerful, or take too large a share of local revenues. And even if this danger is avoided, the local leader has no authority to settle a dispute between an inhabitant of his district and one in another community.

Rome faced this problem in its most acute form. By the end of the Republic it was trying to govern a Mediterranean empire with the institutions of a small city-state. It did not have the administrative structure, or the trained personnel to rule directly the hundreds of city-states, vassal kingdoms, and subject peoples that were under its control. Each unit had its own customs and its own form of local government, but this system, or lack of system, made it difficult to apply uniform policies throughout the Empire. It was equally difficult to settle disputes that arose between men or communities that had different customs and the difficulty increased as trade among the peoples of the Empire increased, and as subjects moved from one region to another. There was a clear need for a set of laws that would override local differences, but these laws had to be acceptable to the inhabitants of the Empire, or at least to the ruling classes. When they were formulated and accepted, they made up for some of the weaknesses of the administrative system; litigants who were asking for the intervention of the central government needed less supervision than those living in isolated communities.

Three factors stimulated the growth and the reception of Roman law. First, the Romans were in no hurry. The law, and the application of the law to the peoples of the Empire, developed slowly; to use it was a privilege, not an obligation. The expansion of Roman law began in the first century B.C.; the classical formulation of the basic principles of Roman law came only in the second and early third centuries A.D. The law was accepted because it seemed to be just and useful, not because it was imposed on conquered peoples. Second, as the growth of imperial power barred citizens from active participation in politics, able men who were interested in the work of government found an outlet for their interests in the study and practice of law. By 200 A.D. the most important intellectual activity in Rome was the work of the jurisprudents. Third, in annexing the Hellenistic states, Rome also annexed Greek philosophy, and for the Roman ruling class the most acceptable school of philosophy was Stoicism. A basic doctrine of Stoicism was that there was a law common to all men, a law which all men could understand by the use of right reason.[6] This doctrine gave Roman lawyers confidence in their work, and also helped to make their work acceptable to the upper classes in the eastern part of the Empire which was dominated by Greek culture.

The importance of law and of lawyers in the Empire scarcely needs to be demonstrated, but the importance of law in Roman society does not mean that the concept of the rule of law was fully developed. Roman jurisprudence was not quite clear on this point, and even if it had been, there were differences between the theories of the lawyers and the practices of the rulers.

The emperor was above the law ("legibus solutus") but he was also a maker of law, since it was agreed that the Roman people had transferred their power of making law to the *princeps*.[7] He was a maker of law in another way; he could give instructions as to how a particular case should be decided, either on his own initiative, or because one of his officials had asked his opinion, or because one of the parties had asked him to intervene. Naturally most of these cases were actually decided by officials at the imperial court, and even when the emperor made a personal decision, the wording was apt to be that of a subordinate who would try to make it conform to accepted forms. No emperor could bind his successor, but if there was an accumulation of imperial rescripts dealing with a particular legal problem there would be some tendency to follow earlier decisions. Nevertheless, if the emperor was above the law, and if he could interpret or change the law at will, then how can it be suggested that there was any concept of the rule of law in the Empire?

First of all, one must reckon with the extreme conservatism of Roman officials and Roman lawyers. Even imperial intervention did not change the law very rapidly; in fact it probably changed the law less rapidly than it should have done. Second, during the formative period of Roman law the bureaucracy was still underdeveloped. It was easier to follow accepted rules than to refer every problem to the emperor and his small staff of advisers. Third,

---

6. This idea had been accepted in the last century of the Republic; see Cicero, *De legibus* I, 33, "Quibus (all men) enim ratio a natura data est, isdem etiam recta ratio data est, ergo etiam lex, quae est recto ratio in jubendo et vetando; si lex, jus quoque . . . jus igitur datum est omnibus."
7. R. W. and A. J. Carlyle, *A History of Mediaeval Political Theory in the West* (6v., Edinburgh and London, 1930-1936) **2**: pp. 64-69.

it was agreed that the emperor should respect the laws, even if there was no way to compel him to do so. As a famous passage in the Code says: the emperor should admit that he is bound by the law because his authority comes from the law.[8]

Thus the law was reasonably stable and the outcome of a lawsuit was reasonably predictable because there was not excessive interference from above. Even when there was intervention by the emperor and his advisers, it usually took the form of an interpretation or an equitable modification of the law, not an arbitrary decision that had nothing to do with the merits of the case. In this sense, the Romans of the Late Empire could boast that they were free men, not slaves like the subjects of the kings of the barbarians.[9] In the same way, the French of the eighteenth century could argue that they were free, while the Russians were slaves. Bossuet said that there was a great difference between absolute and arbitrary government, especially when it came to the administration of justice, and he asserted, like the Roman lawyers, that the ruler was morally bound by the law, even if no coercion could be used against him.[10] This is not exactly the rule of law as we understand it, but it was a step in that direction. Roman emperors and Bourbon kings had to pay some attention to the law, even if they could circumvent it when they felt that it was necessary. And in the case of the Roman Empire in the West, it was the law that survived, and not the absolute power of the emperor.

There was not much law and even less law enforcement in the confused period that followed the collapse of the western part of the Empire. But the feeling that there ought to be law — written law — and that the possession of such laws was the mark of a decently organized, self-respecting people persisted. This was partly due to the influence of the Church, which had been profoundly influenced by its close association with the Empire. The Church

---

8. *Code* I, 14, 4 "Digna vox majestate regnantis legibus alligatum se principem profiteri: adeo de auctoritate juris nostra pendet auctoritas" (Rescript of Theodosius II and Valentinian III).

9. Carlyle, *op. cit.* 1: p. 163, "reges gentium domini servorum sunt, imperatores vero reipublicae, domini liberorum." The phrase comes from Pope Gregory the Great, but, as Carlyle says, it has the ring of a traditional saying.

10. Jacques Bénigne Bossuet, *Politique tirée du propres paroles de l'Ecriture sainte*, ed. Jacques Le Brun (Geneva, 1967), p. 92, "plusieurs affectent de confondre le gouvernement absolu et le gouvernement arbitraire. Mais il n'y a rien de plus distingué, ainsi que nous le ferons voir lorsque nous parlerons de la justice." See also pp. 96-97, his comment on the phrase: "Les rois ne sont pas . . . affranchis des lois."

accepted without question the idea that there was a natural law (derived, of course, through reason from the divine law) in which all people should participate. Law was good because it had a divine origin. Rulers were good if they dispensed justice to their people; in fact, this was their chief duty. Besides the influence of the Church, there was the prestige that was associated with the Roman intellectual inheritance. Law was good because the Romans had made it and written about it. Thus, Roman law, in simplified form, remained the law of large numbers of people living in Italy, southern France, and Spain. Some of this law was codified by Germanic kings, some of it eventually became unwritten customary law. But the learned law was not entirely forgotten. For example, the seventh-century encyclopedist, St. Isidore of Seville, picked up many phrases, directly or indirectly, from the great lawyers of the Empire. There are other tantalizing references to men who read or wrote on Roman law in the early Middle Ages, but it is not important to decide how extensive their knowledge was. What is important is that every educated man knew that Rome had been great, and that Roman law had been part of that greatness.

The teaching of the Church and the Latin intellectual tradition were reinforced by practical necessity. When the dust of the Germanic migrations had settled, most kings found themselves ruling over many peoples, and each of these peoples wanted to preserve its own customs. Thus it was not only religiously and intellectually desirable to have written laws; it was politically expedient. Hence the great burst of codifying and expanding ancient customs that began with the Visigoths, reached its peak in the Carolingian Empire (a multi-nation state if there ever was one), and tapered off with the eleventh-century dooms of Canute in England. None of these codes was complete, and most of them had rather short lives as actual enforceable law. They did keep alive the idea that law, and writing about law, formed an essential element in western society.

These codes also show some of the Germanic concepts that modified ideas inherited from Rome and the Church. First, as was true in most other societies, early Germanic law was almost entirely criminal law. This would have been dangerous to Roman emphasis on civil law had it not been for one peculiarity; the Germans treated most crimes as if they were torts, that is, civil offenses that led to payment of damages and not to afflictive punishments. It was not wrong for men to fight and to injure or kill each other, nor was it wrong for an injured man or a bereaved family to seek vengeance. But if a man or his family wanted to avoid a feud they could pay damages for a killing or a maiming. A great part of early Germanic law was composed of tables of damages. There was no element of criminality in being asked to pay damages, no loss of reputation (any more than in a fender-bending accident today). In fact, in many cases it was considered honorable to offer to pay. What was dishonorable was to continue a feud when a peaceful settlement had been arranged.

This last point illustrates another characteristic of Germanic law; its main purpose was to stop, or prevent, a fight. This is true, to some extent, of all law, and especially of civil law. There is nothing inherently just in any particular form of contract or any particular rule about inheritance: what is important is to be perfectly clear about the elements of a valid contract, or the fraction of the husband's property that must be left to a widow. Law can go beyond this and seek to do justice, or to remedy social problems, but the Germans were not concerned with such matters. As that most German of all Germans, Martin Luther, said in the sixteenth century: "Peace is more important than justice, and peace was not made for the sake of justice but justice for the sake of peace."[11] (This is in his treatise on marriage, a particularly appropriate place for such a remark.) The compilers of Germanic customs would have agreed wholeheartedly with Luther; the main business of the law is to end feuds and obtain peace, not to search for absolute justice. This attitude prevailed during the most creative period of the development of medieval law. As we shall see, one of the key ideas in this development was the protection of possession, a rule that did not always lead to a just decision, but a rule that certainly helped to prevent fights.

The early burst of medieval compilation of law codes was followed by a prolonged slump. Most of the Germanic kingdoms had short lives. The southern kingdoms were conquered by the East Roman Empire and by the Moslems. The northern kingdoms (except for England and Scandinavia) were absorbed into the Frankish Empire, but Charlemagne's attempt to turn the Frankish Empire into a revived West Roman Empire was a failure. Both the administrative and the economic structures of Western Europe

---

11. M. Luther, Von Ehesachen (1530), vol. 30-III of the Weimarer ed., p. 223. "Sintemal friede gilt mehr denn alles recht, und friede ist nichts umbs rechts willen, sondern recht ist umbs frieden willen gemacht."

were too weak to make such a state viable. During the ninth and tenth centuries, the Frankish Empire distintegrated. In Feuchère's phrase, the empire split into kingdoms, the kingdoms into principalities, the principalities into counties, and the counties into castellanies.[12] Fragmentation did not go quite so far in England or in the little kingdoms that held a strip of northern Spain against the Moors; but even in these countries, local lords did much of the work of government.

Fragmentation of political power, and the conception of political power as a private possession seem to me to be the essential elements in feudalism, but fortunately we do not have to discuss that thorny problem in this place. The point is that fragmentation had a disastrous impact on law and on law courts. Each district, even if it were very small, began to develop its own customs, often quite different from those of neighboring districts. Each district had its own court held by the lord of that district. These courts could judge disputes among, and wrong-doing by, peasants; but they had very little authority over the military class of lords and retainers. They were essentially police courts, and they were most effective in the area of criminal law, which means that they had very little impact on basic social relations. These local courts had great difficulty in dealing with suits for land or for rights annexed to land. Even if both parties to a civil suit appeared, which was unlikely, clean-cut decisions were rare. The usual outcome was arbitration leading to a compromise. If the parties did not appear, the chances were fairly good that there would be raids and reprisals, leading to a private war. Civil law could not develop very far under these conditions.

Nevertheless, there were forces working for stability behind the disorders of the tenth and eleventh centuries. The Church, whose possessions were threatened by the aggressions of secular lords, was naturally in favor of institutions that would give it greater security. The greater lords were threatened by the fact that a lesser lord, through a series of successful private wars, might build up his power to a point where he could become a dangerous rival. The weakest lords, who had very little military strength, were at the mercy of their more powerful neighbors or superiors. The more intelligent members of the ruling classes, whether clerics or laymen, great

---

12. P. Feuchère, "Essai sur l'évolution territoriale des principautés françaises," *Le Moyen Age* **58** (1952): pp. 85-86.

barons or humble knights, realized that their income was decreased every time their peasants, artisans, and merchants were impoverished by the raiding and pillaging that accompanied private war.

Thus there was a widespread desire to lessen disorder and violence. It was an effective desire, because it was supported by the leaders of western European society — by bishops and abbots, by kings, dukes, and counts. These leaders could count on the support of the lesser members of the military caste, who might be weak individually, but who collectively were far more numerous than the chief trouble-makers — the possessors of castles. There was hard fighting in some areas, notably around Paris, where Louis VI had to wage a long series of campaigns against the castellans of the Ile de France. Elsewhere, as in Normandy, pacification came earlier and with less effort. But by 1200 there had been a notable increase in security over much of western Europe.

Pacification, however, was only a beginning. Private wars had often been caused by legitimate grievances; every private war had in turn created new grievances. If self-help and violence were barred, how could these grievances be remedied? The only possible solution was to increase the activity of the courts and to work out a new body of law — civil law — that would be acceptable to the upper and middle classes.

This task was begun in the twelfth century and reached a climax in the thirteenth century. These two centuries were one of the most legal-minded periods in western history. The study of Roman law was revived; the basic texts of canon law were compiled; and the classical works on the law of England (Glanville and Bracton), France (Beaumanoir), Germany (the Sachsenspiegel of Eike von Repgow), and Spain (the Siete Partidas of Alfonso X) were written. Almost every pope from Alexander III to Boniface VIII (the period 1159–1303) had been trained in canon law. The dominant school of theology stressed the reason, not the will of God, and pointed out that man, as a rational creature, has a share of the eternal reason, and that law is a result of this participation.[13] In this atmosphere, it was natural that the rulers who were trying to build new states out of the wreckage of the tenth and eleventh centuries relied on law, and on more effective administration of the law, to increase their authority.

The basic idea, especially in English and French law, was the

---

13. Thomas Aquinas, *Summa Theologica*, qu. 91, art. 2, 3; qu. 95, art. 1, 2.

protection of possession. Very few people had an unassailable right
to their landed property or to the rights annexed to property, such
as jurisdiction, tolls, and market-dues, or monopolies (as on
milling). This paucity of sound titles was one of the reasons why
law courts had been so ineffective; they could not give definite
rulings because they did not have the facts. But the fact of
possession was easy enough to prove, and the rule that peaceful
possession was to be protected until legal justification could be
produced for disturbing it gave security to a very considerable part
of the population. It prevented fights by making self-help and
violent eviction unlawful and unprofitable. It was an easy rule
to understand, and, therefore, a relatively easy rule to enforce.
Respect for the courts increased because they could reach useful
and acceptable solutions. The ruler gained the support of the
numerous but individually weak groups of lesser lords and knights,
because he could protect their holdings. At the same time, he made
it difficult for the greater lords to increase their power by waging
private war. The net result was an impressive increase in the
cohesion and organization of the budding states of western Europe.

There were other devices for increasing respect for royal courts,
such as forbidding local lords to hear certain kinds of cases, or
encouraging appeals from baronial courts to the king's court. But
details of procedure are not important: what is important is the
fact that the European states of the thirteenth century were law-
states. The ruler's authority was based on the effectiveness of his
courts of law; sovereignty was defined as the right to give final
judgment,[14] not as the right to make law, or as the possession of a
monopoly of force.

In these circumstances, it was natural that the idea of the rule
of law would begin to take shape. The Roman emperors had
admitted that they derived their authority from the law; this was
historically true, but it had no practical significance in the Late
Empire. But for a thirteenth-century king of England or France
it was true, both in theory and in practice, that authority came from
the law. There was no police force, no standing army. If the
decisions of the courts were not respected there was no way of

---

14. For example, in bringing semi-independent lords of the South under control, the king of France insisted that he had "superioritas" and final right to
hear appeals; see, for example, the settlement of a long dispute with the bishop
of Mende in J. Roucaute and M. Saché, *Lettres de Philippe le Bel relatives au
pays de Gévaudan* (Mende, 1897), pp. 177, 179.

carrying on the work of government, short of the long and expensive process of summoning subjects to the army and waging an internal war. This drastic step had to be taken occasionally, but it was financially and politically impossible to send out military expeditions every year. On the other hand, subjects who had enjoyed a period of relative tranquility lost some of their taste for internal war. They could procrastinate, quibble, protest, and appeal, but in the long run they usually accepted the rulings of the courts. They preferred a legal decision to a fight.

In a law-state, kings were bound by law. They were bound in conscience, as the Roman emperors had been, but the obligation was much more explicit and much more effective, since it was formulated by the Church. An unjust king was no king, but a tyrant.[15] Kings in their coronation oaths swore to do justice; in England they swore to keep and defend the laws of their predecessors and "the laws that the community of the realm shall have chosen."[16] The laws were not simply a tool of government; they were a possession of the people, and this possession was to be preserved just as much as possession of real property. There was no constitutional machinery to defend the laws, but the right to resist a law-breaking king was generally recognized. In Magna Carta, King John was forced to promise that he would henceforth obey certain quite specific definitions of the law. A hundred years later provincial leagues in France secured charters binding the king and his officials to observe local customs, and both Magna Carta and the French provincial charters became part of the law of the land.

One particularly difficult problem arose in the law-states of the thirteenth century. The law protected possession and the income derived from possession. Did a king break the law when he asked for taxes, and thereby interfered with the full enjoyment of the benefits of possession? This was an issue throughout western Europe. Larger and more coherent states were apt to become engaged in longer and more expensive wars. The ordinary revenues of a medieval ruler were very like those of any other landholder. They were inadequate for extensive military operations and they could not easily be expanded. There could be little doubt that taxation was necessary, but was it just? This was a question that was asked

---

15. As Bracton says (following an old tradition), a ruler is a king only so long as he does justice and rules well, if he oppresses his people he is no longer a king but a tyrant. (Woodbine's edition, 3: p. 93.)

16. *Statutes of the Realm*, I, 168.

of popes and theologians (including Thomas Aquinas),[17] of lawyers and of leaders of ruling classes. The answers stressed two points. First, if subjects consented to the tax, it was obviously legal; the only problem was to find a way in which consent could be obtained. Second, in an emergency when the realm was in danger, all subjects were bound to defend the realm, with their bodies or with their money.[18] In England the first principle became dominant because the king had given Parliament such prestige that its consent to taxation was accepted as binding on all subjects. In France (and in most of the other continental states) there were earnest and honest efforts to gain consent, but so many different groups had to be consulted that the process was dangerously slow. Thus, in France, there was a tendency to rely on the duty to defend the realm. In the early years of French taxation this principle was not abused. On the contrary, when a war ceased, the tax ceased, even if very little money had been collected.[19]

About the year 1300, some of the basic ideas of the rule of law had been formulated. "The laws ruled" in the sense that disputes were settled by the courts, not by violence and not by the arbitrary decision of a sovereign. "The people were a party to the laws" in the sense that it was the support of the possessing classes that made the laws effective. And rulers were bound by the law, partly because the Church taught that this was their duty and partly because a ruler who tried to override the laws might find himself faced by organized resistance that he did not have the strength to overcome.

These sanctions of the rule of law lost much of their effectiveness in the troubled times that followed the relatively peaceful and prosperous thirteenth century. The censure of the Church lost a good deal of its sting, and the possessing classes split into factions more interested in gaining political predominance than in upholding the law. At the same time, the idea of "defense of the realm" was turning into the idea of "reason of state." Any act that ensured the safety of the state was justifiable, even if it was against the law. This expansion of the idea of defense (we would say "national

---

17. Thomas Aquinas, "De regimine Judaeorum," *Selected Political Writings* (ed. Passerin d'Entrèves, Oxford, 1948), pp. 90-92. Taxation is legitimate for just cause and the common welfare, as in the case of an invasion.

18. In the bull *Et si de statu*, July, 1297, Pope Boniface VIII allowed the king of France to tax the clergy for defense of the realm. The king claimed this as a basic right, see Archives Nationales, J350 no. 5.

19. E. A. R. Brown, "Cessante cause and the Taxes," *Studia Gratiana* **15** (1972): pp. 565-588.

security") was evident as early as the late thirteenth century. One writer of this period even argued that adultery was no sin if through adultery a woman could be led to reveal a plan to overthrow the state.[20] As dangers to the state increased, the excuse of "reason of state" was invoked more frequently, especially as a justification for arbitrary punishments and increased taxation.

Counteracting the tendency to let the ruler override the law in the interests of security was the steady increase in the percentage of the population that was involved in the political process. This increase was due, in the first place, to the increasing size and greater complexity of effective political units. The affairs of the eleventh-century duchy of Normandy could be settled in informal discussions with ten or twelve men. The affairs of the twelfth-century kingdom of England would require consideration by a somewhat larger group — fifteen or twenty bishops and abbots, and about the same number of earls and barons. If the prelates and magnates agreed, lesser men would follow their lead. By 1300 it was necessary to bring in, if only for propaganda purposes, representatives of the lesser landholders (the knights) and representatives of the towns. To take another dimension, in the thirteenth century, English law courts, both central and itinerant, required the services of no more than twenty to thirty men, most of them professional royal officials.[21] By 1390 there were at least eight justices of the peace in every county,[22] and their numbers grew during the fifteenth century. Thus several hundred men were involved in the task of administering the law. Most of them were country gentlemen, not professional lawyers. They reflected the opinions of their class; if there was much opposition to a government policy in their region, they were not going to make any great effort to put it into effect.

In other countries, assemblies of estates never gained the prestige of the English Parliament, and there was no exact equivalent for the English office of justice of the peace. But everywhere the number of royal officials increased rapidly and these officials tended to form professional, and often hereditary, associations that were very reluctant to make any changes in doctrine or in procedure. The king could overrule them when he was deeply concerned about a particular issue, but he could not interfere with any frequency in the normal procedures of his courts, or of his financial offices.

Another increase in the number of politically conscious subjects

---

20. G. Post, *Studies in Medieval Legal Thought* (Princeton, 1964), p. 305.
21. F. Palgrave, *Parliamentary Writs* (2v., London, 1827-1834), 1: p. 382.
22. Stat. 14 Richard II, ch. 11.

was caused by the growing interference of the state in matters that had been left to other authorities until the late Middle Ages. There had always been some regulation of the economy, but this had been done at the local level, by lords and by towns that controlled markets. By 1300 the state began to take over these regulations, forbidding or encouraging certain kinds of production and certain exports or imports. The urban population was not large (perhaps on the average about 10 per cent of the total), but it was reasonably literate and quite sophisticated politically. Economic regulation affected not only the urban population but also the producers of certain agricultural products, such as wine or wool. Regulations that seemed unwise or that hurt certain interest groups could stir up opposition even if they were justified by reason of state.

Finally, in the sixteenth century, the state began to dictate the religious beliefs and practices of subjects. In a sense, this was nothing new, but in the persecutions of the Middle Ages rulers had acted only as agents of the Church, and not for their own interests. They had also enjoyed the support of the vast majority of their people, except in the case of Bohemia, and Bohemia was the one place where persecution failed. In the sixteenth century, religious uniformity was imposed in the interest of the state, rather than in the interest of either the Catholic or Protestant Churches, and in many countries the dissenting minorities were large, if indeed they were minorities at all. Religion touched all classes — not only those that had long been dominant, but simple peasants and artisans. True, not everyone was equally affected; the tradition of conformity was strong and lukewarm dissenters might prefer to stay out of trouble rather than express their real opinions. But true believers had to face a terrible question: what should they do if the ruler tried to make them accept false doctrine? The answers might differ, but to answer the question at all forced hundreds of thousands of people who had never been involved in the political process to consider the difficult problems of the foundations of authority and the nature of law.

There was bound to be a clash between increasingly powerful states and increasingly politicized subjects. Sooner or later force had to be used to impose a settlement of the dispute, but before force could be used, the issues had to be clarified by arguments about the powers of government, and after a military victory there had to be a settlement expressed in political and legal terms. Thus the sixteenth and seventeenth centuries were a great period for debates on political theory and law. The decisive arguments took place between 1500 and 1700 but the precedents that were cited came largely from the Middle Ages.

Those precedents pointed rather strongly towards the concept of the rule of law. It is true that medieval law was concerned primarily with the protection of possession, but men could possess more than land and houses. They could possess "liberties" (the word is almost always used in the plural), and these liberties could include rights of government (such as the right to hold a local court), and rights that limited government (such as the right to follow local customs that conflicted with generally accepted rules). The most important of these liberties restricted the financial demands of government and prescribed certain procedures in courts of law.

It was precisely in these two areas, taxation and the administration of justice, that the conflict between the more powerful state and the increasingly large body of politically conscious subjects was concentrated. Reason of state could justify any financial imposition, since every European state was in fact endangered by one or more other states, and armies were increasingly expensive. Reason of state could justify extraordinary judicial procedures, since actual rebellion and treason were common, and religious differences had created groups of potential rebels everywhere. Any form of dissent seemed dangerous and any means of discouraging dissent seemed legitimate if the state was to be preserved.

There were naturally protests against arbitrary taxation and arbitary punishments, and these protests raised a new issue that had not appeared before — the problem of civil liberties. In the Middle Ages, when only a few dozen men in each state were concerned with the affairs of the whole community, there was no need to worry about freedom of speech or freedom of assembly. It was easy enough for a handful of prelates and magnates to get together in private and talk over their troubles. If they felt that they had to fight to redress their grievances, they did not need to mount a propaganda campaign; they simply summoned their retainers. Obviously, before the invention of printing, freedom of the press could not be a matter for controversy. Books were suppressed, but this affected only a few scholars; it was not through books that the medieval state was threatened. Again, with most of western Europe thoroughly Catholic, freedom of religion was no problem. Even the Cathars, probably the largest heretical sect in the West before the Hussites, were troublesome mainly because they were supported by nobles seeking to preserve the political and cultural independence of southern France, not because anybody thought that freedom of religion was a basic liberty.

All these conditions changed with the large increase in the politically active part of the population, the dissemination of controversial printed material, and widespread differences over economic and religious policy. More people found more to criticize in the operations of the state, but this criticism could not be effective without public assemblies, and wide distribution of books and pamphlets. The old liberties of due process and consent to taxation could not be defended unless the new liberties of assembly, speech, and printing could be used to make protests effective. But the new liberties were distasteful to many members of the upper classes who had been protected by the old liberties, and they were slow to see that a connection between the old and the new was necessary. Even in England, where the old liberties had survived better than on the continent, Robert Cecil could speak with disgust about the fact that "parliament matters are ordinary talk in the street."[23] Parliament could defend itself; it did not seem, in 1600, to need outside support. Thus there was no close alliance between different groups that were annoyed by the growing power of the state, and as a result the medieval idea of the rule of law was weakened.

In most of western Europe, the result was a fairly close approximation to the standards of the Late Roman Empire, as was suggested above.[24] The king was bound in conscience by the law, and ordinarily the strict rule of law was followed in cases among private parties. When, however, the state needed money, or when its security was threatened, the ordinary rules of law had no effect. Once more we can take an example from England, where royal power was considerably more limited than in France or Spain. Yet an English judge could say in 1606,

> The king's power is double, ordinary and absolute. The ordinary is for the profit of particular subjects for the execution of civil justice . . . in ordinary courts . . . and these laws cannot be changed without parliament . . . . The absolute power of the king . . . is most properly named policy and government. . . . This absolute law varieth according to the wisdom of the king for the common good.[25]

---

23. S. D'Ewes, Journals of all the Parliaments during the Reign of Queen Elizabeth (London, 1682), p. 651.

24. See above, note 10.

25. T. B. Howell, *A Complete Collection of State Trials* (33v., London, 1816-1826) **2**: pp. 382-394.

In this particular case it was ruled that the king could use his absolute power to impose customs dues without the consent of Parliament, since the king had full control of foreign policy, and regulation of foreign trade was a part of foreign policy.

Many of the politically conscious people of seventeenth-century Europe would have accepted this statement as a reasonable and even generous definition of the rule of law. It was not so accepted in England. The English administrative system was based on the justices of the peace who were local notables and not professional bureaucrats. By the sixteenth century many of them had had some training in the common law at the Inns of Court; they revered that law and were suspicious of the law expounded in Star Chamber and other offshoots of the king's Council. These same local notables sat in the House of Commons, the only assembly in a major European country that still controlled internal taxation. The king could juggle customs dues, impose forced loans, and demand money for the upkeep of his fleet, but he could not get enough to support any active policy without a vote of the Commons. England was a remarkably literate country,[26] and also a country that was sharply divided in its religious beliefs. (Germany, of course, was even more divided, but Germany could scarcely be called a country.) Again there was an overlap with the local notables, many of whom were both highly literate and critical of the ritual or doctrine of the established Church. But literacy and dissent went far deeper than country gentlemen and city merchants; the artisans of London and the villagers of East Anglia were Bible-reading Puritans, as were many other people in the more densely populated areas of England. Therefore, as the conviction spread that the foreign policy, the financial policy, and the religious policy of James I and Charles I were usually wrong and frequently illegal, it was easy to organize an opposition. There was a large group of capable leaders with experience in government and knowledge of the law, and an even larger body of disgruntled subjects who were willing to follow these leaders, even to the point of civil war.

At first it seemed possible that the worst abuses could be removed without resorting to violence. Charles I had no effective army, and, at first, not much support from the ruling classes. He had to accept the abolition of all the substitutes for parliamentary taxation that had been devised since the end of the Middle Ages and

26. Lawrence Stone, "The Educational Revolution in England, 1560-1640," *Past and Present* 28: (1964): pp. 44-80.

the destruction of courts that had not followed the rules of common law. These proved to be permanent gains, but no one could be sure that they would last, and some leaders felt that they were not enough. So, as was to happen again in other countries, moderate reform led to radical revolution, and revolution to dictatorship. Neither the radical nor the dictatorial governments were able to gain the support of the majority of the politically conscious people of England, and one reason for this failure was the fact that they could not reconcile, any more than their predecessors, the old and the new liberties. Free speech, a free press, and religious freedom seemed, as they often do, to threaten the accomplishments of the revolution. There was, in fact, more freedom of discussion and more religious diversity than under the Stuarts, but this offended both the dominant group in the Parliament, and the radical minority that seized power from Parliament. It also offended Cromwell, who was trying to preserve some of the old liberties (Parliaments and courts of common law), and who found his efforts thwarted by what seemed to him to be a factious and wrong-headed opposition. And just as Cromwell was unable to reconcile the old and the new liberties, so he was unable to gain the support of either the old or the new political elites. He did not trust the local notables, many of whom were Anglicans, and only a small fraction of the dissenting Protestant leaders trusted him. As a result, his regime collapsed after his death.

The Restoration was as much a restoration of the old ruling classes as it was a restoration of the monarchy. But the old ruling classes were firmly attached to the rule of law, which protected their religious and political dominance as much as it did their property. The limitations on royal power that had been imposed before political opposition turned into armed rebellion were preserved. The law that ruled was not a very just law, and the judges who enforced the law were often abusive and prejudiced, but the English jury system made it possible for public opinion (in the sense of the opinion of the politically conscious population) to mitigate the harshness of the law and the brutality of the judges. Thus in 1670 a London jury refused to convict William Penn of holding an illegal public meeting, in spite of bullying by the court, and when the judge sought to punish the jury for disobeying his instructions he was overruled by the Chief Justice of England.[27]

---

27. W. S. Holdsworth, *A History of English Law* (12 v., 4th ed., London, 1927) 1: p. 345.

It is not surprising that Penn had a good opinion of the rule of law "when the people are a party to the laws." And Penn's case did not stand alone; there was, in fact, more freedom of speech, publication, and religion, under the later Stuarts than a strict interpretation of the law would have permitted.

It is ironical that James II was deposed for trying to suspend or dispense with the same sort of laws that juries often refused to enforce. There was, of course, a great difference between a jury's refusal to convict, which left the letter of the law untouched, and the king's assertion of a right to suspend the effectiveness of a law without the assent of Parliament. But the difference was political as well as legal; James was trying primarily to protect the Catholics, who were considered dangerous by the majority of Englishmen, while the juries in most cases were protecting liberal or radical Protestants who were disliked by the ruling classes, but were not considered dangerous. In fact, the support of the dissenting Protestants was necessary and helpful to the ruling classes in their disputes with the king. Thus the dissenters were willing to join in the Revolution of 1688 in the hope of gaining toleration through an act of Parliament, rather than through an assertion of royal power.

The settlement of 1689, like the Restoration of 1660, was as much concerned with maintaining the political position of the landed and urban oligarchies as in strengthening the rule of law. It did reassert, more strongly than ever, that law could be made and modified only by an act of Parliament, and that no money could be levied by the crown except through a parliamentary grant. It did include a rudimentary Bill of Rights — no excessive bail or fines and no cruel or unusual punishments — and it did contain a strong assertion that the rights and liberties of the people of England were never to be questioned. But the dissenters were rather shabbily treated; they were granted toleration but were still subject to social and political discrimination. Freedom of the press increased because the Licensing Act was allowed to expire, but the legal definition of libel still made direct criticism of the government dangerous.

Nevertheless, the Englishmen of the eighteenth century thought of themselves as freer than any other Europeans and the continental Europeans tended to agree with them. English liberties were protected by law, and that law could not be changed by an arbitrary act of a king or a council. It is true that English law was still inclined to protect privilege and men in power against pressures from the common people and from criticism by liberal or radical thinkers. But there were limits to what the law could do in suppressing opposition, and on the whole those limits were observed.

If this was the situation in England, it is easy to understand why the American colonies could carry the idea of the rule of law even further. They claimed all the rights of Englishmen, and suffered from few of the limitations on those rights. In a land of extreme religious diversity, it was difficult to penalize dissent (though it was attempted in Massachusetts and in Virginia without much success). In a land of great social mobility, and with no hereditary aristocracy, it was difficult to concentrate political power in the hands of a privileged minority. In a land in which most of the people were politically conscious, if only at the level of the local community, it was difficult to suppress criticism of public officials (as the Zenger case of 1733 demonstrated). In fact, since all colonial governments had a definite and recent origin in time, it was difficult to think of government as something so sanctified by age and tradition that it could not be altered or improved. And in a land where all government was based on a charter (royal or proprietarial) the "fundamental laws" were actual written documents, not fuzzy abstractions like the French "fundamental laws," or the English "constitution." The existence of the charters meant that every colony had a constitution in our sense of the word — a document that defined and limited the structure and powers of its government. Thus the concept of the rule of law could be concrete and definite — much more concrete and definite than it could be anywhere in Europe, or even in England.

The American Revolution expressed this overwhelming sense of the importance of the rule of law. Jefferson's magnificent rhetoric should not make us forget that the largest part of the Declaration of Independence is a list of specific charges that George III has broken the law. The state constitutions that preceded the Federal Constitution, the Federal Constitution itself, and the Bills of Rights which were included in, or added to, the constitutions, proclaim the idea of the rule of law. In the Supreme Court, perhaps unwittingly, the framers of the Constitution created the most powerful instrument that the world has ever known to ensure that the rule of law should prevail.

I wish that I could end on this high note. But no solution to any human problem is eternal and no evil is ever completely wiped out.

Reason of state (or national security) is again a danger to the rule of law, all the more so because, in the world we live in, no state can be entirely secure. This danger has so far been averted by the steady increase in the percentage of the population that is politically conscious and is suspicious of reason of state. But the increase has led to another danger; the demands of these politically conscious people are so numerous and so diverse that they could force the government to become arbitrary in spite of itself. As in the sixteenth century, the state is intervening in areas that it had not touched before, but this time it is doing so not because it seeks to increase its power but because it is trying to satisfy its citizens. As in the sixteenth century, the new liberties are not yet merged with the old liberties, and it is difficult to reconcile the two. Is it proper, for example, to interfere with the right of free speech in order to advance the rights of minorities? The rule of law is threatened by the burdens that we place upon the law. We expect the laws to solve our problems when we ourselves have not agreed on acceptable solutions. We expect the laws to impose patterns of common responsibility for the welfare of a society so complex that no one knows what those patterns should be. We expect the laws to make us good, when the most that the law can do is to make it possible for us to seek the good. The result is complication, confusion, uncertainty in understanding the law, and intolerable delays in the administration of justice. This situation invites, as it did in the sixteenth century, arbitrary administrative decisions that by-pass ordinary legal procedures. It would be ironic if the forces that led to the establishment of the rule of law should be forces that lead to the breakdown of the law. But history is full of such ironies, and no society can be sure that it will escape them.

JOSEPH R. STRAYER
Dayton-Stockton Professor Emeritus
of History, Princeton University

The Liberating Influence of
Science in History

W HEN I WAS SURPRISED with the invitation to speak on this occasion, I felt it to be an honor and an opportunity and was rash enough to accept without the hesitation that seemliness would have imposed after a pause to consider the scope of the topic. As a more decent sense of inadequacy set in, I was tempted at several intervals to modify the subject with a view to taking shelter within boundaries defensible out of my own research. I have resisted that temptation, not without assistance (it has to be acknowledged) from President Boyd, whose fearlessness fortifies us all, and I shall ask, together with your indulgence, only that some phrase like "Thoughts on" be prefixed to the title in your mind's eye, or ear. For I do believe that science has been a liberating influence in our history, and it is an appropriate moment to try to think how and in what ways that has been true. One even feels urgency about it, in that prominent among the doubts afflicting the bicentennial is a certain retreat from science, a certain loss of confidence and nerve. The word revulsion may not be too strong. The same is true of liberty, and though I am not going to say that I think they reduce to the same thing at bottom, there probably is some connection between their ups and downs both in history and among the fissures of the present. It may even be that the cracks widening round us here and now on the surface of the past were foretold in the casting of the once and future bell, suspended all inscrutable under its new jar on the wrong side of Chestnut Street.

Time was, and not so long ago, when a historian handling this subject would have spoken mainly of ideas and metaphors: of Jeremy Bentham's ambition to be the Newton of legislation; of the idea of nature presupposed by the Declaration of Independence; of mechanistic images of checks and balances; of an atomistic society composed of the individuals its parts; of the notion of survival of the fittest influential in affairs. I never used to find that approach uncongenial. What with socialization and politicization of scholarship, however, recent fashion has turned toward its reciprocal, thereby emphasizing all that science has drawn from the structure of language, culture and society for its very possibility, and even for certain of its formulations: Darwin's debt to social thought instead of the other way about, Newton's to commercial capitalism, or that of all rationalism to the syntax and vocabulary of classical Greek. That, too, is convincing, to a degree, but even so relatively traditional, younger colleagues might say hide-bound, a historian as myself, one who never went to school to the *Annales,* feels that these verbal connections, so far as they record something real, have largely been made, and that we need to look beneath programs and the recollection of prophecy and scrutinize the ways in which science and the scientific community have actually functioned in the social process.

We are not the first to do so. Among our predecessors ten score years ago there was considerable agreement about the topic I have been asked to discuss. It is epitomized in one of those books so profoundly unoriginal as to be specially precious, the *Sketch for a Historical Picture of the Progress of the Human Mind,* by the Lucretius of the Enlightenment, the Marquis de Condorcet.[1] Most of the accomplishments he chronicles pertain to what we now call science (I acknowledge the anachronism, but do not think it signifies). Spiritually, science is said to have liberated men from ignorance, superstition, religious bondage, and routine. Materially, it is said to have increased the ease and convenience of life and to hold the promise of greater plenty and equality of fortune. The perspective was not, on the whole, a political one, except insofar as agents of despotism, and notably priests, are said to have kept oppressed communities in ignorance in the interests of those wielding power. Our political leaders did not need to await Condorcet to be taught this outlook. It was theirs already, though less dogmatically and simplistically held and attended by such differences in emphasis as vary any set of intelligent opinions. I would myself, for example, discern two fairly distinct traditions at work in forming the early American expectations of science, one rationalist, Encyclopedist, largely French in derivation, centering on natural history and arts and trades, emphasizing education and exploitation

---

1. *Esquisse d'un tableau historique des progrès de l'esprit humain* (Paris, 1795).

of nature, and epitomized in Jefferson; the other Baconian, experimental, largely British in derivation, centering on physics and the investigation of new phenomena, valuing ingenuity and self-education, more democratic somehow, epitomized by Franklin in colonial times and re-emerging in Jacksonian America in the career of Joseph Henry. If that is anywhere near the mark, it is amusing that Franklin went down far better in Paris than Jefferson ever did.

However that may be, I have to confess to an even larger measure of agreement with what the rationalists of the eighteenth century thought of science than that which I also feel with the intellectual historians of the last generation. Their position has, of course, been subject to criticism, of which I shall mention two stages. They are said, in the first place, to have been unaware of unconscious mental operations and of the capacity for irrational feelings to issue in irrational conduct. I doubt whether that is altogether correct, but even if it were, I cannot see that accommodating it would require anything other than an enlargement of their sense that science is the most reliable educator of humanity and healer of its ills. The followers of Freud have not, after all, welcomed imputations that their findings are merely introspective and their practice an exorcism, and they do not intend psychoanalysis to be an apology for irrationality any more than seismology is for earthquakes or vulcanology for eruptions.

A second set of reservations has arisen more recently and is more serious. It is signaled by the taboo that anthropologists have placed upon the word "primitive." I have just heard a brilliant young French historian give a paper on death. More precisely, his subject was the manner whereby authorities of the Church in olden times went about to persuade Christians that making a good death was the end of life in both senses. At one point he had to apologize for inadvertence in using the word "superstitious." He acknowledged it to be a ridiculous term but in the heat of discussing those practices was unable to think of any other. Now then, attitudes like his clearly amount to more than an injunction to suspend disbelief for the purpose of penetrating in imagination the inwardness of one's subject. They bespeak a systematic defection from the notion that there is any reason given by the nature of the world itself for preferring one representation of its processes or structure over another, the Newtonian over the Aristotelian, the Darwinian over the Taoist, the quantum mechanical over the Navajo, since each of them is merely an epiphenomenon of a particular culture serving the purposes, economic or political, of a particular society at some certain stage.

Another colleague, this one concerned with the ancient civilization of India, recently told me at a seminar held in that country that it makes as much sense to say "magic works" as it does "science works." Such relativism is bound to be, and is meant to be, fatal to any notion that science holds a privileged place in history, the dimensions of its growth being those of the progress of knowledge. It is difficult for me, at least, to refrain from replying *ad hominem* to such observations, or in the latter case *ad feminam*, considering that neither she nor any other participant, though never so mystical and Persian, had flown to our meeting place on a carpet. But serious cultural as well as crass technological evidence demonstrates the greater survival value that science has manifested in the social process throughout all history. In no society on any continent have other, indigenous systems of belief about nature withstood its introduction. For whether it be in developed, developing, or degenerating societies, science has had an unvarying effect. It has dissipated, it is not too much to say it has corroded, tradition. If magic and folklore, however charming to tourists, persist, the measure is in inverse ratio to education, except where revivals appear to occur; and they always start among embers fanned from on high by sentimentalists and dissidents, and never descend far, perhaps because real fires seldom burn down. Whether this situation is to be regretted is a matter of opinion, as it also is whether the dissipation of what the eighteenth century knew for superstition is to be called a liberation. It is self-evident that the effect is not one that could have been desired ahead of time by those among whom it happens.

In a sector of more concern in 1789, and just afterwards, than in 1776, and equally to us in recent years — that of civil liberties and freedom of conscience — the part of science has probably been smaller and has certainly been more ambiguously judged than is usually supposed, particularly among scientists. There is no preponderance of historical evidence to show that science either requires political liberty in order to flourish or directly favors its realization. The connections that can be made out are indirect and circumstantial, though none the less interesting for that. In the eyes of liberals, the two classic cases involving science with conscience have been the trial of Galileo before the Roman curia and the conflict between Darwinism and Biblical Christianity. It has been disconcerting in one such pair of eyes, my own, to learn repeatedly that neither Galileo nor Darwin is even a sympathetic, much less a heroic, figure when viewed from farther left, and for the same reason: it is as unacceptable to the new and social, as it was to the old and cosmic, teleology that laws of nature or statements of fact should be irrelevant to the realization of goals. At least Cardinal Bellarmine had the welfare of mankind in view according to his lights, and not mere physical relations paraded as nature while really serving interests of class, race, or nation. The matter of Robert Oppenheimer was different from the crime of Galileo, of course, except that his travail too was one over which the far Left has subtly ceased to agonize.

Among the writers of the eighteenth century, it was Voltaire who put his finger most directly while most lightly on the point at issue between Newtonian science and its detractors. Here is his summary in a single sentence: " 'But there is no such thing as better or worse in things that are indifferent,' say the Newtonians; 'But there are no things that are indifferent,' reply the Leibnizians."[2] And Voltaire took his stand with Newton, who in his account only purported to say how the world is in fact made in contrast to Leibniz and Descartes and philosophers before them who said how it must be made in order to satisfy their metaphysics. The triumph of fact over dogma: that is what Voltaire saw in science. Liberty is emancipation from dogma and acceptance of facts. Candide has to learn that by experience. Mankind has science, however, experience worked up into knowledge. But once emancipated, we are on our own morally. It is no good looking there for comfort or guidance. Before Micromégas, the giant space voyager from Sirius, returns from our blob of mud to his celestial home, he leaves a book from the Universe with the permanent secretary of the Academy of Sciences, a book that will show men the good in things. That official opens it after Micromégas is gone, and the pages are blank. And I do think that the history of liberty in its relation to science has borne out Voltaire's perception. Science may indeed have had nothing to do with freedom in itself, but only with nature. That was also Kant's problem. It was not itself libertarian, but it conduced to the liberty that is possible in requiring a better distinction than has ever been made in any other way between actuality and wish, fact and dogma. For facts need not

2. *Elémens de la philosophie de Neuton* (1738), Part I, Chapter 3.

be restricted to physical nature. In Voltaire's sensibility, the more
interesting facts were not. It may, of course, be said that science
has produced its own dogmas no less luxuriantly than other modes
of thinking, belonging, and believing. A historian is bound to
agree, and yet to suggest what I find a saving difference. It is
that scientific dogmas finally yield to science. In that they are like
other pathologies of science, for example technologically produced
pollution, or (we have no choice but to hope) nuclear weapons,
and they are unlike religious, political, racial, or national dogmas,
which never yield to internally generated analysis and criticism, but
only to force, to time — or to science.

Despite Voltaire, Pangloss never died, however, and neither have
other echoes of his Master's voice, for it may be that science has
appeared to be a liberating influence mainly in the eye of the
beholden. All the cultural soul searchings and breast beatings of
recent years bring home to us once again that for certain temperaments in all circumstances, and perhaps for all temperaments in
certain circumstances, science is rather a set of bonds confining
the imagination in its prison house. The revulsion we have been
sensing these days is compounded of a complex set of attitudes,
the elements of which are readily itemized: a radicalism that scorns
reform and cries transfiguration; an externalization of faults, not
to say sin, from human nature to society; a consequent transvaluation of values, such that in so-called anti-social actions the victim
is really to blame for his complicity with society and the perpetrator
really innocent for having been victimized; a glorification of will
over mind and of action over analysis; a fascination, sometimes
horrid, with the transcendental and occult; an assertion of sexual
liberty going beyond free love to the validating of homosexuality,
the promotion of pornography, and the dabbling in diabolism;
an experimentation with drugs and other modes of altering perception and consciousness; a repudiation of exact and mathematical
science in favor of a vitalistic biology, and of a rationalized technology in favor of traditional crafts of artisans working by hand.

Perhaps these remarks do in some measure come out of my own
research, for a historian of science living through the recent past
will recognize in this secularized antinomianism the re-emergence
of a mentality with which I, at least, first became acquainted in
studying what might now be called a counter-Enlightenment in
the late eighteenth century, and not only in France. Almost twenty
years ago I delivered and then published a paper about science

and the French Revolution.[3] It developed a finding that had surprised me, which was the existence of a strain of virulent hostility to abstract, theoretical science among the Jacobin left. Despite what seemed to me the clearest evidence, I failed conspicuously to convince my more progressively minded colleagues that there could have been any conflict between science and political radicalism. In those days such a thing was unthinkable in principle, and they attributed the undeniable suppression of the Academy early in the Terror rather to its elitist form. Nowadays when that paper is read by scholars and students at the same end of the political spectrum, they accept the findings as self-evident and disagree with me only in thinking that the left was right to distrust science.

For my part, however, I have come to think that the question goes deeper than ordinary political differences into regions where the extremes touch. Others have discerned the features of a similar mentality in proto-Nazi aspects of the culture of Weimar Germany.[4] In all these contexts, America in the last ten years, France in the 1780's, and Germany in the 1920's, as well as in more partial and personal instances, a sense of the failure of institutions and of corruption in high places produced the diagnosis of a sick society, which appears to have been connected with these manifestations in consequence of the breakdown of legitimate authority. It is certainly a feature of the scientific enterprise that it has always needed to draw upon authority, externally for funds and institutionalization, and internally for the maintenance of standards, standards of rigor and of discipline, and also for motivation to work. I do not think that these necessities are inconsistent with liberalism. The legitimacy of the authority is the limiting factor. But to the rebellious temperament, authority and discipline are anathema, and we can understand why it often finds science uncongenial. For what defines that temperament is that it refuses all limitations upon human personality and will, and denies the validity of any boundary separating one aspect of existence from another: whether that boundary separates man from man (hence

---

3. "The *Encyclopédie* and the Jacobin Philosophy of Science," *Critical Problems in the History of Science*, ed. Marshall Clagett (Madison, Wisconsin, 1959), pp. 255-289.

4. Notably, Paul Forman, "Weimar Culture, Causality, and Quantum Theory, 1918-1927," *Historical Studies in the Physical Sciences* 3 (1971): pp. 1-115. Peter Gay, *Weimar Culture* (New York, 1968); G. Lukács, *Die Zerstörung der Vernunft* (Berlin, 1954).

equality and fraternity, the get-it-all-together spirit, though not necessarily liberty); whether it separates man from woman (hence, increased sexuality and decreased distinction between the sexes); whether it separates virtue from vice (hence, the transvaluation of value); whether it separates natural from supernatural (hence, reversion to the magical and miraculous); whether it separates man the maker from what he makes (hence, health in craftsmanship and dehumanization in externally powered machinery); whether it separates consciousness from nature (hence, yearning for a world alive, and the would-be substitution of psychology and biology for mathematics and physics as the ordering sciences); whether, finally, such a boundary separates science from its object (hence, nature is to be known through penetration and sympathy, not through analysis and abstraction). In Blake's demonology, Newton measures, and divides.

Some years ago I had occasion to argue that one's sense that science generally pertains to progressivism historically, while telling against conservatism and tradition, has to do neither with the political implications of laws of nature, for they have none, nor with the political actions of professional scientists, for whatever their private opinions, their civic role has normally been to provide the state with powers, an act of partnership rather than partisanship, while drawing authority and resources from the state for science. Instead, the progressivism of science has to do with its orientation toward new knowledge and the future, and of scientists toward novelty, change, and social mobility.[5] Thinking on this disposition leads me to a larger, not inconsistent reflection, with which I shall close. Perhaps it falls into the class of those things that go without saying, and that therefore (as I have heard a wise dean observe) need to be said.

We find ourselves here on this continent, not merely nor even mainly in consequence of an assertion of liberty in the city of Philadelphia, but as an instance of the most integral and most ineluctable process in the history of our civilization, the expansion of Europe. The voyages that brought European men to the Americas north and south belong in the early chapters — Morison just got them written, fortunately — of the history of a movement that is first systematically recognizable in the fifteenth century, when it acquired the *vis viva* that half a millennium later carried

---

5. "Remarks on Social Selection as a Factor in the Progressivism of Science," *American Scientist* **56** (1968): pp. 439-450.

spacecraft to the moon. What differentiated those voyages and all their sequels from the random travels of antiquity and of other civilizations, which produced only adventure, legend, or commerce, is that they have always been involved with, I deliberately do not say motivated by, the problem of how the world is made, in a word with knowledge. They were animated by the same instinct that informed the works of a Brunelleschi, a Leonardo, a Machiavelli, and later a Galileo: namely, that knowledge finds its purpose in action and action its reason in knowledge, that if a problem can be solved it should be solved, that if something can be done it should be done. In my belief, those were the behavior patterns that made of the culture of the Renaissance in Italy the matrix wherein ancient and scholastic learning and technique were converted into modern engineering and science.

Thus, it seems to me an extraordinary blindness in the historiography of science that its purview, though expanded recently to embrace all sorts of esoterica, has given little prominence to mapping and discovery. Historians at large are no less blinkered in that they have failed to perceive, or at least to act on, what was evident in another way to Condorcet, that the history of science can be thought the most comprehensive aspect of western history, and no narrow specialty. Both comprehensive and distinctive, for surely the two most general sets of fact about our history are one at bottom: first, that Europe with America came to exercise a dominant power in the world until yesterday; and second that, also until yesterday, modern science has been an artifact of European civilization and of it alone among all the others that the world has seen. A little over a century ago, Walter Bagehot wrote an essay on a subject very like mine today, calling it *Physics and Politics.* Apropos of the former of these considerations, he observed, "The progress of the military art is the most conspicuous, I was about to say the most *showy,* fact in human history." Though liberal, he was never one to blink a fact. Apropos of the latter, and "omitting the higher but disputed topics of morals and religion," Bagehot located the superiority of Englishmen over Australian aborigines in "their greater command over the powers of nature. This power is not external only: it is also internal. The English not only possess better machines for moving nature, but are themselves better machines."[6]

---

6. New York edition (1873), pp. 44, 208.

Clearly, whether science has been a liberating or an enslaving influence in history depends upon whose history you study. At all events, it certainly liberated the European genius from confinement within the spherical triangle bounded in the fifteenth century by the Adriatic, the Portuguese littoral, and the Irish Sea. It is, moreover, the one aspect of our civilization that the others have wanted to adopt. They have never wanted our political or economic systems, our religions or philosophies, our arts or letters. Beginning with the Japanese, they have wanted science, and they can acquire it and operate it just as well as we do, in order to liberate themselves from constraints of many sorts, including us. So perhaps there is a final sense in which science may be seen as liberating, one combining the personal and social aspects. Though created out of personality and in culture, it is not then bound by personality or culture. It is impersonal and universal. I can think of nothing else of which that may be said.

There have been those who have seen that as the highest liberation of all.

CHARLES C. GILLISPIE
Dayton-Stockton Professor of History,
Princeton University

The European Enlightenment in its American Setting

W E CALL THE EIGHTEENTH CENTURY the age of Enlightenment because the people of that time believed that theirs was a peculiarly enlightened age. They were conscious of possessing a new and better kind of knowledge, more reliable than the often mistaken and trivial knowledge of the past, and closely associated with natural science. The very words "science" and "knowledge" were still not quite distinct in the various European languages. It was believed that this new knowledge, or philosophy, should now be put to use for the improvement of human life in the everyday world. The very name of the American Philosophical Society, "held at Philadelphia for promoting useful knowledge," comes to us as the clear voice of the Enlightenment itself.

That there was an Enlightenment in both Europe and America is evident, but a few problems arise with the conception of a European Enlightenment in its American setting, a title devised by the program committee for the present occasion. If the thought of human beings is a historical product, formed by surrounding conditions, as it surely is, then how could the Enlightenment of sophisticated Europe exist in the more simple environment of the American colonies? Was the American Enlightenment the same as the European? Did it have the same origins, the same tone or content, and the same effects? If so, what were the similarities, and if not, what were the differences? To deal with such questions in thirty minutes requires drastic simplifications.

Let us suppose that there were two kinds of Enlightenment, one primarily scientific, the other political; an Enlightenment of thought and one of action; or simply Enlightenment I and Enlightenment II. They might exist in the same person, and it need hardly be said in the present company that such a person was Benjamin Franklin. He was described by a French admirer,

Turgot, in a verse which became famous, and which in these learned halls can be quoted in the Latin, *Eripuit caelo fulmen, sceptrumque tyrannis.* That is, "He snatched the lightning from heaven and the scepter from tyrants." The reference, of course, was to Franklin's experiment with his kite and to his role in the American Revolution. To snatch the lightning from heaven was Enlightenment I; to become politically active to the point of revolution was Enlightenment II.

In Enlightenment I the Europeans and Americans had much in common, and the European Enlightenment found an easy home in the American setting. It was the Enlightenment of science, both of actual science and of science in the more extended sense in which verifiable or organized knowledge was preferred to customary or authoritative ideas. In this Enlightenment the former heavens had been replaced by Newtonian cosmology and violent electrical phenomena in the atmosphere. Discovery, exploration, and scientific expeditions pushed the boundaries of knowledge ever farther throughout the earth. Collections were made of rocks, plants, insects, and animal bones. They were studied by learned men in America as in Europe. The past no longer had any persuasive power in its own right. Ancient fables and even reputable historians were subjected to criticism. The old belief in witches had faded, along with other superstitions. No enlightened person feared the devil. Miracles, oracles, and lives of the saints were viewed with suspicion, and the Bible itself was not beyond doubt. There was a distaste for mystery, the very negation of knowledge. Revealed religion was a source of embarrassment, and natural religion was thought to be enough, a kind of placid deism in which belief in the Deity and in a future state for departed human beings was recommended.

In this kind of Enlightenment, Europe and America were not very different. Real science knew no inherent regional or national limits, for anyone who could understand it, or who had the equipment, could participate. Franklin's experiment with his kite could be duplicated anywhere else. Observations of the transit of Venus in 1769 were made in Europe, Hudson Bay, and the Pacific Ocean, and also at Philadelphia, and about twenty other places in the British American colonies. The best of these American observations were internationally reported. There was an international network of correspondence on scientific and related matters, carried on among academies and seats of learning. At a more popular level, which if not strictly scientific at least claimed to be rational, the American Enlightenment seems also to have resembled the European, or perhaps even exceeded it. A surprising percentage of Americans at the time of the Revolution were not members of any church. There seem to have been a great many popular free-thinkers. For example, on what was then the frontier, in Vermont before it even became a state, the celebrated Ethan Allen, in 1784, published a highly deistical work, called *Reason the Only Oracle of Man.*

For Enlightenment II, however, the political or activistic Enlightenment, we may ask to what degree European ideas could or did exist in an American setting. The two Enlightenments, indeed, might flow together. To reject the past as a source of reliable knowledge might go with rejecting it as a source of lawful authority. To have doubts on revealed religion might lead to a demand for religious toleration or neutralism on the part of the state. Men of science might throw themselves into humanitarian causes, as when the French Academy of Sciences worked to improve the Paris hospitals in the 1780's. Medical doctors, especially, were prominent in the two Enlightenments of science and of action. Four physicians were among the signers of the American Declaration of Independence, and almost thirty of them sat in the first assembly of the French Revolution.

Yet Enlightenment II remains conceptually distinct. It was carried on by publicists and pamphleteers, or in Europe by men of letters and *philosophes* who were not exactly philosophers, and in America by men like Jefferson who, while having a serious understanding of science, did their important work in other fields. In this kind of Enlightenment, America and Europe were less alike.

The big difference is that enlightened Europeans, in the sense of Enlightenment II, were generally dissatisfied with their existing institutions, and felt the need for sweeping reform, whereas the Americans, even before the Revolution, were more content with the circumstances in which they lived. Another difference is that in Europe, or at least on the Continent, under what is somewhat misleadingly called enlightened despotism, governments undertook a variety of enlightened reforms, and reformers looked to a central government to achieve their aims, whereas in America the governments seldom took such initiatives, and not much was expected of government anyway. For Europe, a long list could be made of enlightened servants of the executive power, from the Emperor

Joseph II through the French Turgot and others in the German states, Spain, and even Naples. In America, at the end of the century, Alexander Hamilton was more like a European in this respect than were his Jeffersonian adversaries, but the Jeffersonians may have been more typical of the Enlightenment in America.

In Europe, the burden of thought in Enlightenment II was opposed to the feudal and ecclesiastical institutions inherited from the Middle Ages. It was against the society of legal estates and orders, personified by nobles and bishops. It opposed the fiscal and other privileges of avowedly privileged classes. It was against the extravagance of the rich and the destitution of the poor, the burdensome and unfair taxation, the chronic wars, the professional armies, and the wastefulness and incompetence with which public business was all too frequently conducted. It questioned the very principle of religious orthodoxy, or of association of the state with an established religion, as still existed even in England and Holland, where full civil rights were enjoyed only by those within the politically favored church. Where state and church protected themselves by censorship, as in France, enlightened thinkers became devious and sometimes even dishonest. Hostile to so much in the present, they rejected the past and scoffed at tradition. They engaged both in a profound rethinking of the foundations of society and in everlasting superficial polemics. The Enlightenment in Europe produced the passionate depths of Rousseau, the mockery of Voltaire, the virulent irreligion of Helvétius, and the concealed and elusive radicalism of Diderot and the Encyclopedists.

Little of all this existed in America. To document Enlightenment II in America we have no vast and rich literature as in France, but a body of *ad hoc* materials: the four hundred pamphlets in the controversy preceding the Revolution, so fully studied by Bernard Bailyn; the Declaration of Independence; the state constitutions written during the revolution, with their accompanying declarations of rights; the federal constitution of 1787 with the accompanying Federalist papers; together with a few works like Jefferson's *Notes on Virginia,* appropriately called "Notes," since hardly anything written in America between 1760 and 1790 was actually intended to be a book.

When John Adams heard of the Stamp Act, he published in the *Boston Gazette* some thoughts which came later to be known as his *Dissertation on the Canon and Feudal Law.* As a diatribe against feudal and ecclesiastical institutions, it might have been written by a French *philosophe,* and indeed Adams had recently been reading Rousseau's *Social Contract* with much approval, so that we might say that we have here a piece of the European Enlightenment in an American setting; but as such it had a strange or negative relevancy, for Adams was not attacking these deplorable institutions in his own country, where he boasted that they did not exist, but expressing the suspicion that beyond the Stamp Act there might be a conspiracy to introduce them into an America that had always been free of them. There was no nobility in America, feudal or otherwise; but many Americans were afraid that there might be, and several of the first state constitutions, as well as the federal constitution of 1787, contained clauses prohibiting the creation of a nobility which had never existed. There were no bishops in America until after the Revolution, but there was an uneasiness at what might happen if bishops were introduced. Central government was minimal and far away, but there was a fear of a growing central power. There was really no standing army, and British regulars had been stationed in the colonies for only a few years; but there was an alarm about standing armies. Taxes were low, virtually non-existent by European standards; but there was a dread of possible future taxes, and the whole dispute with England originated in such apprehensions.

Enlightenment II in America was thus a comparatively bland affair. It was essentially defensive. It was not as anti-religious as in Europe. In America there was no anguished rethinking of the foundations of human society. There was a sense of continuity with the past, not rejection. Until independence from England produced a series of new problems, the political Enlightenment was not even very innovative; it was the British government that was accused of innovation. Even after independence, the pre-existing civil and criminal law was largely retained, the new state constitutions were hardly as novel for Americans as were the French revolutionary constitutions for France, and the institution of slavery, denounced by virtually all enlightened Europeans, persisted untouched in most of the American states.

In saying that Enlightenment II in America was not very innovative, we are in effect saying that the Americans, in what is called the Age of Enlightenment, drew their ideas from other and older sources. One of these was the Greek and Latin classics; another, the English Whig tradition of 1689; a third, especially powerful, the memory of the English Puritan revolution of the 1640's, and of the short-lived English republic or commonwealth, which had failed in England, but whose principles were perpetuated into the eighteenth century by a small group of political writers in England, and were kept alive in America. But mainly the Americans drew on their own experience. Emigration and settlement, the abandonment of an old society and creation of a new one, had already done in America what in Europe was to be attempted by aggressive Enlightenment and violent revolution. The European past, so oppressive in Europe, was in America only a shadow. The American past was a source of pride and satisfaction. Social stratification was simple, with no such wealth or poverty, or legal rank, as existed in Europe; and as Edmund Morgan has argued, the fact that much of the most menial or dirty labor devolved upon blacks allowed whites to enjoy a sentiment of equality with each other. In the famous aphorism of Tocqueville, the Americans had been born equal, and needed no revolution to become so. Like most truths, this one had only a relative application, but Tocqueville meant it only as a means of contrasting America with France and Europe.

The thought of Enlightenment II, on both continents, ultimately expressed itself in the language of liberty and equality, the rights of man, the sovereignty of the people, and constitutional government, with delegation and restriction of power under explicit written constitutions. Enlightenment II, like Enlightenment I, was indeed an international and transatlantic movement. But if the origins of Enlightenment II in Europe and America were different, so too was its impact. In Europe such ideas were a challenge that undermined the existing order, and to a great extent eventually replaced it. In America they codified what already existed. They raised American familiar practices to a higher plane. They turned custom into reason. This thought has been better expressed by Bernard Bailyn than by anyone else, when he says that the American Revolution, which was the consummation of Enlightenment II in America, gave a universal significance to what had formerly been parochial, or that it made the Americans, who had formerly thought of themselves as provincials, a simple plain people who had not yet attained the refinements of the Old World, now believe that theirs was the civilization of the future, or that they were in fact more enlightened than Europeans. I would only add to what Bailyn has said that a great many Europeans, not only in France from Lafayette to Tocqueville and beyond, but also in Great Britain,

Germany, and elsewhere, by their praises of America, helped to give Americans this favorable picture of themselves. America, from being a colonial backwater, was now assigned a momentous place in world history.

These observations have been exceedingly general, but they can be illustrated from the life of a former foreign member of this Society, whose marble bust has long been installed in this very room, and appropriately surveys the present discussion from the regions of philosophical immortality — namely the Marquis de Condorcet. Condorcet, fully as much as Benjamin Franklin, combined the two Enlightenments in his own person. Like Franklin, he showed the relationship between Europe and America. He was the only one of the more notable *philosophes* who lived to play a leading part in the French Revolution. He won fame at first as a mathematician, and became permanent secretary of the French Academy of Sciences in 1776, but from an early age he was also consumed, as Keith Baker puts it in his new book on Condorcet, by a "passion for the public good." He was in fact elected twice to membership in the American Philosophical Society, once in 1775 and again in 1786. It appears that in the confusion of the Revolutionary war the Society may have forgotten in 1786 that it had already elected him in 1775.

Condorcet, knowing Franklin as a fellow scientist, in 1774 wrote him a letter containing five questions, which he asked Franklin to submit to the Society at Philadelphia. The questions were purely scientific. Condorcet wanted to know how the magnetic needle behaved in America, what the height of mercury in the barometer was, whether American rocks included any basalt, whether fossil bones had been discovered and if so at what depths below the surface and at what altitude in the mountains. He asked also whether there were any "free Negroes who have *not* mixed with whites," and if so what their children were like, and whether "men of genius or parts have been observed among them." Here, too, his purpose was probably scientific, to gather evidence on the effects of heredity and environment, but probably also he was already inclined to believe in an underlying equality in the distribution of talents among the races. The Society appointed two committees to reply to these questions, and elected him to its membership.

Then came the American Revolution, with which Condorcet enthusiastically sympathized. He wrote an essay, published in

1786, "On the influence of the American Revolution on Europe." Its tenor may be shown in a few quotations. "The spectacle of a great people among whom the rights of man are respected is useful to all others. . . . It shows that these rights are the same everywhere." Or again: "The spectacle of equality which prevails in the United States, and which assures their peace and prosperity, can also be useful to Europe." He went on to argue that, because of this equality, in the absence of social ranks, legal estates, and false ambitions, the Americans "would produce almost as many men occupied with adding to the mass of knowledge as all of Europe, that they will at least double the progress of knowledge and make it twice as rapid. This progress will embrace both the useful arts and the speculative sciences." Condorcet thus firmly joined America and Europe in a common Enlightenment, and simultaneously expressed what I have called the two Enlightenments of science and of public service or action. The American Philosophical Society again elected him to its membership. It is tempting to think that he had first been elected as a spokesman of Enlightenment I, and the second time for his contributions to Enlightenment II.

The French Revolution soon followed, in which Condorcet favored a radical course. He was overtaken, however, in the crisis of 1793, by those more radical than he was. The great equalitarian was accused of elitism, and the exponent of progress denounced as reactionary, sentenced to arrest, and forced into hiding. He died before his pursuers could find him. During his concealment he completed the work for which he is best remembered, his *Sketch of the Progress of the Human Mind*. This was essentially a world history, or at least a history of what a later writer called the rise of the spirit of rationalism. In the later phases of this long and troubled story the Americans occupied a distinguished place. The American Revolution, said Condorcet, had shaken all Europe from the Neva to the Guadalquivir. It had taught Europeans to know and to demand their rights. Yet the American Revolution was less violent than the French, he added, and less profound or sweeping, not because American ideas were different from those of Europe, but because these ideas were already largely realized in America even before the Revolution. Long before 1776, he said, the Americans understood better than Europeans "What were the common rights of all individuals of the human species." It was because they already had enlightened institutions that their revolution was less revolutionary. They were content with the civil and criminal laws that they had received from England, and had no need to reform a vicious system of taxation, nor to destroy feudal tyrannies, hereditary distinctions, rich and powerful privileged corporations, or a system of religious intolerance; and so they could limit themselves to establishing new political powers as a substitute for those which the British nation had previously exercised over them.

I think that these sentiments of Condorcet, as well as his life and death, illustrate what I have tried to say, and help us to understand what is meant by the European Enlightenment in its American setting. So far as the Enlightenment was a matter of pure science, of barometric readings, magnetic needles, and correspondence among the learned, it was much the same sort of thing on both continents. America at the time was of course less developed than Europe, but Americans and Europeans engaged in a common enterprise, with common scientific standards, common goals and a ready exchange of each other's findings. But so far as the Enlightenment was a design for the transformation of society there was a difference. The sharing of goals or ideals, the common use of words such as liberty, equality, and rights of man, could not obliterate the difference, nor conceal it even from such a visionary as Condorcet. It was after all easier, or less controversial, to snatch the lightning from heaven than to wrest the scepter from tyrants. "Tyrant" was not a scientific conception; it was more of a value judgment, or even an epithet; the liberal of today might find himself called the tyrant of tomorrow. In such matters various interests, temperaments, forces, and social classes aligned themselves differently. Struggle and violence followed. It was the good fortune of Americans to possess already what Europeans had to make greater efforts to obtain. If Enlightenment II was more bland in America, it was because grievances were less inveterate and class conflicts less deep-seated. The American Revolution, unpleasant as it was for the Tories, was mild compared to the French. Yet it gave the colonies not only independence but a universal significance. America became a showpiece of the European Enlightenment, pointed to by Condorcet and others as an illustration of what they had in mind. America had been called the "new world" since the days of Columbus. The words now took on another sense. It was a "new world" in that it was a new society, a new kind of civilization, a new order or harbinger of a better future.

ROBERT R. PALMER
Professor of History, Yale University

Diversity in Religion as a Force for Liberty: A Quadricentennial View of the Problem

T HE TITLE OF THIS ESSAY was assigned by the American Philosophical Society, but the sub-title, following the inevitable colon, is my own. Given this long and wide focus, many sweeping generalizations and painful abridgments of the story became necessary, and the result may seem pontifical in spirit. Yet I hope the reader will share with me Kenneth Burke's wily retort: "to pontificate; that is, to make a bridge."[1] What I shall link with my verbal arches are various remotely separated spots of time which must be given a common connection if we are to understand some major idiosyncrasies of our national history—and perhaps even ourselves. It will in due course be seen that I share Sacvan Bercovitch's concern for "the Puritan origins of the American self."[2]

A statement on the assigned topic, however, should probably begin with the observation that diversity in religion has not usually conduced to the increase of human liberty. Religious pluralism has existed in diverse contexts through all of recorded time, but the enjoyment of liberty on a general basis has been rare. Western civilization, moreover, has created serious barriers to the very freedoms it has so often professed to enlarge.

A semi-philosophical explanation of this fact can also be offered. Because religious convictions have a transcendent reference and are by definition matters of ultimate concern, they are, except over very long reaches of time, relatively non-negotiable. People do not put their ultimate value structures up for auction. Religious diversity, more often than not, exposes differing cosmological con-

---

1. Kenneth Burke, "I, Eye, Ay—Emerson's Early Essay 'Nature': Thoughts on the Machinery of Transcendance," in: *Transcendentalism and its Legacy*, Myron Simon and Thornton H. Parsons, eds. (Ann Arbor, University of Michigan Press, 1969). p. 5.
2. Sacvan Bercovitch, *The Puritan Origins of the American Self* (New Haven, Yale University Press, 1975).

ceptions and divergent ethical systems. Struggles for power and the oppression of the weak are a common result. If we had to choose between Thomas Hobbes's dark picture of mankind in the "state of nature" as against Rousseau's idyllic rendering, we should choose Hobbes. We are advised, therefore, not to approach the question with undue optimism. Only under unusual circumstances should we expect to find any widespread commitment to liberty in a social or political system wherein there were various subgroups with contrasting beliefs and mores.

Yet it is a fact that in England to a degree, and in America to a far greater degree, diversity in religion and libertarian practice did come into existence more or less simultaneously and in a manner that was quite literally epoch-making, at least so far as Western civilization is concerned. Indeed this phenomenon occurred under circumstances so unusual and in a manner so dialectical that a repetition or recurrence of the process is not easily imagined. During the era of world-wide imperial conflict which beheld the flowering of American libertarianism the idea of a government dedicated to the democratic way of life was an exhilarating novelty.

Two hundred years later, however, the world's concern seems to have shifted — even in the truly free nations — toward problems of distributive justice, equality, resource conservation, ecology, and sheer human survival. There are vast multitudes throughout the world who truly and freely believe that the "libertarian era" was at best a way-station on the road to a better world. During this time of Bicentennial observance, therefore, we are somehow bound to ask how a country that has persistently proclaimed itself as God's New Israel came into an ideological legacy which in some ways reversed the dominant tendencies of Christendom.

The word of the Lord that comes to us through the Hebrew Scriptures is the most uncompromising of the major world religions. The Lord God of Israel is a jealous God, visiting his wrath unto successive generations of those who turn to other gods or who follow not his commandments. Long before the emergence of Christianity, the Hellenizing successors of Alexander the Great felt the force of Israel's austere monotheism, its detestation of polytheistic or syncretistic religion, and its relentless accent on the urgency of time's inexorably linear movement from Creation to Consummation — and perhaps above all its convenantal conception of Holy peoplehood, its sense of being God's Chosen People and a holy nation (Exodus 19:6).

Yet it was not Israel itself that would finally conquer and transform Classical civilization, but the Christian Church, which explicitly identified itself as the New Israel.[3] In New Testament times, of course, the church was a persecuted pilgrim community; but with a rapidity that was often regarded as miraculous Christianity conquered the empire. By A.D. 325 the emperor Constantine had no other recourse than to rule the empire as a Christian and to guide the church to a settlement of its doctrinal controversies. Before another century had passed, the emperor Theodosius had closed the pagan temples and made Christianity the religion of the empire. Except for elements of Graeco-Roman or other then flourishing "Eastern" religions which were absorbed and perpetuated in the Roman Catholic Church, the celebrated religious diversity of the Roman empire was stamped out.

Then followed the great medieval millennium — say from Alaric's sack of Rome in the fifth century to the Reformation's repudiation of the Roman Catholic Pontifex Maximus in the sixteenth century. During this long period of Catholic Universalism the old tendency to syncretistic accommodation continued. Most important, perhaps, was the degree to which Neo-Platonic and gnostic forms of otherworldliness were sustained and institutionalized. In this context many diverse sorts of Christian expression arose; yet a vigorous concern for heresy also remained. Many inquisitions and crusades were launched against heretical offenders.

With the disruption of papal religious hegemony and the emergence of various sharply defined Protestant and Catholic churches the accent on orthodoxy and heresy also increased. With the gradual decay of feudal structures and the rise of more absolutistic forms of monarchy, the pressures for strict orthodoxy grew stronger. An age of religious wars ensued, some of them between Catholic and Protestant powers, others as civil wars. Among Protestant kingdoms, however, it was England which endured the longest and most turbulent struggle to determine what form its Protestantism would take. Amid drastic alternations of circumstance eight monarchs and a lord protector strove for a settlement — and two kings lost their thrones. Yet oddly enough, it was out of this long travail that libertarian theory and praxis first emerged — in a context of extreme religious diversity. This experience, moreover, is closely linked with various American developments. In both cases these

---

3. See especially I Peter, 2:1-10.

complex processes are intimately related to the emergence of increasingly radical forms of Puritanism.

Puritanism has become the more or less established name for the religious movement which arose in England among those committed Protestants, many of them returned exiles from Queen Mary's oppressive regime, who sought to bring the English church and people into accord with the Reformed or "Calvinistic" system of doctrine set forth in the Forty-Two Articles of Religion first promulgated under Edward VI (1547–1553) and then repromulgated as the Thirty-Nine Articles after the accession of Queen Elizabeth (1558–1603). Because it was a time when the threat of the Catholic Counter-Reformation was at a maximum, the movement's prime conviction was its identification of the Roman Church as the Anti-Christ. Almost as strong was its insistence that in the providence of God it was now England's assigned role to be the palladium of evangelical truth in a war-torn world where the Protestant cause was at bay. An essential corollary of this stance was an abhorrence of all policies, beliefs, and practices associated with the Church of Rome, and therefore, of many traditional features of English church order and popular behavior. Very early this led to demands for eliminating popish vestments, ornaments, ceremonies, and even the fundamental hierarchical structure of a national church, of which the sovereign was supreme head or governor.

In the correction of popish errors Puritans were determined to provide sound Biblical grounds, but in carrying out such a program of reform they discovered that consensus as to the precise meaning of God's word in scripture was not easily gained. Consequently a wide range of sectarian sub-division began to occur. In due time, therefore, England became more Protestant, but the price was an increase of controversy and strife which opened the way for Voltaire's latter-day observation that England was a land of a hundred religions, but, alas, of only one sauce.[4] This process of sectarian sub-division probably reached its most rampant stage during the Cromwellian period, especially in the New Model Army; but before dealing with that revolutionary period we must take account of a culminating development in the formation of the Puritan spirit.

---

4. Puritan strictures against extravagance and self-indulgence may also have contributed to the dearth of sauces.

The crucial phase of Puritan development can be located during the later years of Elizabeth's reign when the intensely felt religious needs of earnest laity, Puritan pastors, and several leading theologians led to increasing concern regarding the nature of justification by faith and the grounds for Christian assurance in the light of the classic Reformed doctrine that everything in this world and the next is under the absolute sovereignty of God.[5] This is, of course, a grand and somber view of the divine order. It was also a comfortable doctrine in that it took people out of the constant uncertainties of a complex penitential system and turned them to the tasks of life in this world.[6] Yet it also created problems. If nothing in the world happens by chance, and if every autumn leaf falls to its appointed place, and more importantly, if God did before all worlds decree who would and would not be called in due time to his eternal glory, then how do I know whether I am included among the saints of God? Here, indeed, is an existentially relevant question: How do I know if or when God has called me unto salvation?

To deal with these momentous questions was to recur to the fundamental issues around which the writings of St. Paul whirl, and with which Augustine, Luther, and Calvin had wrestled. Now in a new context, amid urgent social and political tensions, it arose again. What are the essential marks of a Christian? Then out of the discussions and debates between Puritan and Episcopal theologians (most of them from Cambridge University), there emerged what can be called the classical Puritan answer — an answer which without any modish stretching of the term can be seen as a veritable revolution in Christendom. It was set forth with power during the 1590's by William Perkins and then developed further by William Ames, Richard Sibbes, John Cotton, and many others during the tension-filled reigns of James I and Charles I, reaching its culmination, perhaps, during the days of Cromwell.

Even after the Restoration, however, this form of piety received further deepening in the preaching and writings of Richard Baxter, John Bunyan, George Fox, and countless others. What emerged from all of this was a new kind of pastoral counsel which moved toward the view that the only sure way in which God's effectual

---

5. The "Calvinistic" character of England's Articles of Religion is often not fully appreciated. In order to placate Puritans even the conformity-minded Archbishop Whitgift in 1595 supported the publication of the nine Lambeth Articles which made the predestinarian position even more explicit.

6. Even Ralph Waldo Emerson in his essay, "Fate," comments on the profundity of this view: "The foresight that awaits/Is the same Genius that creates."

call could be known, the only route to assurance, was an inward experience of God's redeeming grace, or through what later generations would call a conversion experience.

This may seem to many an innocent and pious resolution — especially if seen through the gentility of a Billy Graham revival; but in seventeenth-century England these new doctrines intensified the already serious questions that were arising with regard to the admission, disciplining, and excommunication of church members, as well as questions pertaining to the access of merely professing Christians to the sacraments, especially the Lord's Supper. More ominous still was the growing desire among many for a church consisting only of "visible saints," and therefore strong opposition to the commitment of the Established Church to the indiscriminate baptism of infants — and hence to the very idea of a comprehensive national church. In fact, to adopt these spiritual views was to repudiate a tradition that dated back to the early Middle Ages, a tradition, moreover, that the magisterial forms of Protestantism (Lutheran Reformed and Anglican) had more or less maintained. In this sense strenuous Puritans were probably correct in seeing the accomplishment of such reforms as spelling the end of the Constantinian apostasy of the Church and the restoration of the New Testament Christianity.

Most radical of all was the way in which the cumulative effect of this new conception of faith and assurance was the steady proliferation of conversions that met these rigorous standards of piety and which summoned converts to a new and austere mode of personal behavior. What gradually came into existence was a large Puritan constituency that included the likes of the lord protector Oliver Cromwell, not to mention the founders of several commonwealths in the New World. Because conversion committed individuals to a new counter-cultural mode of living and acting in this world, the new Puritan constituency was also marked by a deep-going transformation of values and morals. Individualism in religion led inexorably to its corollaries in the social, political, and economic realms. After 1640 this new constituency, with the aid of various allies, would bring down the old monarchical order of England.

Still another revolutionary dimension of these developments in Puritan piety has to do with the way in which the acceptance of an inward warrant of God's effectual call opens the road to subjectivism in matters of religion and hence to the rise of modern religious ideas and the subversion of orthodox dogmatism. More directly pertinent to the present essay, however, are the ways in which this subjective principle leads directly to the emergence of a broader view of Christian fellowship which tends, in turn, to mitigate the impact of sectarian division. Indeed, it was the Puritan emphasis on conversion that opened the way to modern "denominationalism."

The essence of denominationalism is the recognition of an over-arching unity-in-the-spirit of persons who agree to disagree on other less essential doctrines. And one can concur with Winthrop Hudson that its "real architects . . . were those seventeenth century Independent divines . . . whose most prominent representatives were the Dissenting Brethren in the Westminster Assembly," who though disagreeing in part with the Assembly's Confession of Faith did not deny their opponents the name of Christian.[7] In a more thoughtful, but also more radical manner of interpretation, this line of thought also brought Roger Williams to the institu-tionalization of religious freedom in Rhode Island. More celebrated still was the religious freedom granted under Cromwell. Even in the Massachusetts Bay Colony, despite official counsels to the contrary, one finds many similar tendencies.[8] In 1691 Increase Mather, while in England, arranged an accord between Congrega-tionalists and Presbyterians, while his son Cotton, in a famous gesture of fellowship in 1718 even participated in a Baptist ordination service in Boston. Then during the great evangelical awakenings of the eighteenth century in both America and Great Britain this new attitude became a commonplace of church practice, finally even overleaping the walls that separated "Calvinists" and "Arminians." Indeed it is John Wesley's declaration of fellowship with all "real Christians" who fear and love God that becomes the classic statement of the denominational idea. By this time the same spirit had also made much headway among the pietists on the Continent, whence many immigrant groups brought it to America, most notably in the person of Count Zinzendorf.[9] With these passing references to American events, however, it becomes appropriate to shift our focus entirely to the New World.

---

7. Winthrop S. Hudson, *American Protestantism* (Chicago, University of Chicago Press, 1961), pp. 33-48.
8. See E. Brooks Holifield, "On Toleration in Massachusetts," *Church History* 36, 2 (June, 1969).
9. On the links between English Puritanism and Continental Pietism, see E. Ernest Stoeffler, *The Rise of Evangelical Pietism* (Leiden, E. J. Brill, 1971).

The oft-told story of England's colony-founding on the North American continent need not be recounted yet again in this essay, but one must emphasize that the Puritan impulse was decisively planted on this far shore by means of a series of firmly led intentional communities and then continued by the migration of many like-minded people. The first of these colonies, to be sure, was flawed from the start by the pecuniary interests of its stockholders, the nondescript settlers they recruited, its early commitment to black chattel slavery, and the rise of a far-flung plantation system. Nothing much better can be said of the proprietors or royal governors of the other southern colonies, for they also encouraged the rise of a paternalistic, slave-holding society. Unlike Virginia, however, they did allow the free exercise of religion to all who came.

It was thus in New England, first at Plymouth and then in a half dozen other areas, that the most cohesive, theologically informed, and thoughtfully governed commonwealths came into existence. On the other hand, it was the Quaker, William Penn, who toward the century's end projected the last great venture in Puritan statecraft; and his Holy Experiment rapidly became the pluralistic paradigm of the future United States.

Before long, however, even Pennsylvania lost its distinctiveness as migration from Britain and the Continent as well as intercolonial migration began to transform the entire area of British settlement. The process was undramatic in the extreme: New Englanders pushing their frontiers westward and to the north, or founding towns in New Jersey; Quakers and Baptists drifting south to the Carolinas; Germans of various religious persuasions and Scotch-Irish moving west in Pennsylvania or down into the southern back-country. Nearly all of these people, moreover, were consciously or unconsciously participating in the creation of a new kind of social order. The king was far away; local authority was weak. People were acquiring land, becoming merchants, founding churches as they pleased, and participating in local or commonwealth politics according to their highly various desires. When the Glorious Revolution erupted in England, many of these Americans participated in disturbances in each of the American colonies — and in the process became more concerned about gaining more secure guarantees of the liberties they were enjoying.

What this steady, seemingly nondescript process accomplished was historically momentous. These common people were creating a social order such as the world had never before seen. It was not only unique, but revolutionary. In leading their routine lives on farms, in villages, and in small but growing cities, these Americans were constituting themselves as the social vanguard of Western civilization. Karl Marx would refer to their accomplishment as the bourgeois revolution. And as their numbers increased, they would be able to resist even the most strenuous efforts of the British government to limit their freedoms. Eventually even the slave system would be seen as an unacceptable contradiction of their ideals. Only when their anti-Catholicism, their xenophobia, or their racism was aroused, would they seriously compromise their libertarian set of mind.[10]

Then during the 1730's and 1740's this inchoate and slumbering but broadly Reformed and Puritan population was to a considerable degree awakened by a "great and general revival" which swept through the colonies from Georgia to New Hampshire, with George Whitefield as its chief exciting agent and Jonathan Edwards as its leading American exponent. What that great spiritual convulsion did was to reinvigorate every Puritan conviction and prejudice and bring into being a selfconscious and intercolonial evangelical constituency which would challenge the standing order of the churches wherever they existed. Before long they would reduce religious establishments to a shambles. The Baptists would emerge as major bearers of the Puritan tradition, though they were soon to be challenged by the Methodist movement which even then was rising in Britain. Religiously speaking, something new had entered into history.

Only against this background can we understand the astounding judgment of Isaac Watts, the learned and cosmopolitan leader of English dissent, when he first heard the details of the little frontier revival that had surprised the ministry of Jonathan Edwards in the town of Northampton. Watts declared that "we have not heard of anything like it since the Reformation, nor perhaps since the days of the apostles."[11] The odd thing is that Watts's statement is not

---

10. Supporting this delineation of a bourgeois revolution is a vast theoretical and historical literature that has been stimulated above all by Karl Marx and Max Weber. Selected major works are listed in sections 5, 16, and 17 of the bibliography in my *A Religious History of the American People* (New Haven, Yale University Press, 1972; New York, Doubleday-Image edition, 2 v., 1975).

11. Clarence C. Goen, ed., *The Works of Jonathan Edwards: The Great Awakening* (New Haven, Yale University Press, 1972), p. 36 (on Watts), pp. 353-358 (on Edwards's millennial expectations).

wildly extravagant: the Great Awakening was indeed a sign of spiritual vitality that could easily be interpreted as a momentous sign of God's providence. When Edwards himself declared that he saw in these marvelous events the signs of the coming of the Kingdom of God in America, he was saying more than he knew. Least of all could he appreciate the positive effect of the revivals on the national selfconsciousness of the American people — and hence on the rise of the revolutionary spirit.

Within a year after Edwards's death British victories would have won the transfer of New France and the Spanish Floridas to Protestant rule of England — a blow to the Anti-Christ that would have loomed almost as large in Edwards's mind as the Reformation itself. A quarter-century later his grandson, Timothy Dwight, would be writing an anthem to the glory of a new republic that was "the last of time."[12] A quarter-century after that his son Jonathan would be joining Dwight in the joys of a Second Great Awakening. By that time the notion of the United States as God's New Israel had become a settled element of the nation's patriotic piety. The Founding Fathers who in the providence of God had, as it were, given this new society the full political equipment of a sovereign nation, were entering into legend and hagiography. Now, two hundred years later, not even the most cynical observer can deny that the revolutionary generation of leaders did an enduring work that made libertarian principle the foundation stone of their deed.

The federal constitution, the bill of rights, and particularly the first amendment, were by no means simply pragmatic concessions to the pluralism of the American religious situation. One must also concede that the "Enlightened" assumptions of many of those who guided national affairs during the revolutionary era are reflected in the great deeds and documents of the age, perhaps especially in the realm of political and constitutional theory. It is by no means coincidental, moreover, that Adam Smith's *Wealth of Nations* was published in 1776. The basic fact nevertheless remains: the Declaration of Independence and the creation of a federal republic institutionalized and gave enduring form to a social revolution that had been profoundly inspired by the Puritan Revolution in England and by the gradual shaping of a new kind of social order

---

12. Dwight's paean to the nascent republic was written in 1777: "Columbia, Columbia, to glory rise,/The queen of the world, and child of the skies:/Thy reign is the last, and the noblest of time. . . ."

on the North American continent. One must agree with John Adams's settled conviction that the "real revolution" in America stemmed from the great Puritan migration and was chiefly constituted by a change in the feelings, sentiments, and affections of the people that had taken place long before the outbreak of military hostilities.[13] Underlying this change is a profound dialectic of Puritan piety and sectarian diversity that is part and parcel of the rise of libertarian ideals. We may say, in fact, that liberty and religious pluralism are two sides of the same ideological coin.

We must recognize, however, that this new libertarian coinage circulated freely only in a White, Protestant-dominated world. It failed to fill its function during that long period of tumultuous national growth when the population was swelled by the immigration of more than fifty million Europeans, and when the progeny of four million emancipated slaves became part of the body politic. During this entire period — if, indeed, not throughout our entire history — many Americans have felt the brunt of nativism, racism, and counter-subversionary pressures.[14] If we move into the realm where we count the poverty-stricken, the hungry, and the hopeless Americans, we discover that our libertarian coinage functions even less satisfactorily. These are the circumstances which lead Robert Bellah to speak of America's "Broken Covenant."[15]

In terms of the major theme before us, we are thus led quite inexorably to the view that, however inalienable a right, and however priceless a boon, and however historically achieved, the principle of liberty is not a social panacea or a sovereign good. It can lead to cruelty, oppression, and injustice. And in the United States it has. When libertarianism is further stimulated by the arrogant view that the American republic is an Elect Nation with a manifest providential destiny, oppression can easily be extended beyond our borders.

When Americans reflect on their past and evaluate their legacy,

13. Bernard Bailyn, *The Ideological Origins of the American Revolution* (Cambridge, Harvard University Press, 1967), pp. 19-21.

14. The long history of these shortcomings is surveyed in Ray A. Billington, *The Protestant Crusade* (New York, Macmillan Company, 1952); John Higham, *Strangers in the Land* (New Brunswick, Rutgers University Press, 1955); Edward D. Baltzell, *The Protestant Establishment* (New York, Random House, 1964); P. L. van den Berghe, *Race and Racism* (New York, John Wiley & Sons, 1967); David B. Davis, *The Fear of Conspiracy: Images of UnAmerican Subversion from the Revolution to the Present* (Ithaca, Cornell University Press, 1971).

15. Robert N. Bellah, *The Broken Covenant: American Civil Religion in Time of Trial* (New York, Seabury Press, 1975).

therefore, it is very important that they recognize that public tranquility cannot be assured and the general welfare cannot be provided for unless a lively dialectic of liberty and equality becomes the central reality of our social existence. On the other hand, if that double legacy were realized, the resentment, alienation, and cynicism that haunts our national life would be vastly reduced. If the seeking of justice became our first concern, Jefferson's and Lincoln's vision of this republic as the last best hope for the world would not be so remote from our everyday life together.

SYDNEY E. AHLSTROM
Professor of American History
and Modern Religious History,
Yale University

The Efforts of William Penn to Lay a Foundation for Future Ages

T HE RISE AND FALL of ancient and modern republics present many problems for narrator and analyst. The balance of environment and period, design and fortuitous circumstance, of external and internal forces, seems impossible to determine with any certainty. Mysteries about change, causation, and motive remain. Some persons, situations, and inventions undoubtedly have affected succeeding generations and occurrences, others seem rather to have anticipated, than directly to have influenced, the future.

Early settlers in North America were laying a foundation primarily for their own, their families' and associates' good. Few foresaw society as it developed in these United States. The majority crossing the Atlantic, if not carrying out official duties, seeking a perhaps temporary refuge from threatening conditions at home, or earning a livelihood by choice or force as indentured servants or slaves, planned a new and better life. William Penn, already involved in New World experiment, sought the Proprietary in order to create overseas a province where people could worship freely, live according to just and merciful laws, and improve their material well-being. By the grant of Pennsylvania, Penn hoped to provide for his own family. He was laying a foundation for freedom as he understood it, offering at once a scheme for better relations and a fairer distribution of imperial obligations between settlements; he probably never conceived of a time when colonies, singly or united, would be independent of the British Empire. Yet much of his accomplishment suggests a foretaste of what was to eventuate.

In the lives and thoughts of members of the Society of Friends, Penn's outstanding prestige, along with that of George Fox and Robert Barclay, is undisputed, and will not be discussed save peripherally. Theological writings were studied. Quakers interested themselves in the republication of individual and collected Quaker memoirs, history, homilies, and maxims. This, and the general curiosity aroused by the Society from its early beginnings, though often interwoven with Penn's posthumous repute, form a separate topic. As the years went by, and until, as we all know, Benjamin Franklin absorbed much of Europe's attention, William Penn and Pennsylvania very nearly monopolized eighteenth-century commentary on British America. Only in 1826 did Philadelphia celebrate the landing of 1682 on the shores of the Delaware. A Russian guest paying tribute, pointed out that the colony was the only one to bear its founder's name.[1] Americans might be slow to recognize achievement, but others had long been fascinated by the reported freedom, riches, and growth of the Quaker state, what Penn did, or wanted to do. The ambience, or significant circumstance he created, was seldom discussed during the revolutionary years, but has relevance in any study of the emergence of the Republic, and of the image it came to present to the world.

During his lifetime, Penn was at once notorious as the rich man's son turned fanatic, and as the consummate courtier politician. Repeated incarceration and harassment for nonconformity, provoking determined arguments in his own and his fellows' behalf, made him well known during the reign of Charles II. Yet before the Merry Monarch died, he had granted the Charter of March, 1681. During the brief rule of James II, the Quaker's influence with the king was sufficiently obvious to make life after the Revolution of 1688 and the royal flight into exile precarious and uncomfortable. Yet again Penn survived; regained, after temporary deprivation, his rich province, and moreover, held onto it during serious attempts at Westminster to substitute royal for proprietary authority. Even imprisonment for debt did not entirely abolish his effectiveness with England's ministers of state. Only ill health in the brief years following release from confinement, just as the successful sale of a colony with which he was disillusioned was being negotiated, ended Penn's extraordinary performance.

This ability to manipulate affairs in his native land makes all the more surprising the fact that in Pennsylvania, during brief visits and long absences, Penn's wishes were constantly ignored or thwarted by those he had expected to be grateful and generous. Penn was a visionary, deeply steeped in much of the most enlightened thought of his day, but he was a poor administrator.

---

1. Zachariah Poulson, *American Daily Advertiser* **55** no. 55568 (Philadelphia, 28 October, 1826): p. 2.

The first Frames of Government — omitting here those earlier, tentative drafts — incorporated ever decreasingly their originator's ideas. They were, in turn, finally replaced by the Charter of Privileges of 1701, reluctantly agreed to by the Proprietor on the eve of his final departure. By this Pennsylvania was to be governed until 1776. Many of Penn's expedients were dropped. Much of that executive initiative he had wished to retain diminished, though to be sure certain dues, quit-rents, exemptions from estate taxes, and rights of appointment to office remained, and did little to promote good relations between the Penns and their colony.

Until 1754 the Assembly was controlled by conservative Quakers during a period called by Thomas Clarkson, over-optimistically, a "Golden Age."[2] Pennsylvania politics, in spite of occasional years of comparative calm, were acrimonious. Little attention was paid to the grievances of newer communities as population increased, became more varied, and spread over a much larger area. Need for representational changes had been foreseen as early as the Frame of 1683, but the Assembly was loath to weaken its power. Up to, and during the critical years, faction proliferated: even Quakers differed among themselves. Bad blood developed between distant regions and the ruling coteries around Philadelphia; in that city the various elements of its society were often at odds. These bitter partisan disputes had, as often noticed, important consequences. Internal preoccupations and jealousies, as well as the religious scruples of the Friends, and the expectable reluctance of wealthy citizens to incur the risks of military involvement, were to be responsible for the comparatively minor and delayed part taken by Pennsylvania in the activities of the sixties and seventies. The role, indeed, that can be found, was largely that of a small knot of men — immigrants like Benjamin Franklin, James Wilson, and Charles Thomson — though others like Benjamin Rush and John Dickinson must always be remembered.[3] The apparent neglect of Penn by the Founding Fathers is surely due to the complexity of the political scene within the colony, as well as to the form which his contribution had earlier taken.

Penn lived in an age of seminal political writing. Speculations of all kinds were published. The return of the Stuarts in 1660 ended for the time being experiments in government, but did not

---

2. Thomas Clarkson, *Memoirs of the Private and Public Life of William Penn* (2 v., Dover, N. H., 1820), p. 172.

3. See list of works on Pennsylvania politics appended to this article.

inhibit the production of major works like those of John Locke and Algernon Sidney, of their lesser near contemporaries like Henry Neville, Walter Moyle, John Somers, and John Trenchard, and of many tracts, thereafter frequently cited on both sides of the Atlantic, by the first earl of Shaftesbury, Andrew Marvell and others. To this literature Penn added nothing comparable in popular appeal. Reports of the trial in 1670 of Penn and William Mead for preaching in Gracechurch Street were freely circulated and widely known. The accused had defended their rights as Englishmen, the freedom lawfully accorded the jury, and had quoted appropriate legal authorities. Eventually, in spite of the judge's attempts to intimidate the twelve men, their verdict of not guilty was upheld by Chief Justice John Vaughan, and was to be regarded as a landmark in developing English liberties. *An Historical Review of the Constitution and Government of Pennsylvania,* published in London in 1759, otherwise very critical of the proprietor, was to praise Penn's interpretation of Magna Carta, and *England's Ancient and Just Liberties,* as one account of the trial was called.[4] Possibly Franklin himself had read the Great Charter in the copy said to have been deposited in the colonial archives by Penn. He may even have read the commentary on it and other statutes in *The Excellent Priviledge of Liberty and Property* brought out in 1687 by William Bradford at Penn's behest, if we may believe David Lloyd's statement in 1728. If Penn was also responsible for an earlier compilation published in London in about 1681, whose first forty pages are almost the same as the first part of *The Excellent Priviledge,* then he had a share at the beginning of a convenient compendium of constitutional material. This, in its many and often enlarged versions, enjoyed an extensive circulation in both England and America up to the Revolution. *England's Liberties* [later *British*] *Or the Free-born Subject's Inheritance* was often attributed to a Quaker, Henry Care, before others took it over in later editions. Winthrop S. Hudson has examined the possibility that Penn was responsible for initiating the series, which was to afford apt quotation for orator and polemist, too busy to search dusty law books.[5]

---

4. *An Historical Review of the History of the Constitution and Government of Pennsylvania* was reprinted by Jared Sparks in *The Works of Benjamin Franklin* 3 (Philadelphia, 1840): pp. 116-531; reference to Magna Carta, p. 157; Carl Van Doren, *Benjamin Franklin and Richard Jackson* (New York, 1945) discusses the work in relation to anti-proprietary activities.

5. Winthrop S. Hudson, "William Penn's *English Liberties:* Tract for Several Times." *William and Mary Quart.* 3rd ser., **26** (1969): pp. 578-585.

With these possible exceptions — reports of the trial and parts of *England's Liberties* in which his share is at least uncertain — Penn's political pamphlets found comparatively few readers. *The Great Case of Liberty of Conscience* (London, 1670), was twice reprinted in that year. *England's Present Interest* (London, 1675), went into five editions and a couple of reprintings by 1702. Tracts written to support candidates for Parliament, who, if elected in 1679, could be trusted to seek relief for dissenters, and addresses to Protestants and against Popery, were by their nature, ephemeral, if sometimes eloquently phrased. A two-folio volume collection of *Works* came from a Quaker press in 1726. Selections from it, discarding matter that had become untimely, were republished in London in 1771, 1782, 1825. American reprints of any kind but theological items before 1776 cannot be traced.[6] Penn's political philosophy must in great part be derived from inspection of documents connected with the establishment of Pennsylvania. Celebrity was the result of the colony's success.

Not surprisingly then Penn was, as noted, seldom cited during the discussions of the last quarter of the eighteenth century. Allusions to him are almost non-existent. Of course, he was not a revolutionary; he was the friend of kings, and himself of aristocratical proclivities. Unlike Locke and Sidney, Moyle and Trenchard, he provided no phrases appropriate to speeches urging resistance to tyranny. Even Quakers, arrested in 1777, and suspected of Tory sympathies, quoted in their own defense, not Penn, but Charles Secondat, Baron de Montesquieu.[7] Yet one of those exiled in Virginia without proper trial, James Pemberton, owned a copy of the *Selected Works* of 1771 sent him not long before by Dr. John Fothergill of London.[8] Nor could Penn's authority be used to support separation. By the time independence was in the air, Americans, long increasingly aware of their own identity, as Carl Bridenbaugh has so eloquently shown us, were ceasing to

---

6. Edwin B. Bronner of Haverford College Library is preparing a bibliography of Penn's works to which I have kindly been allowed access.

7. *An Address to the Inhabitants of Pennsylvania of these Freemen of the City of Philadelphia who are now confined . . .* (Philadelphia, 1777), unnumbered page following title, quotation from *The Spirit of the Laws,* Book XI, c. vi; I am indebted to Edwin B. Bronner for this reference.

8. Betsy C. Corner and Christopher C. Booth, *Chain of Friendship, Selected Letters of Dr. John Fothergill* (Cambridge, Mass., 1971), p. 331.

stress status as Englishmen.[9] Penn's role in the history of the appearance of the United States is complex and indirect. I used the word ambience earlier. Through his colony Penn created an environment, and made familiar certain conceptions often later associated with America. Others of the thirteen colonies contributed a quota of distinctive republicanism, a demonstration of democratic government, an activist opposition to British policies, and of men of decision in times of crisis. With Penn, long dead, the case is different; in his works are to be found suggestions afterwards adopted without acknowledgment, and possibly even knowledge of their existence.

Scholars have often examined the encomiums awarded by Frenchmen and others to Founder and Province — praise focused less upon what the Proprietor said or wrote, than upon the privileges and wealth enjoyed by the settlers. Voltaire lauded wise legislation. Montesquieu dubbed Penn a modern Lycurgus, an epithet often used thereafter.[10] The Abbé Raynal spread the fame of the Holy Experiment far and wide, while another abbé, Mably, struck a more critical note in finding Penn's system useless, since it could scarcely survive without external protection.[11] Crèvecœur, who had, unlike most other foreign commentators, visited the province, also extolled the good laws of that "simple but illustrious citizen."[12] Edmund Burke, disdainful of the moral and divine works, declared that all mankind should honor the legislator.[13] John Adams reflected upon Penn's avarice for land.[14] Franklin, like Dr. Benjamin Rush, admired the Founder much more than his descendents, was well acquainted with his laws, belief in liberty of conscience, and good treatment of the Indians. Franklin, however, did not discourage Richard Jackson's disparagements in *An Historical Review,* which, on account of its anti-proprietary tone,

---

9. Carl Bridenbaugh, *The Spirit of '76* (New York, 1975), *passim.*

10. Edith Philips, *The Good Quaker in French Legend* (Philadelphia, 1932), *passim* for material on these and many others especially pp. 91-132.

11. John H. M. Salmon, "The Abbé Raynal, 1713-1796," *History Today* 26 (1976): pp. 109-117; Professor Salmon also gave me the reference to *Oeuvres complètes de l'Abbé de Mably* (Lyons, 1796) 9: pp. 87-89.

12. J. Hector St. John de Crèvecœur, *Letters from an American Farmer* (London, 1793; edition used, London, 1904), p. 182.

13. Edmund Burke, *An Account of the European Settlements in America* (London, 1757) 2: p. 189.

14. Zoltain Haraszti, *John Adams and the Prophets of Progress* (Cambridge, Mass. 1952), pp. 131, 133.

was often attributed to his rather than the Englishman's pen.[15] Only it seems when Philadelphia was preparing for a celebration of the landing, already mentioned, were tributes from founding fathers, sought by the city authorities, forthcoming. James Madison accepted membership in the Society for the Commemoration of the Landing of William Penn then being established, and referred to Penn as lawgiver and philanthropist. Thomas Jefferson, approached before his death, congratulated the community on the creation of an annual festival in Penn's honor, and declared the Quaker the greatest lawgiver mankind had ever seen.[16]

Failure to produce popular or important political treatises, and contradictions and vicissitudes in private life, do not of course diminish the effect of a demonstrably thriving Pennsylvania. Penn's efforts for good government, concern for just laws, determination to encourage economic progress and a population large enough to promote it, are part of the history of the Commonwealth. His fundamentals were threefold: people should be governed only by laws to which they had assented; all should share in the juridical process—that is should serve on juries, and, if accused, be judged by a jury of the neighborhood; conscience should be free, diversity rather than uniformity strengthened the state. Penn also outlined tentative plans for federal organization. He declared that he had no preference for any particular model of government, and knew none that time, place and "singular emergency" might not alter. There must be a rule of law. Good citizens were essential to public welfare. People must be secured from the abuse of power. Only with that security could they attain the agreed end of all government, happiness and prosperity.

Penn's first Frame provided for a bicameral legislature consisting of elected assembly and council. Voting was to be by ballot and office was to rotate. These provisions were swept aside in 1701, and a single chamber was established, the only one in the colonies. Though the Proprietor kept some power, he was obliged to give up much that he had wanted. The Charter afforded the possibility, especially at the beginning, for a good colonial government, but this was in large part due to the liberty of conscience secured, and

---

15. *The Papers of Benjamin Franklin,* edited by Leonard Laboree *et al.* 6 (New Haven, 1963): pp. 301-303; 8 (1965): p. 266 and *passim; Autobiography of Benjamin Rush,* edited by George W. Corner, Memoirs Amer. Philos. Soc. 25 (1948): p. 285; *Letters of Benjamin Rush,* edited by Lyman H. Butterfield, Memoirs Amer. Philos. Soc. 30 (2 v., 1951): pp. 1046-1047, 1089.

16. See note 1 above.

the excellent laws drawn up by the Founder, and although somewhat amended, still as enlightened as any in contemporary America. Situation and policy combined to encourage the economy.[17]

As a young man Penn studied at the Inns of Court. He was familiar with the protection he and many of his contemporaries believed English law, if properly observed, should afford. When he obtained the Charter in 1681, he drew up, besides concessions intended to encourage colonists, laws under which they would live. In December, 1682, at Upland, or Chester, his Great Code, longer than the laws agreed upon in England, was approved, and, during the following spring, revised and amended. As the years went by many further changes were made. Punishments became less lenient after 1718; the requirements for oaths and affirmations were modified. Locations and jurisdictions of local courts were altered. Though they could still worship as they pleased, Catholics were excluded from office after 1705. There are some studies of crime and punishment in Pennsylvania, but there is a good deal still to be learned about Penn's Great Code. Penn was undoubtedly aware of contemporary discussions of law reform; detailed scrutiny might yield interesting results. Nor is much known of the effect, if any, of his innovations upon the reformers in late eighteenth-century Pennsylvania, even if their debt to Cesare Beccaria and John Howard has been investigated. The first volume of the Pennsylvania *Statutes at Large* has still to be published, though a couple of nineteenth-century versions of laws and charters, 1681–1700, exist. Laws were published in Penn's lifetime and thereafter as the Assembly directed — the folio collection printed by Franklin in 1742 being perhaps the best known. The inhabitants of Pennsylvania and other English-speaking areas could study colonial law; but it is difficult to find out whether all those continental observers studied Penn's legislative contribution, or based their judgments on reports at large.[18] That the much-praised

---

17. *Charters and Laws of Pennsylvania, 1682-1700,* edited by Staughton George, *et al.* (Harrisburg, 1879), pp.81-90; The Charter, pp. 91-99, The Frame, pp. 99-103. The Laws agreed on in England, and also second and third Frames. For the Charter of 1701 a convenient source is in *Remember William Penn* (Harrisburg, 1944), pp. 98-103.

18. Two useful articles: Herbert William Keith Fitzroy, "Crime and Punishment in Pennsylvania," *Penn. Mag. History and Biography* 60 (1936): pp. 242-269; Gail McKnight Beckman, "Three Penal Codes Compared," *Amer. Jour. Legal History* 10 (1966): pp. 148-173; Herbert Levi Osgood, *The American Colonies in the Seventeenth Century* (3 v., New York, 1904) 2: pp. 277-308 useful on the courts.

legislator would have been horrified at the transformation of his work by 1783 is certain.

Penn wished to ensure that the due process traditionally asserted in the Great Charter of 1215, enlarged and confirmed in later enactments, should be available to all inhabitants of Pennsylvania. He had himself continually been deprived of those rights he declared to be those of all Englishmen. How much in his Code was prompted by the well-known English belief in the excellence of their laws, how much by the suggestions of reformers during his lifetime, and by the principles of the Society of Friends is difficult to say. Personal experience in court and prison undoubtedly enforced his pronouncements.

In the province, justice was to be open, speedy, and the proceedings in English. Charges were to be stated. Sufficient witnesses were to be called, copies of indictments made available to the accused. Verdict, of course, would be by the jury. Not only were punishments more merciful than in England, but prisons were free, and, a new note perhaps, reformation of the criminal was to be attempted. Procedure in many matters — marriage, inheritance, and so on, was to be simpler. Reasonable treatment of debtors, and of the property rights of the families of suicides and the condemned was provided for. Registers of vital statistics should be kept. The New World and almost palatine privileges allowed Penn to decree certain long-desired improvements in the English system. Also of course, Puritan prejudices with respect to taverns, Sunday observance, "uncleaness" in moral and social behavior, dictated some prohibitions and limitations. Fame as a legislator was deserved, but should possibly rest today upon more detailed scrutiny, than upon reports at large as in the years after the establishment of Pennsylvania.[19]

Penn recognized that forms of government and laws inevitably changed, but he never admitted that anything short of liberty of conscience could be allowed. He inserted in the Charter of 1701, so much of which was not of his devising, phrasing almost the same as in earlier frames and laws, the guarantee of religious liberty. In spite of disputes and bad feeling between the growing variety of denominations, as the original Quaker majority shrank to less

---

19. Staughton George, as in note 17, pp. 107-155, The Great Code as delivered 7 December, 1682, and amended 10 March, 1683; George has historical notes in an appendix pp. 472-482 discussing failure to print the code, the titles of its chapters, etc.

than a third of the population, the colonists continued to affirm their faiths without serious persecution. That such liberty existed was more important than any theory developed in Penn's writings. The late Henry Cadbury could discover nothing original in the Founder's thought, derived in part from the convictions of the Society of Friends, and in part from arguments being put forward by others.[20] Penn's friend George Villiers, second duke of Buckingham, in a speech to the House of Lords in 1675, declared that dissenters should be relieved of penalties, since conscience was involved in an Englishman's property or propriety in his person, a thing he was known to value most highly.[21] When Thomas Jefferson was promoting the cause of religious liberty in Virginia he did not refer to Penn, but remarked on the absence of disturbances in those settlements lacking established churches.[22] In a rather different vein, critics of the new constitution of Pennsylvania in 1776 noticed favorably that the Founder had restricted office to Christians, while, under the new order, they feared rule by Deists, Mohammedans, and Jews.[23]

Economic progress in the Delaware valley astonished observers, and is surprising to the student of Penn's incompetent, even disastrous, management of his personal finances. Losses were never in his lifetime compensated for by profits from the colony. Yet he showed imagination and acumen in decisions for city and province. The good fortune the colony experienced was by no means entirely due to the settlement of an exceptionally fertile region. Penn fought the claims of Lord Baltimore lest they should effect any diminution in the advantages enjoyed by Philadelphia's excellent geographic situation; and pushed forward enlightened and innovative urban planning. Men were land-hungry; Penn knew it and skillfully promoted purchase on attractive terms, doing all that he could to attract men who would generate and expand trade. The privileges granted the Free Society of Traders, incorporated into the early laws, though they did not result precisely as expected, reveal Penn's awareness of the need for conscious encouragement of investment and enterprise. A wide acquaintance among the

20. Henry Joel Cadbury, "Persecution and Religious Liberty," *Penna. Mag. History and Biography* 68 (1944): pp. 359-371.

21. *State Tracts . . . printed in the reign of Charles II* (London, 1689), p. 62.

22. Thomas Jefferson, *Notes on the State of Virginia,* edited by William Peden (Chapel Hill, 1955), pp. 160-161.

23. J. Paul Selsam, *The Pennsylvania Constitution of 1776* (Philadelphia, 1936), p. 218.

well-to-do merchants of London, Bristol, and elsewhere, was employed to further these objectives. Moreover, though taxation was never to be imposed without the consent of a majority of the legislators, its exactions tended to favor the rich rather than the poorer ranks of society, and this was also true of the qualifications required for voting, liberal though these were by contemporary standards.[24]

Development not only demanded a judicious appraisal of possibilities, and the attraction to the colony of those capable of fulfilling them, it also needed a growing population. This Penn did his best to stimulate. Good relations with the Indians were brought about; he even learned a few words of their language the better to establish communications of a friendly kind. Few of the legends which surround his name are better attested, and Pennsylvania profited. The scattered inhabitants — English, Swedish, Finnish, and Dutch, already in the province in 1681 — were afforded easy naturalization, and the fair treatment being promised to newcomers. Many contacts made during earlier missionary tours in Western Europe were used to induce emigration. Quakers of course were welcomed, but so were other sects. Elsewhere in British North America, a mixture of peoples could be found, but no one individual as deliberately as Penn did more to encourage different nationalities to settle. In colonial times Pennsylvania was often singled out as an asylum for the oppressed. In the last two centuries millions have found a similar refuge in the United States.

Federalism as it emerged in America developed a form peculiar to a situation in which union seemed necessary. Penn formulated no theory of federal state or republic. He made two most interesting suggestions, for colonial union and a European diet, which seem to have been neglected by eighteenth-century Americans. While the Articles of Confederation of 1774–1782 included most of Penn's Brief Scheme of 1696,[25] neither its architects nor the earlier participants at Albany gave any evidence they knew his work.[26] While in retirement caused by government harassment, Penn wrote *An Essay towards the Present and Future Peace of Europe*, published in London in 1693, and twice reprinted before 1702. In

---

24. Selsam, as cited, pp. 32-33.

25. Merrill Jensen, *The Articles of Confederation, 1774-1781* (Wisconsin, paper, 1970), pp. 107-108.

26. Frederick B. Tolles and E. Gordon Alderfer, *The Witness of William Penn* (New York, 1957), p. 135; "A Plan of Union," follows, pp. 136-137.

this he planned a diet of European nations which would adjudicate disputes and prevent wars. This and his promotional *Account of the Province of Pennsylvania* published twice in differing versions in 1681 are his only writings to have a niche in the *Old South Leaflets* [nos. 75 and 171]. In 1696 Penn presented to the Lords of Trade and Plantations a scheme for the union of certain American colonies. By this, arrangements were to be made for meetings, presided over by a royal official, and to be held at intervals to allocate the raising of funds, to determine other measures for defense, as well as to seek peaceful resolution of problems arising between settlements. The plan inspired Charles Davenant to précis its contents and expand its theme in a work published in 1698. This in turn evoked two rebuttals in 1701, both concerned to condemn the idea that each colony, whatever its size and population, should count equally in decision-making. Once again Penn anticipated, if he did not directly influence, future operations.[27]

The most original aspect of Penn's political philosophy may be found in arguments for a balance of disparate elements in state or community. Others theorized on the matter in his day, but he had a chance to experiment practically. Differences, he wrote, to Henry Bennet, later Lord Arlington, in 1669, did not always make trouble; kingdoms containing a balance of parties had remained secure. Only civil disobedience, lack of industry, or disloyalty could justify correction.[28] Force created hypocrites; diversity could not be prevented or suppressed. No one group monopolized all the wisdom, wealth, numbers, sobriety, and resolution. Physicians varied medicine given according to the admixture of distempers. Divers languages, laws, customs, and religions did not result in mutiny among Italy's invaders. Hannibal's army, containing a variety of men, suffered fewer disturbances than the more uniform hosts of Rome. The conviction that absence of uniformity brought strength rather than confusion[29] lay behind Penn's emphasis on the rights of dissenters, of Indians, of people of different origins. He tried to provide in the province for their varied needs.

Historical sequence is complex. Ordinary circumstances and hidden forces accompany, or give rise to great events. Even extra-

---

27. Hampton L. Carson, *History of the Celebration . . . of the Promulgation of the Constitution . . .* (2 v., Philadelphia, 1889) **2**: pp. 449-460, Penn, Davenant & rebuttals.
28. William Penn, *Select Works* (London, 1771), pp. v-viii.
29. William Penn, *England's Present Interest* (London, 1675; edition used, 1698), pp. 98-101.

ordinary accomplishment cannot always be positively credited with later decisions. Many of the virtues associated with the Quaker colony came in the future to be attributed to the whole United States. The legacy William Penn left to Americans lies in the realization of the value of diversity. "Many Inquisitive Men into Humane Affairs," he wrote in 1675, "have thought that the Concord of Discords hath not been the infirmest basis Government can rise or stand upon."[30]

CAROLINE ROBBINS
Professor Emeritus of History,
Bryn Mawr College

BIBLIOGRAPHY

DUNN, MARY MAPLES. 1967. William Penn: *Politics and Conscience* (Princeton).

HANNA, WILLIAM A. 1964. *Benjamin Franklin and Pennsylvania Politics* (Stanford).

HUTSON, JAMES H. 1972. *Pennsylvania Politics, 1746-1770* (Princeton).

ILLICK, JOSEPH E. 1965. *William Penn the Politician* (Ithaca).

LINCOLN, CHARLES H. 1901. *The Revolutionary Movement in Pennsylvania* (Philadelphia).

NASH, GARY B. 1968. *Quakers and Politics 1681-1726* (Princeton).

SELSAM, J. PAUL. 1936. *The Pennsylvania Constitution of 1776* (Philadelphia).

SHEPHERD, WILLIAM R. 1896. *History of Proprietary Government in Pennsylvania* (New York).

TOLLES, FREDERICK B. 1948. *Meeting House and Counting House, 1682-1763* (Chapel Hill).

Useful reprints of Charters in:

TOLLES, FREDERICK B., and E. GORDON ALDERFER. 1957. *The Witness of William Penn* (New York).

WILLIAM PENN TERCENTENARY COMMITTEE. 1944. *Remember William Penn.* (Harrisburg).

The Statutes at Large of Pennsylvania in the Time of William Penn, 1680-1700 (New York, 1976), edited by Gail McKnight Beckman. [unfortunately this will appear after my paper is given, and I have thus been unable to make use of it.]

---

30. Penn, as cited in note 29, pp. 100-101.

Tentative Moves Toward Intercolonial Union

My PAPER should please those who like to see experts proven wrong. For at the time of the American Revolution all of the experts, Whig and Tory, domestic and foreign, believed that a lasting union of the American colonies was impossible. "Were the colonies left to themselves tomorrow," predicted Patriot James Otis, "America would be a mere shambles of blood and confusion."[1] "Leave the colonies to themselves," warned Loyalist Thomas Chandler, and "we should soon see province waging war against province, and our country would be involved in such misery and distress as are beyond all our present conceptions."[2] "Union," declared the Founder of The American Philosophical Society, "is not merely improbable, it is impossible."[3] Turgot, Frederick the Great, and the best minds in Europe agreed with Franklin. The conclusion of the cognoscenti was summed up by the Dean of Gloucester, Josiah Tucker: "their Fate seems to be — a Disunited People, till the End of Time."[4]

The experts based their conclusion on solid evidence: the inability of the colonies before the advent of the American Revolution to unite on anything for any time. One reason for their repeated failures was the great differences between them. Most, it is true, were settled by seventeenth-century Englishmen, but settlement occurred under various auspices — principally under trading companies and proprietors — was propelled by different motives, and was affected by men with passionate differences over politics

---

1. John C. Miller, *Sam Adams Pioneer in Propaganda* (Stanford, 1960), p. 98.

2. Edwin G. Burroughs and Michael Wallace, "The American Revolution: The Ideology and Psychology of National Liberation," *Perspectives in American History* 6 (1972): p. 225.

3. Albert H. Smyth, ed., *The Writings of Benjamin Franklin* (10 v., New York, 1907) 4: p. 71.

4. Gerald J. Ghelfi, "European Opinions of American Republicanism during the 'Critical Period,' 1781-1789" (unpublished manuscript), pp. 14, 19, 36.

and religion. Settlement occurred, moreover, in different climates and physical environments, which produced different social and economic systems. Diversity was the colonies' common denominator.

The settlers of North America brought with them from England two ideals, both of medieval origin, which informed all early attempts at union. One of them Professor Charles McIlwain described in writing about James I: "the key to the political thought of the time is the fact that all men still held the medieval conception of the necessity of uniformity."[5] The same key opens the spiritual thought of the time, for English Reformers were committed to uniformity in the ecclesiastical realm, none more fervently than the Puritan divines who settled New England.[6] Uniformity, then, was one ideal which the settlers brought to America.

The other was what a recent writer has called "localism."[7] The "great majority" of seventeenth-century Englishmen, Joan Thirsk writes, were gripped by an "almost morbid anxiety to preserve the traditional fabric of local society."[8] Charles I and his ministers, in an effort to increase the power of the monarchy, intruded into all manner of English local institutions. In the opinion of Timothy Breen, the assault from the center was one of the principal factors which propelled the Puritan migration to New England; so great was the Puritans' commitment to localism that they traveled 3,000 miles to "preserve a customary way of life."[9]

A simultaneous commitment to uniformity and localism appears to be one of those incompatible mixtures which Americans at the time of the Revolution called solecisms in politics, but the early settlers attempted to incorporate both ideals into their unions. Consider, in this regard, the first attempt to form an American colonial union, the experiment which resulted in the formation, in 1643, of the United Colonies of New England.

Proposed by Connecticut to Massachusetts at a synod in 1637, a union would, its promoters hoped, prevent the "further 'alienation'

---

5. Charles H. McIlwain, ed., *The Political Works of James I* (New York, 1965), p. XVII.

6. Perry Miller, *Orthodoxy in Massachusetts 1630-1650* (New York, 1970), chapter 1.

7. Timothy H. Breen, "Persistent Localism: English Social Change and the Shaping of New England Institutions," *William and Mary Quart.* 32 (1975): pp. 3-28.

8. *Ibid.*, p. 16.

9. *Ibid.*, p. 17.

of religion" in the area. Accordingly, in 1643, the Puritan colonies — Massachusetts, Connecticut, Plymouth, and New Haven — confederated. Rhode Island, which had become a haven for dissenters from orthodox practices, was emphatically excluded from the union on the grounds that it was anarchical and heretical.[10] Union, for the New Englanders of 1643, was possible only where there was uniformity.

The New England Confederation was also designed for defense against the Indians, who were rumored, in 1642, to be combining to annihilate the English. In this respect, the Confederation was characteristic of later colonial efforts at union, the great majority of which were initiated in response to external threats. The Indian threat caused the Articles of Confederation of 1643 to be written as "a firm and perpetual league of friendship and amytie of offence and defence." The localistic passion of the confederates was incorporated into the compact by a stipulation that each member state retained its sovereignty; officials of the confederation were expressly forbidden from "intermeddling with the government of any of the Jurisdictions which . . . is preserved entirely to themselves."[11] The preservation of local sovereignty was a constant feature of later plans of union. So, too, were other aspects of the New England Confederation: equal representation of each colony, a presiding officer elected by delegates to the Confederation, meeting places revolving among member colonies; powers delegated to commissioners to set quotas of men and money and to request, but not to coerce, the members to meet them, powers delegated to settle disputes among members, to negotiate with foreign powers and Indians, and to apprehend fugitives.[12]

Because of the similarity of the New England Confederation to succeeding plans of union, some historians have alleged that it inspired not only the Albany Plan of Union of 1754, but even the Articles of Confederation of 1781 and the Federal Constitution of 1787.[13] No evidence has been produced to support these claims, although some has been fabricated — it has been stated, for example, without any foundation in fact, that in composing a draft

10. Harry M. Ward, *The United Colonies of New England* (New York, 1961), pp. 32, 36, 42.
11. *Ibid.,* p. 387.
12. *Ibid.,* pp. 384-397.
13. *Ibid.,* p. 376.

of articles of confederation in the summer of 1775 Benjamin
Franklin "scribbled on it his analysis of the Articles of Confederation of 1643."[14] The similarity of the Articles of 1643 to later plans
demonstrates no more than a consistent failure of the creative
imagination: colonists contemplating union were so committed
to the preservation of local interests that they could not see beyond
devices designed to protect them like equality of representation
and non-coercive requisitioning; hence these devices became staples
of colonial thinking on union.

The New England Confederation foundered in 1652 on the rock
of localism. All members save Massachusetts wanted to attack the
Dutch, but, since there was no means to compel concerted action
and since Massachusetts stood out against her partners, the union
became virtually inoperative. It flickered to life again in 1672,
but was snuffed out in 1686 by the next notable attempt at colonial
union, the Dominion of New England.

The Dominion was an extension to American soil of the policy
of Stuart centralization, which had sent the colonists fleeing across
the Atlantic a half-century earlier. The objective of the Dominion
was to force New England to take its appointed place in the
imperial commercial system which had begun to be forged, in
earnest, after the Restoration of Charles II. The means chosen
to accomplish this was to unite the New England colonies under
one government. Devoted to the concept of uniformity, James II
and his advisers proposed to reduce all the New England colonies
to the same constitution by abolishing their charters. The charter
of Massachusetts was, in fact, vacated on October 23, 1684, and
writs of *quo warranto,* vacating the Connecticut and Rhode Island
charters, were issued the next year. With individual distinctions
effaced in New England, James II gave the colonists a government
of uniform tyranny. Sir Edmund Andros was appointed captain
general of New England in 1686 (New York and New Jersey
were added to his control later). Representative assemblies were
abolished; town meetings were restricted; land titles were challenged; the press was muzzled; and the Congregational religious
establishment was modified — a progressive step, actually, in the
direction of liberty of conscience, but one which the Puritans

---

14. *Ibid.*, p. 397. Ward's documentation for this statement is L. K. Matthews,
"Benjamin Franklin's Plans for a Colonial Union," *Amer. Polit. Sci. Rev.* 8 (1914):
pp. 393-412. Mrs. Matthews offers no substantiation whatever for his statement.

regarded as being contrived by the "bloody Devotees of Rome" to produce the "Extinction of the Protestant Religion."[15]

The Stuart assault on local New England institutions in the name of uniformity was, of course, enormously unpopular. When word reached Boston that William of Orange had overthrown James II, the natives rose in revolt against James's creature Andros, took over the government, and threw him and his associates in jail. At about the same time England and France declared war and the conflict, as European wars always did in the colonial period, spilled over into America. In 1689 the French in Canada, ably led by Count Frontenac, launched a three-pronged offensive against the British colonies, thus opening the half-century of conflict for control of the North American continent. The frontiers of New Hampshire and Massachusetts were ravaged. New York was invaded and the important outpost at Schenectady was destroyed (February 9, 1690).

In response to the French threat, the English colonies tried to unite. On March 19, 1690, the government of Massachusetts called for an intercolonial congress at New York City. Jacob Leisler, a military usurper governing New York at the time, reiterated the call on April 24, sending invitations to New England, to the colonies as far south as Virginia, and to Bermuda and Barbadoes. Only Massachusetts, Connecticut, and Plymouth sent delegates to New York. An invasion of Canada, planned by the delegates, turned into a fiasco, because of poor coordination between New York and Connecticut. The campaign ended with Leisler arresting Connecticut's military commander and then caving in to threats from Connecticut and releasing him.[16]

The next year Leisler's successor, Sloughter, stressing the need for "a hearty union among us," called another intercolonial congress. No one attended. Connecticut intimated that New York ought to carry the burden of opposing the French alone: "you have a large trade; we have not. We live by hard labor at the earth." Virginia, taking a position which was characteristic of her in colonial times, pleaded poverty and declared that her security, in any case, was not dependent on that of New York.[17] Fletcher, Sloughter's successor,

15. Michael G. Hall, *Edward Randolph and the American Colonies* (Chapel Hill, 1960), p. 114; see also Viola Barnes, *The Dominion of New England* (New York, 1960), p. 441.

16. Herbert Osgood, *The American Colonies in the Eighteenth Century* (4 v., New York, 1924) 1: pp. 80-81, 87-88.

17. *Ibid.*, pp. 233-234, 345.

tried to call another intercolonial congress in 1693, but received as little cooperation as his predecessors. The "English colonies," he declared in exasperation, "were as badly divided as Christian and Turk." They "are become, and do in a manner treat each other, as foreigners," complained a New Englander three years later.[18]

Despairing of help from her neighbors, New York petitioned the crown, "asking that the power of the home government be used to compel the other colonies" to join together to repel the French.[19] Imperial officials tried to oblige by annexing Pennsylvania to New York in 1692 to strengthen her. Since to British officials union meant uniformity, William Penn was removed as proprietor, so that both jurisdictions could be run as royal governments. In the same year, William Phips was appointed royal governor of Massachusetts with control over the militias of Connecticut, Rhode Island, and New Hampshire. When the colonists frustrated both of these experiments in centralization, the Lords of Trade, on August 21, 1694, attempted to dictate by royal fiat quotas of men which each colony would supply for the common defense. This order, royal officials ruefully observed later, was "very uncertainly and imperfectly complied with," because, in their opinion, the American colonies were "so crumbled into little governments and so disunited in their interests."[20]

In 1695 the customs official and imperial busybody, Edward Randolph, proposed a series of regional unions in America: South Carolina and Barbadoes would be united, for example, as would Virginia and North Carolina, Pennsylvania and West New Jersey, New York, East New Jersey, and Connecticut, and Rhode Island and Massachusetts. That uniformity would prevail in each jurisdiction, Randolph proposed the abolition of the proprietary and charter governments and their conversion into royal governments.[21] In the same year, the Lords of Trade, hankering after the uniformity of the Dominion of New England, proposed its resurrection.[22]

18. Evarts B. Greene, *Provincial America* (New York, 1905), pp. 117-118; J. W. Fortescue, ed., *Calendar of State Papers, Colonial, 1696-1697* (London, 1904) 15: p. 134.

19. Winfred T. Root, *The Relations of Pennsylvania with the British Government 1696-1765* (New York, 1969), p. 260.

20. J. W. Fortescue, ed., *Calendar of State Papers, Colonial, 1696-1697* (London, 1904) 15: p. 165.

21. Michael G. Hall, *Edward Randolph and the American Colonies* (Chapel Hill, 1969), pp. 157-158.

22. J. W. Fortescue, ed., *Calendar of State Papers, Colonial, 1693-1696* (London, 1903) 14: p. 541.

But the Dominion was an idea whose time had passed. The Revolution of 1688, which banished the Stuarts from England forever, signaled the final acceptance in British politics of the indispensibility of the representative assembly. The House of Commons was now unassailable in the mother country and its replicas across the Atlantic, the representative assemblies, were now accepted as a permanent part of the colonial scene. No longer could they be blotted out by a James II or an Andros. The American representative assemblies had become, over the years, palladia of localism, and to accept them, differ though they might from each other, meant to accept the prevalence of localism in America. This development defeated imperial officials in the 1690's. "The importance and advantage of . . . union for mutual defense and common security is on all sides agreed on," the Board of Trade reported in 1697, but it was apparently unobtainable, because "the different forms of government in the various Colonies render all union . . . impracticable."[23]

Despite the record of repeated failures, the colonists continued to hope that union could be achieved. But they were emphatic that their local interests should not be sacrificed in the process. On June 13, 1695, for example, Peter de la Loy of New York wished that the king "would place a Generall Government over New England, New York, and the Jerseys, so as the Assemblys, Courts of Judicature and Laws of the respective colonys may remain and be kept separate and entire as they now are."[24] De la Loy's plea was repeated by other colonists who wanted union as long as "no breach be made on any of the Grants and Privileges of the several provinces in their Civil affairs."[25] On February 1, 1697, a petition was read before the Board of Trade from "several proprietors and inhabitants of the Northern Colonies of America" which stated what had become the colonial position on union in a way which revealed that an intellectual revolution was taking place. "We wish," the petitioners requested, that "some good form of government may be established by uniting the many interests occasioned by the divers and separate Governments . . . we do not conceive the thing may be impracticable in itself, but

---

23. *Ibid.* 15: pp. 384-385.
24. William Hull, *William Penn A Topical Biography* (Freeport, New York, 1971), pp. 237-238.
25. Winfred T. Root, *The Relations of Pennsylvania with the British Government 1696-1765* (New York, 1969), p. 260.

that a single Governor may be so established over the provinces
as to ensure to each its civil rights, properties, and customs."[26]

With these words — with the conviction that a union of diverse
elements was possible — we hear one pillar of the medieval world
collapsing in America. The American experience of different
sovereignties up and down the Atlantic coast conditioned the
colonists to accept diversity — pluralism, if you will — as a fact
of life and to try to turn it to their advantage. If they did not,
in 1697, know how to construct a system at once united and
diverse, they did not dismiss it as an impossibility. What was
impracticable in England was practicable in America. New possibilities were being glimpsed in a New World. A distinctive
mentality, a distinctive character, was in the process of emerging
in America in the 1690's.

The system toward which Americans were groping was, in fact,
given a form in 1697. William Penn, whose life had been devoted
to preserving a separate existence for what official England regarded as an exotic and distasteful people, presented to the Board
of Trade on February 8, 1697, a plan of union for the North
American colonies from "Boston," as he called Massachusetts Bay,
to "Carolina," which preserved the autonomy of the individual
members. Penn's plan, which was proposed as an alternative to
the royal order of 1694, dictating military quotas for the colonies,
was a short, unsophisticated document — no more than a sketch.[27]
It contained many of the features of the New England Articles of
Confederation of 1643: equal representation for each colony, commissioners empowered to settle intercolonial disputes, to apprehend
absconding criminals, and to set and request, but not coerce,
"Quotas of men and Charges." A feature which would appear in
later plans of union was the appointment by the king of an executive officer for the confederation. Penn's plan was made known
to the colonists by the political writer Sir Charles Davenant, who
published it and praised it in 1698 in his *Discourse on the Plantation Trade.*[28] Despite the claims of Penn's admirers, however, there
is no evidence that his plan, any more than the New England

---

26. J. W. Fortescue, ed., *Calendar of State Papers, Colonial, 1696-1697* (London, 1904) 15: p. 653.

27. Penn's *A Briefe and Plain Scheam* . . . is reprinted in William Hull, *William Penn A Topical Biography* (Freeport, New York, 1971), pp. 236-237.

28. Charles Whitworth, ed., *The Political and Commercial Works of that Celebrated Writer Charles D'Avenant* . . . (5 v., London, 1771) 2: pp. 40-41.

Confederation of 1643, inspired the Articles of Confederation of 1781, the Constitution of 1787, or any subsequent plan of union.

War with France, temporarily ended by the Treaty of Ryswick in 1697, was resumed as soon as the combatants had refreshed themselves. From 1702 to 1713 colonial Americans fought colonial Frenchmen in what was called Queen Anne's War. Once again, the French threat produced plans of union. In 1701 Robert Livingston of New York imitated Randolph in proposing three regional unions — a northern, middle, and southern — in all of which proprietary and charter governments would be abolished in favor of uniform royal rule.[29] In the same year an anonymous Virginian,[30] aroused both by rumors that the French were settling "upon the Mouth of the River Meschasipe" and by Davenant's essay, which he considered an insult to the Old Dominion, published a plan of union under the title, *An Essay upon the Government of the English Plantations on the Continent of America.* The anonymous author took one step forward — he proposed proportional representation for member colonies in an intercolonial assembly — and one backward — the elimination of all charter and proprietary governments as a preliminary of union.

That both Livingston and the anonymous Virginian insisted on uniformity as a precondition of union demonstrates the strength of the concept in the Anglo-American world. On the other hand, in no subsequent plan of union proposed by an American — not even in the plans of the conservative future Loyalists, William Smith and Joseph Galloway, of 1765 and 1774 — was uniformity advocated.[31] British officials, however, never weaned themselves from the concept. In 1715, for example, Colonel Caleb Heathcote, surveyor general of the North American customs, proposed the abolition of the charter governments as the first step toward a

---

29. See Hampton L. Carson, ed., *History of the Celebration of the . . . Constitution of the United States* (2 v., Philadelphia, 1889) 2: p. 459.

30. Variously identified as Robert Beverley, Ralph Wormeley, and Benjamin Harrison III. Louis B. Wright, ed., *An Essay upon the Government of the English Plantations on the Continent of America* (San Marino, Cal., 1945): Virginia W. Fitz, "Ralph Wormeley: Anonymous Essayist," *William and Mary Quart.* 26 (1969): pp. 586-595; Carole Shammas, "Benjamin Harrison III and the Authorship of An Essay upon the Government of the English Plantations on the Continent of America," *Virginia Mag. History and Biography* 84: (1976): pp. 166-173.

31. Robert S. Calhoun, "William Smith Jr.'s Alternative to the American Revolution," *William and Mary Quart.* 22 (1965): pp. 105-118; Julian P. Boyd, *Anglo-American Union; Joseph Galloway's Plans to Preserve the British Empire, 1774-1778* (Philadelphia, 1941).

union of the colonies. In the 1720's, writes a student of imperial relations, "the main efforts of British policy to bring about uniform government in the colonies were concentrated in quo warranto proceedings and attempts to secure an act of Parliament to abolish the charters of the corporate and proprietary colonies . . . the Board of Trade recognized the royalization of all the colonies as the basis for effective union."[32] As late as 1764, the royal governor of Massachusetts, Francis Bernard, in drafting a plan for colonial reorganization, proposed reducing all colonies to the same form of government. "Bernard insisted on uniformity," writes Professor Edmund S. Morgan.[33]

The threat of war with Spain in 1721 produced another crop of plans of union. The Board of Trade devised a union of all colonies from the Bahamas northward; over it would preside a captain general appointed by the king — the position was offered to the Earl of Stair, from whom the plan derives its name — who would act in conjunction with a "general council," consisting of two members from each colony, which would set quotas of men and money and requisition, but not compel, them. In 1722 Daniel Coxe of New Jersey proposed a similar plan: a chief executive, appointed by the crown, to preside over a "great council" of two delegates from each colony, whose powers were confined to setting quotas of men and money and requisitioning them.[34]

The outbreak of the War of Jenkins's Ear in 1739 produced more plans of union; a vague one from a former governor of Pennsylvania, Sir William Keith,[35] and a detailed, innovative one from a member of the Board of Trade, Martin Bladen, which contained, apparently for the first time, a bicameral intercolonial legislature.[36] But Bladen's plan seems never to have been transmitted to, or made known in, America and, therefore, it had no influence on subsequent developments.

By 1750 a decisive struggle with France for control of the North American continent was looming. The French were beginning to move into the Ohio Valley, intending, as Benjamin Franklin feared,

---

32. Harry M. Ward, *"Unite or Die" Intercolony Relations 1690-1763* (Port Washington, New York, 1971), p. 9.

33. Edmund S. and Helen M. Morgan, *The Stamp Act Crisis Prologue to Revolution* (Chapel Hill, 1953), pp. 13-14.

34. For the Stair and Coxe plans, see Hampton L. Carson, ed., *History of the Celebration of the . . . Constitution of the United States* (2 v., Philadelphia, 1889) **2**: pp. 460-464, 465-466.

35. *Ibid.,* 467.

36. Jack P. Greene, "Martin Bladen's Blueprint for a Colonial Union," *William and Mary Quart.* **17** (1960): pp. 516-530.

to coop the British up forever within the confines of the Allegheny Mountains. In 1751 Archibald Kennedy, a transplanted Scotsman residing at New York, proposed that commissioners from all the colonies meet yearly to coordinate military efforts against the French.[37] Franklin warmly endorsed Kennedy's ideas; a union of the colonies, he believed, was both necessary and possible.[38] As French designs became more ominous, the Board of Trade, on September 18, 1753, ordered the governor of New York to call an intercolonial assembly to deal with the problem. Virginia refused to attend, even though the French were occupying her western lands; New Jersey also absented herself. Pennsylvania and Maryland, however, sent strong delegations to Albany, New York, where they were joined by equally strong delegations from the New England colonies.

In deliberations from June 19 through July 11, 1754, the delegates forged the Albany Plan of Union.[39] Based on a sketch submitted by Franklin, the Albany Plan created a "Grand Council" of delegates, elected by colonial assemblies, presided over by a "president general," appointed by the crown; proportional representation was established in the Grand Council, which was given a broad mandate, covering military matters, Indian affairs, and the settlement of western lands; most importantly, the Grand Council was given the power to tax constituent members.

Aware of the failure of previous efforts at union, the delegates to the Albany Congress had no illusions that their handiwork would be adopted voluntarily.[40] Localism was too potent, they knew. The colonies, Franklin observed, had "particular interests to manage, with which an union might interfere and . . . they were extremely jealous of each other." Therefore, the delegates recommended that the crown impose union on the colonies. This the crown declined to do. Submitted to the assemblies of the individual colonies, the Albany Plan was rejected by all of them.[41]

---

37. Proposals for intercolonial cooperation were coming from all quarters at this period, especially from Pennsylvania. George Thomas, Thomas Penn, and Richard Peters were proponents of union. Julian P. Boyd, *Indian Treaties Published by Benjamin Franklin, 1736-1762* (Philadelphia, 1938), pp. lxi-lxii.

38. Franklin to James Parker, March 20, 1751, in Leonard W. Labaree, ed., *The Papers of Benjamin Franklin* (19 v. to date, New Haven, 1959-) 4: p. 118.

39. *Ibid.* 5: pp. 345ff.

40. Lawrence H. Gipson, *The British Empire before the American Revolution Zones of International Friction* (13 v., New York, 1936-1967) 5: p. 142.

41. Franklin, "Remark," Feb. 9, 1789, in Leonard W. Labaree, ed., *The Papers of Benjamin Franklin* (19 v. to date, New Haven, 1959-) 5: p. 417.

The repudiation of the Albany Plan, intelligently drawn and sponsored by men of stature like Franklin and Thomas Hutchinson, created deep pessimism among Revolutionary statesmen about the possibility of uniting the colonies. It was to the fate of the Albany Plan that Franklin alluded in 1760, when he wrote that the colonies' "jealousy of each other is so great, that however necessary an union . . . has long been, for their common defence and security against their enemies, and how sensible soever each colony has been of the necessity, yet they have never been able to effect such an union among themselves, nor even to agree in requesting the mother country to establish it for them."[42] But the pessimism of Franklin and his colleagues was excessive, for they did not perceive how far the colonies had come by the 1760's toward the possibility of union. Over a century of colonial history had implanted in Americans the habit of trying to unite in the face of external threats. And, more significantly, over a century of life in America had destroyed the medieval conception, which the colonists had brought to the continent with them in the seventeenth century, that uniformity was necessary for union; given the diversity of the American colonies, the persistence of this concept would have prevented union forever. On the other hand, after a century, the colonists had not made much headway against the medieval legacy of localism. In fact, their failure before it obscured, for Franklin and his contemporaries, the progress on other fronts.

The plan of the British Parliament in 1765 to take the property of Americans without their consent by imposing a Stamp Act produced the usual attempt at a united response, which in view of some of union's earlier miscarriages succeeded remarkably. Delegates from nine colonies met in New York in October, 1765, and adopted petitions to the king, House of Lords, and House of Commons, protesting against British policy.[43] Balancing this victory for cooperation, however, was the halting effort to orchestrate a united response to the Townshend Acts of 1767. Colonial leaders called for a unanimous, intercolonial non-importation agreement, but different colonies acted at different times and the agreement collapsed in 1770 amidst mutual recriminations. When the British passage of the Intolerable Acts in 1774 produced the meeting of the First Continental Congress in which twelve colonies participated

---

42. *Ibid.* 9: p. 90.
43. Edmund S. and Helen M. Morgan, *The Stamp Act Crisis Prologue to Revolution* (Chapel Hill, 1953), pp. 103-113.

with hitherto unexampled cooperation, American leaders believed that they had beheld a virtual miracle. Wrote Samuel Adams to Samuel Cooper: "The Boston Port Bill suddenly wrought a union of the Colonies which could not be brot about by the Industry of years in reasoning on the necessity of it for the Common Safety."[44] But the Revolutionary leaders had no illusions about the difficulty of perpetuating the union thus achieved: it would, wrote John Adams on May 15, 1776, be "the most intricate, the most important, the most dangerous, and delicate business of all."[45] And, of course, Adams was right. On June 7, 1776, Richard Henry Lee moved his famous resolution, that the United Colonies declare themselves independent, make foreign alliances, and form a confederation. To accomplish the first objective required less than a month; the second slightly over three months. To confederate took five years.

The Articles of Confederation, which were finally ratified in 1781, were in the nature of a treaty between independent states, each equally represented, each reserving to itself the essential elements of sovereignty. The Articles were an abdication of statecraft, for they represented no advance in conception or imagination over plans of union conceived a century earlier. That six years later some of the same men who formed the Articles could convene in Philadelphia and frame the American system of Federalism is almost unaccountable. But acts of genius, whether individual or collective, usually are.

The national government created by the Constitution began to show north-south fracture lines from its inception. But the threat of regional separation would have been infinitely worse had it not been for the one great act of creativity of the Congress of the Confederation: the Northwest Ordinance. By repudiating colonialism and creating a system under which the western areas could enter the union on equal terms with the east, the Confederation Congress aborted one of the most ominous threats to union. For during the colonial period of American history those regional differences which erupted into violence were always east-west, never north-south. Thus, in forestalling east-west conflicts, the Confederation Congress took a decisive step toward preventing the bloody Balkanization of the American continent which the pessi-

---

44. Samuel Adams to Samuel Cooper, April 30, 1776, transcript in editorial files of Letters of Delegates to Congress, 1774-1789, Library of Congress.
45. To James Warren, May 15, 1776, *ibid*.

mistic experts predicted. The Cassandras, of course, had their hour in 1861. But the union survived the Civil War and today, when our oldest friends in Western Europe seem to be coming apart, when Britain, Spain, and even France threaten to devolve into their medieval components, we take our union as much for granted as the air and water.

Eighteenth-century experts said that union in America was impossible. But the American people were not listening. Today's experts tell us that everything is impossible: population control, continued economic growth, a clean environment, racial justice — the list is endless. Let us hope that once again the American people are not listening.

JAMES H. HUTSON
Coordinator, American Revolution Bicentennial Office, Library of Congress

The Problem of Popular Sovereignty

WHEN THE FIRST ENGLISH COLONY was founded in America, England was ruled by a king who claimed that his authority came directly from God. By that divine authority he empowered his subjects to settle colonies in the New World. And when the first colonists had time to talk about the nature of government, they traced its origin either to their God-given king or directly to God himself. Even in Massachusetts Bay, where the governor owed his position to annual elections by the freemen of the colony, Governor John Winthrop explained to them that they must not think themselves the source of his authority: "It is yourselves who have called us to this office," he acknowledged, but "being called by you, we have our authority from God, . . . the contempt and violation whereof hath been vindicated with examples of divine vengeance."[1]

A hundred years later the divine right of kings was no more than a quaint fiction in England; and the divine right of colonial governors, if occasionally affirmed by ardent ministers of the gospel, was no longer seriously claimed by those who held public office. In place of God, the people had made themselves the fountain of authority. The conversion was by no means complete at the time of the American Revolution. Until 1776 there remained in both England and her colonies vestiges of power that was not derived from the people, and in England, of course, these lasted into the nineteenth century. But in 1776 Americans began creating governments that rested wholly on popular choice and that justified their actions as the will of the people. It was the beginning of a change that would sweep the rest of the world: the establishment of governments that repudiated hereditary authority, divine authority, and every authority not derived from the people.

It is possible, of course, to see the change as merely the substitution of one fiction for another, the will of the people for the will

---

1. John Winthrop, *The History of New England from 1630 to 1649,* James Savage, ed. (2 v., Boston, 1853) **2**: p. 280.

of God. But I believe the difference was real. Although government has always rested ultimately on the consent, however obtained, of the governed, both Englishmen and Americans in the seventeenth and eighteenth centuries sought to make government by the people a reality. They confronted, before the rest of the world did, the problems that we still face in trying to make the will of the people not merely the excuse for government but the operating force in government. In this paper I wish first to examine some of those problems as they emerged with the growth of popular government in the seventeenth and eighteenth centuries and then consider what happened to them during the American Revolution, when Americans discarded every basis of authority other than the popular will.

In order to understand the problems we have to recognize the early growth of a popular base of government in England and America. The most striking development that signalized the arrival of popular power, apart from the dramatic surges of civil war and revolution, was the growth of the electorate, the number of people participating in the choice of the men who made their laws. In England, as J. H. Plumb and W. A. Speck have shown, the voters who elected the members of the House of Commons more than doubled in the century before 1715, while the total population increased by only about 25 per cent.[2] In America all the English colonies had representative legislative assemblies by the end of the seventeenth century, and most adult males shared in the right to choose the members. The existence of so many voters, more than any other development, gave substance to the claim that government rested on the people.

The people's sense that they mattered was also encouraged by the development of a political philosophy which appeared to discourage fictions, a philosophy that relied on Aristotle rather than Plato, on Machiavelli rather than Augustine, a philosophy whose prescriptions were derived not from divine commands but from observed facts. It was a philosophy that made sense or seemed to make sense out of the rise of popular participation in government,

-----

2. J. H. Plumb, "The Growth of the Electorate in England from 1600 to 1715," *Past and Present,* no. 45 (1969): pp. 90-116; W. A. Speck, *Tory and Whig: The Struggle in the Constituencies 1701-1715* (London, 1970), pp. 13-32. By modern standards, of course, the proportion of voters to total population remained small. Half the population was excluded automatically by sex, another large segment by age, and another by servitude or poverty. But in spite of these exclusions there were probably a quarter-million voters in England by 1715.

not as something to be desired or sought after on moral grounds but rather as something inevitable, the natural consequence of social and economic changes that had developed over a century. The principal founder of this philosophy in England was James Harrington, whose *Oceana,* appearing in 1656, explained to Englishmen what had happened to them and their government in the preceding century. Political power, Harrington believed, rested on economic power, and economic power at that time, for practical purposes, meant ownership of land. In England, he explained, property had become so widely distributed among yeoman farmers by the middle of the seventeenth century that only a popular government was feasible. Hence when the king tried to act contrary to the popular will, the people simply removed him. Harrington had watched them do it in 1649. They did it again in 1688, and in 1776 the Americans did it. And with each revolution Harrington's proposition seemed to be demonstrated.[3]

As the electorate grew in both England and America, so did the conviction that the legislative branch of government was superior to the other branches and that the legislature itself was simply a substitute for the people. The people could have exercised the power to make laws themselves, but it was more convenient for them to turn the job over to men they chose specifically for that purpose. Even before Harrington wrote, remonstrances to Parliament reminded the members that they were a mere convenience, agents of the people, holding power in a revocable trust.[4] And by the eighteenth century members of Parliament had come to accept this position as axiomatic.[5] We are all familiar with Edmund Burke's lofty rejection of it in his address to the electors of Bristol who had chosen him to represent them in Parliament.[6] But at the time when Burke spoke, in 1774, his view was not the common one. The common one was that the people had the right

---

3. On the Harringtonian tradition see Caroline Robbins, *The Eighteenth-Century Commonwealthman* (Cambridge, Mass., 1959).

4. See, for example, *A Remonstrance of Many Thousand Citizens, and other Free-born People of England to their owne House of Commons,* reprinted in William Haller, ed., *Tracts on Liberty in the Puritan Revolution* (3 v., New York, 1934) 3: p. 353: " . . . we possessed you with the same Power that was in our selves . . . wee might justly have done it our selves without you, if we had thought it convenient. . . . Wee are your Principalls, and you our Agents. . . . "

5. The passage cited in note 4, which was written by Richard Overton, a leveller, was reprinted with approval in 1739 by *Common Sense* (no. 141, Oct. 13, 1739), an organ of Lord Bolingbroke's "Country Party."

6. *Works* (Boston, 1866) 2: p. 95.

not only to choose the men who made their laws but also to tell
them what laws to make. And voters of a particular constituency
sometimes met to formulate instructions for their representatives.
Those of Bristol had announced in 1701 that "it is no doubt to us
that we have a right to direct our Representatives," and the instructions that followed the announcement were printed along with
several from other constituencies to their members (requiring support of the Protestant succession to the throne) in a pamphlet re-
minding every member that "the power with which he is intrusted,
must be larger and fuller in the People who chuse and give him that
Trust, than it can be in Him, their Delegate and Substitute."[7] By
voting in elections and by instructing their representatives between
elections, it was thought the people could make government truly
their creature, their substitute.

The attention that members of Parliament gave to public opinion
supported the supposition that they were indeed substitutes. In
debate they told each other that "we ought to see with the same
eyes our constituents see with," that "we are, properly speaking,
the attornies of the people."[8] Members upon receiving instructions
frequently replied with due humility, "We thankfully acknowledge
your Commands, and with Joy receive your Renewal of a Fundamental Right." "I shall never," said a member from Coventry,
"think myself at Liberty to act contrary to your Representations."[9]
In debate a member from Tewkesbury admitted that he would vote
for a particular bill because "I am required so by my constituents,
who, I think have a right to direct those that represent them."[10]
Even in the House of Lords a minority could protest that a bill
should have been passed because of instructions given to the
Commons by their constituents, "whose voice, we think, ought to
have some weight even here."[11]

Just as the individual member of Parliament was a substitute
for the people of his particular constituency, Parliament itself, the

---

7. *The Electors Right Asserted with the Advices and Charges of Several Counties, Cities and Boroughs in England to their Respective Members of Parliament*
(London, 1701), pp. 2, 13.

8. William Cobbett, ed., *Parliamentary History of England, from the Earliest
Period to the Year 1803* (London, 1813) 11: p. 353; 13: p. 1060.

9. *Great Britain's Memorial Containing a Collection of the Instructions, Representations etc. etc. of the Freeholders and other Electors of Great Britain, to
their Representatives in Parliament, for these two Years past* (2 v., London,
1741-1742) 2: pp. 60, 92.

10. *Parliamentary History* 11: p. 380.

11. *Ibid.,* 12: p. 6.

aggregate of representatives, was a substitute for the whole people. As such it should mirror the interests and wishes of the various constituencies and be, in effect, a scale model of the whole. "The parliament," said Charles James Fox, "is only a substitution for the community at large, in which her delegates are stationed and ordained to act as one aggregate body, to hear her united dictates, and without consulting their own, to adopt them as principles of action."[12] Even Edmund Burke, four years before his declaration of independence from the electors of Bristol, insisted that the people ought to keep the House of Commons "as dependent upon themselves as possible." "The virtue, spirit, and essence of a House of Commons," he said, "consists of its being the express image of the feelings of the nation."[13]

In the colonies the very manner in which representative assemblies originated demonstrated that the members were simply a substitute for the people, deputed to exercise powers that the people could have exercised by themselves if they had chosen to do so. In Massachusetts representative government began because the charter of the colony, originally issued as the charter of a joint-stock trading corporation, required the directors, known as the governor and assistants, to obtain the consent of the stockholders, known as freemen, to the company regulations. When the trading company transported itself, lock, stock and barrel, to the colony which it had been empowered to found and govern, the government of the Company was transformed into the government of the colony. One of its first actions was to admit a large number of settlers to freemanship, and it continued to do so regularly thereafter. These freemen could have performed in person the functions assigned them in the charter. But since there were too many to meet together conveniently they chose "deputies" from each town to do the job for them, the name signifying the status.[14]

In Maryland the character of the representative branch was even more apparent from its origin. The Maryland charter allowed the proprietor, Lord Baltimore, to make laws for the colony only with the consent of the freemen *(liberi homines)* who settled there. In

---

12. As quoted by an admirer in Maryland, in Melvin Yazawa, ed., *Representative Government and Revolution: The Maryland Constitutional Crisis of 1787* (Baltimore, 1975), pp. 165-166.

13. *Works* 1: pp. 492, 536.

14. E. S. Morgan, *The Puritan Dilemma: The Story of John Winthrop* (Boston, 1958), pp. 84-114.

the early years the freemen who assembled to give or withhold their consent frequently carried proxies from neighbors who had found it inconvenient to attend. In 1639 the assembled freemen agreed to regularize this procedure by holding elections in the different centers of settlement. Thenceforth their assembly was to consist of persons chosen "to supply the places of all the freemen consenting or subscribing to such their election" together with "such other Freemen" as cared to attend, "not haveing consented to any the Elections as aforesaid." In other words, the majority of freemen in a neighborhood would henceforth give their consent through a representative who shared their views. But the dissenting minority could either attend in person or assign a proxy. This new arrangement, perhaps inadvertently, gave an undue weight to the dissenting voter who showed up for the assembly carrying a parcel of proxies, because the holder of a proxy could cast it as a separate vote in the assembly, apparently equal to the vote of an elected delegate. In 1642 Giles Brent carried seventy-three proxies and constituted a majority of the assembly all by himself. In order to avoid this kind of politicking, in later assemblies the governor prescribed that no one could hold more than two proxies. Thereafter the assembly was gradually transformed into a wholly elective body, but the fact that representatives were the agents of those who appointed them could scarcely have been made more clear.[15]

It went without saying that in assemblies thus constituted the electors could give instructions to their representatives as English constituencies did. The fragmentary early records of the colonies do not contain many examples, but those of Boston show that the town instructed its representatives in the Massachusetts assembly on at least eighteen different occasions before 1689. In the eighteenth century when a Massachusetts royal governor tried to get the assembly to vote him a permanent salary, instead of a year-to-year grant, the towns sent instructions telling their deputies to do no such thing, and in 1754 an excise tax prompted another set of instructions. Outside New England instructions were less common, because representation was usually by county rather than town, and it was difficult to assemble the voters to decide what instructions to give. Nevertheless the practice was not unknown, and with the onset of the quarrel with England, Americans in counties and

---

15. *Archives of Maryland* 1 (Baltimore, 1883): pp. 81-82, 168-169, 259, and *passim*.

towns throughout the colonies became sufficiently agitated to assemble and direct their representatives in the assertion of colonial rights. By that action they gave the lie to the British ministry's claim that Americans were virtually represented in Parliament. If Americans had appointed no representative to express their will in Parliament, it seemed to them a palpable piece of nonsense to argue that the members who served as the agents of English constituencies were by some magical process transformed into their agents also. A representative was someone you could give directions to, and a representative assembly was a substitute for the people who chose it.[16]

Thus when the American colonists revolted from England and established governments which rested entirely on popular choice, they were carrying to its logical conclusion an idea that had long been familiar. The Revolution produced many new affirmations of the idea, especially in the constitutions of the independent states, which generally began with assertions that the government rested wholly on the popular will. The Massachusetts constitution, for example, stated specifically that "All power residing originally in the people, and being derived from them, the several magistrates and officers of government, vested with authority, whether legislative, executive, or judicial, are their substitutes and agents and are at all times accountable to them." And to protect the right of the people to supervise their government and to act outside it, Massachusetts and other states affirmed the people's right "to assemble to consult upon the common good," and to "give instructions to their representatives."[17]

To all appearances, then, the American Revolution confirmed and completed the subordination of government to the will of the people. The American Revolution, like the English Revolution of 1688, became a benchmark of government, a standard to which subsequent statesmen and politicians must refer in order to justify their actions. The principles of the Revolution must be the basis of government, and the principles of the American Revolution,

---

16. The best discussion of instructions in the colonies is Kenneth Colegrove, "New England Town Mandates," Colonial Society of Massachusetts, *Publications* **21** (1919): pp. 411-449.

17. F. N. Thorpe, ed., *The Federal and State Constitutions, Colonial Charters, and other organic laws* . . . (7 v., Washington, D. C., 1909) **3**: pp. 1890 and 1892. For other states: **3**: pp. 1686-1687; **4**: pp. 2453-2454; 2457-2474; **5**: pp. 2787-2788; 3082-3084; **6**: pp. 3762-3764; **7**: pp. 3812-3814. The first constitutions of Massachusetts, New Hampshire, North Carolina, Pennsylvania, and Vermont all provided for the right of instruction.

even more than the English, seemed to make the authority and authenticity of any government action or policy depend upon the accuracy with which government reflected the will of the people.

But the will of the people is far more visible in revolution than it can be in the day-to-day operation of government. It was easy enough to say that the officers of government must be the agents of the people, that a legislature is a substitute for the people themselves, that the members must subordinate their own views to those of their constituents. These were the principles established in revolution. But how was the will of the people to be known when the revolution was over? The question has agitated statesmen, philosophers, and politicians since the seventeenth century and still remains a burning question, for no one has yet found a satisfactory answer to it.

In the eighteenth century the people seemingly could make their will known in two ways: by electing representatives and some other officers of government and by giving instructions to them between elections. Why there should have been any uncertainty about either way may begin to be apparent if we pause to consider how the voting population came to be as large as it was in both England and America by the eighteenth century. Contrary to the usual assumption, most of the great number of people who gained the vote did so without asking for it. The expansion of the electorate in England came about largely because of monetary inflation that reduced the value of the property qualification required for voting. It was also expanded, in ways too complex to dwell on here, by contests within the government, between king and Commons, and between Whigs and Tories.[18]   But it did not result from popular demand. In the colonies the large electorate came into existence largely because of the abundance of land, which made it possible for most adult males to meet the traditional property qualifications. There are instances in the colony records of unenfranchised groups demanding representation or the right to vote, but much more common is legislation requiring people to exercise their vote, fining them for failure to vote, and fining towns for failure to send representatives to an assembly.[19]   In short the expansion of the electorate,

---

18. See note 2.

19. See, for example, Max Farrand, ed., *The Laws and Liberties of Massachusetts* (Cambridge, Mass., 1929), p. 23; W. W. Hening, ed., *The Statutes at Large; Being a Collection of all of the Laws of Virginia* (Richmond, 1809-23) 1: p. 334; Thorpe, *Federal and State Constitutions* 2: p. 780.

which helped to give substance to the claim that government rested on the will of the people, came about for the most part, both in England and America, without benefit of any express wish of the people for it.

If we examine the elections for which there are records of persons voting, the will of the people as expressed at the polls looks equally faint and obscure. In England the number who actually voted in a given election was only a fraction of the eligible voters. There was no point in tallying votes if only one candidate was running for office, and this was the situation commonly faced by most of the electorate. For rarely more than a third of the seats in Parliament was there any choice between candidates or any poll of the voters.[20]

Where a choice was available and a vote taken, the poll books reveal a curious volatility in the composition of the electorate. For example, in the county of Northamptonshire in 1702, 4,517 persons voted; in 1705, 4,876 voted, but only 2,875 voted in both elections.[21]

In the colonies, where the potential electorate probably exceeded that of England by the last quarter of the eighteenth century, the same phenomenon occurred. The American voters generally did have a choice between candidates, but usually not much more than half of them cared to exercise it. In Rhode Island in the

---

20. In eighteenth-century England and Wales there were 270 parliamentary constituencies. The number of these in which a poll was taken in elections before the American Revolution was as follows (figures compiled from A. S. Foord, *His Majesty's Opposition 1714-1830* [Oxford, 1964] and Speck, *Tory and Whig*):

Year	Counties	Boroughs and Cities	Total
1701	20	72	92
1702	20	66	86
1705	26	83	109
1708	18	79	97
1710	25	105	130
1713	13	82	95
1715	18	93	111
1722	15	88	103
1727	12	65	77
1734	14	71	85
1741	8	61	69
1747	4	42	46
1754	8	50	58
1761	4	37	41
1768	9	56	65
1774	13	68	81

21. Speck, *Tory and Whig*, pp. 19-20.

1760's, for example, in spite of heated election contests, attendance varied from 34 per cent to 52 per cent of the qualified voters.[22] And in the colonies as in England the people who voted in one election might be considerably different from those who voted in the next one. In the New York City elections of 1768 and 1769, 37 per cent of those who voted in 1768 failed to vote in 1769, and 25 per cent of those who voted in 1769 had not voted in 1768.[23] In Halifax County, Virginia, in precisely the same years, of the 545 people who voted in the two elections, only 214 voted in both years.[24] Similarly in Burlington, New Jersey, in elections held in 1783 and 1787, a total of 502 persons voted, but only 96 voted in both elections.[25]

With such an inconstant electorate, the outcome of an election could be determined by persons who had not bothered to vote at all in the preceding election. The volatility of voters can be strikingly seen in an election that took place in 1757 for Boston's four representatives in the Massachusetts assembly. On the morning of May 10, 528 voters cast their ballots, and the polls closed at noon. Upon counting the ballots, the selectmen found that only three candidates had received the necessary majority. The selectmen therefore announced that the polls would again be open at 3 P.M. for one hour to choose the fourth representative. By 3 P.M. aspiring candidates for the position rounded up 754 voters, an increase of nearly 43 per cent over the morning turnout.[26] It would appear, therefore, that the expression of the popular will in elections could be affected by radical shifts in the composition and number of voters not only from year to year but from hour to hour. When the will of the people was the will of one group one year, and when that group remained silent the next year while the will of a substantially different group became the will of the people, then there was reason to wonder whether the will of the people as expressed in elections was not sometimes a will of the wisp, or

22. D. S. Lovejoy, *Rhode Island Politics and the American Revolution* (Providence, 1958), p. 17.

23. Roger Champagne, "Liberty Boys and Mechanics of New York City," *Labor History* 8: (1967): p. 129.

24. R. E. and B. K. Brown, *Virginia 1705-1786: Democracy or Aristocracy?* (East Lansing, Michigan, 1964), p. 161.

25. The poll list for 1783 is in AM Papers 1715, State Library, Trenton, New Jersey. That for 1787 is in H. C. Shinn, "An Early New Jersey Poll List," *Penna. Mag. History and Biography* 44 (1920): pp. 77-81.

26. *A Report of the Record Commissioners of the City of Boston Containing the Boston Town Records, 1742 to 1757* (Boston, 1885), pp. 304-305.

whether at any rate it did not depend to a degree no one wished to admit on the manipulation of different segments of the population by ambitious politicians.

When we turn to the instructions by which constituents directed their representatives after they were elected, the impression of manipulation becomes even stronger. Although it was possible for instructions to originate locally, out of popular concern about government policy, the instructions that were likely to affect policy generally resulted from a coordinated campaign conducted by persons within the government seeking popular support for measures under dispute in the legislature. One case that can be particularly well documented in England is that of the instructions in the years 1739–1741, calling for Parliament to pass a bill limiting the number of seats that could be occupied by placeholders, that is, persons holding offices of profit in the government. The opposition had been trying for years to get such a "place bill" through Parliament in order to reduce the influence which Robert Walpole wielded in the House of Commons by his power to appoint members to such offices and remove them. In 1742 Walpole was forced to resign and a place bill finally went through the Commons, after instructions from all over England and Scotland made it embarrassing for the members to refuse it.[27]

It would be difficult to assess precisely what role these instructions played in the unseating of Walpole or in the passage of the bill, but it is not impossible to assess the validity of the ministry's charge that the instructions had been originated, not by the constituencies but by the members themselves. The whole thing, the ministry charged, was "a mere juggle . . . the Member first transmits his Notions to his Creatures, and then they, under the name of his Constituents, instruct him, as he first instructed them."[28] When the opposition replied that instructions, however originated, were still the voice of the people, the ministry answered, "that tho' the Voice be Isaac's the Hands are Esau's. It is the People that speak but the Malecontents dictate. A gross piece of State Mummery, wherein A instructs B how B shall instruct A."[29]

That this charge was pretty close to the facts can be demonstrated from surviving correspondence. While the campaign for the place

---

27. The instructions were printed in *Great Britain's Memorial* (see note 9).

28. *A Letter to a Member of Parliament, Concerning the present State of Affairs at Home and Abroad* (London, 1740), p. 6.

29. *The Daily Gazetteer*, Feb. 6, 1740.

bill produced some strong pronouncements of the people's right
to dictate to their representatives, the dictates that the people
ostensibly gave were drafted by a few members of the nobility,
notably the Earl of Chesterfield and the Earl of Stair, and were
adapted to the needs of a Parliamentary faction in search of
power.[30] Probably few of the instructions given representatives in
the colonial assembles were so clearly the product of a legislative
party looking for leverage. But the most conspicuous example
of the use of instructions in the colonial period testifies to the
uncertainty that a highly responsive popular assembly felt about
instructions.

In 1754 the Massachusetts assembly, in which the members from
the farming towns of the interior constituted a majority, laid an
excise tax on rum consumed in households. It was a soak-the-rich
tax, for rum was consumed mainly in the eastern towns where
wealth was concentrated, and the tax affected only large-scale
consumption (in lots of 30 gallons) in private households. The
farmers of the interior who drank cider of their own making and
the ordinary town dweller who bought his rum by the glass or
bottle would be virtually untouched by the tax. The governor of
the colony, who thought the east already paid too heavy a share
of the tax burden, refused to sign the measure until the representatives had consulted their constituents. Town meetings assembled,
especially in the east, and gave the instructions. When the legislators reconvened, they had before them a large collection of
instructions that had been specifically requested for their guidance.
Most of the instructions apparently were against the tax. After
"a large debate" the details of which were not recorded, the assembly refused to consider the instructions and two weeks later repassed
the tax.[31]

---

30. Chesterfield and Stair, leaders of the Country party, organized the movement for instructions, with advice from Lord Bolingbroke and assistance from
the Earl of Marchmont, his son Lord Polwarth, and William Pulteney. The
evidence is scattered through their papers, in J. M. Graham, ed., *Annals and
Correspondence of the Viscount and the First and Second Earl of Stair* (2 v.,
Edinburgh & London, 1875); George H. Rose, ed., *A Selection from the Papers
of the Earl of Marchmont;* Bonamy Dobrée, ed., *Letters of Philip Dormer
Stanhope, fourth Earl of Chesterfield* (London, 1932); and Historical Manuscripts Commission, *Report on the Manuscripts of the Right Honorable Lord
Polwarth* 5 (London, 1961).

31. *Journals of the House of Representatives of Massachusetts, 1754-1755* 31
(Boston, 1956): pp. 60, 63, 101. The controversy is discussed in Robert Zemsky,
Merchants, Farmers, and River Gods (Boston, 1971), pp. 150-151, 166-167,
277-283. I am also indebted to an unpublished paper by Barbara Clark Smith.
There are known records of 24 instructions against the excise and 6 in favor,
but there were over 160 towns entitled to send representatives to the assembly.

The decision to ignore instructions seems to have been the result of a rank-and-file action by members who ordinarily deferred to the leadership of well-to-do easterners. The majority of the assembly evidently felt that on this matter they knew better than their accustomed leaders and perhaps knew better than the people who had sent instructions. One of the more articulate of them explained what they were doing: "the business of a representative," he said,

> is to consult the good of the whole body, and to take particular care that the town he represents, does not pay a greater proportion of the charges of government than it ought to do. . . . I take [this] to be the proper business of a representative, and not to follow the humor of his constituents, when it is evidently contrary to the good of the community.[32]

Not so very different, that, from what Edmund Burke told the electors of Bristol twenty years later. "Certainly, Gentlemen," said Burke,

> it ought to be the happiness and glory of a representative to live in the strictest union, the closest correspondence, and the most unreserved communication with his constituents. Their wishes ought to have great weight with him; their opinions high respect; their business unremitted attention. . . . But his unbiassed opinion, his mature judgment, his enlightened conscience, he ought not to sacrifice to you, to any man, or to any set of men living. . . . Your representative owes you, not his industry only, but his judgment; and he betrays, instead of serving you, if he sacrifices it to your opinion.[33]

Burke was speaking in answer to words of his colleague, elected from Bristol at the same time, who had declared that he would be bound by whatever instructions the electors might give him. The Massachusetts assembly of 1754, like Burke, would not be bound and in its refusal expected to serve the will of the whole people better than by following the will of those who had sent instructions.

Thus, long before the quarrel between England and the colonies began, both Englishmen and Americans had come up against some of the problems involved in resting government on the will of the people. They had seen the volatility of popular participation in the electoral process; they had learned a few doubts about the authenticity and usefulness of instructions; and they had thereby been given cause to wonder whether the property-holding yeomen of their countries actually exhibited the independence of mind and

---

32. Quoted in Zemsky, *Merchants, Farmers, and River Gods*, p. 280.
33. *Works* 2: p. 95.

will that Harrington had attributed to them. They may even have pondered David Hume's arresting observation of Harrington's fallibility. "Harrington," said Hume, "thought himself so sure of his general principle, that the balance of power depends on that of property, that he ventured to pronounce it impossible ever to re-establish monarchy in England: But his book was scarcely published when the king was restored."[34]

The American Revolution, with its renewed and repeated assertions of the sovereignty of the people could not erase the experience of the previous century. When Americans set out to replace their colonial governments with independent state governments that rested entirely on the will of the people, they could not forget the problems they had already encountered with the popular will, and they tried to minimize them. While devising constitutions that proclaimed the absolute power of the people over all branches of government, they retained upper houses in their legislatures, and many removed the upper house from direct election by the people, leaving the choice to the presumably more sophisticated judgment either of the lower house or of an electoral college. The federal constitution similarly placed the election of much of the national government at one remove from the people by assigning the choice of the senate to the state legislatures and the choice of the president to an electoral college.

The federal constitution also provided for less frequent elections, that is, for less frequent consultation of the popular voice, than had been common in the colonies or states. It even restricted the House of Representatives to so small a size that to many people it seemed incapable of reflecting the complex interests of the population which it was supposed to mirror. At the Constitutional Convention although delegates confidently affirmed that representation was "an expedient by which an assembly of certain individuals chosen by the people is substituted in place of the inconvenient meeting of the people themselves,"[35] the same delegates then declined to assign more than one representative to 30,000 people, a ratio that made the first house of representatives smaller than most state legislatures and only one-eighth the size of the con-

---

34. David Hume, *Essays Moral, Political, and Literary*, T. H. Green and T. H. Grose, eds. (London, 1875), p. 122.

35. Max Farrand, ed., *The Records of the Federal Convention of 1787* (4 v., New Haven, 1911-1937) 1: p. 561.

temporary British House of Commons.[36] The federal constitution was designed, as James Madison, its principal author, explained,

> to refine and enlarge the public views, by passing them through the medium of a chosen body of citizens, whose wisdom may best discern the true interest of their country. . . . Under such a regulation, it may well happen that the public voice, pronounced by the representatives of the people, will be more consonant to the public good, than if pronounced by the people themselves convened for the purpose.[37]

Here again we have substitutes for the people knowing what is good for the people better than the people do. And attitudes toward instructions under the new governments showed how disillusioned many Americans had become with this form of popular direction. In Maryland in 1787 a lengthy discussion of the subject filled the newspapers when the state's indirectly elected senate refused to pass a bill for an emission of paper money initiated by the lower house. The lower house adjourned the legislature in order to seek instructions not only for themselves but for the senate too, informing the people that "We . . . hold both branches of your legislature bound by your instructions, whenever you please to give them; on a diversity in sentiment between us and the senate, you alone are to decide, and to you only can there be any appeal. . . ." In answer the senate did not deny the right of the people to instruct them, but argued that, if in practice instructions were to be sought when house and senate disagreed, the senate would in effect be deprived of its function. In other words, the senators might be obliged by instruction to bow to the will of a misinformed people, whose true interest they knew better than the people themselves. And in the end the view of the senate prevailed: the lower house gave up the contest.[38]

At the national level the question of instructions came up in the first session of Congress under the new Constitution. In ratifying the federal Constitution many states had objected to the absence of a bill of rights and had reaffirmed among other popular rights

---

36. There were 65 representatives in the first Congress. The legislatures of New Hampshire, Massachusetts, Rhode Island, Connecticut, New York, Pennsylvania, Virginia, and South Carolina were all larger. The British House of Commons in the eighteenth century had 513 members from England and Wales and 45 from Scotland.

37. Jacob E. Cooke, ed., *The Federalist* (Middletown, Conn., 1961), p. 62.

38. Yazawa, *Representative Government and Revolution,* quotation on p. 35.

the right of instruction.[39] The members of Congress accordingly
made it one of the first orders of business to draft amendments to
the Constitution, embodying a bill of rights. In debate on the first
one, which guarantees the right of the people to assemble, Thomas
Tudor Tucker of South Carolina moved to insert the words "to
instruct their representatives." The debate that followed brought
out all the familiar old assertions of the need for the legislature
to be a mirror of popular wishes. John Page of Virginia, for
example, declared that

> all power vests in the people of the United States. . . . If it were
> consistent with the peace and tranquility of the inhabitants, every
> freeman would have a right to come and give his vote upon the
> law; but inasmuch as this cannot be done by reason of the extent
> of territory, and some other causes, the people have agreed that
> their representatives shall exercise a part of their authority. To
> pretend to refuse them the power of instructing their agents appears
> to me to deny them a right.[40]

But by this time the pitfalls in the practice of instruction had
become too widely apparent for such reasoning to be persuasive.
Thomas Hartley of Pennsylvania expressed the general embarrassment at having to seem to oppose popular control. He wished that
the motion had not been made. But he went on resolutely to argue
that instructions were not a safe or accurate way to determine the
will of the people. "Instructions," he said, exaggerating only a
little, "will never be resorted to but for party purposes, when they
will generally contain the prejudice and acrimony of the party,
rather than the dictates of honest reason and sound policy." They
would elevate local views above the general good. They would
foreclose debate on issues about which the people were uninformed
or misinformed. Other members rose to point out the impossibility
of securing bona fide instructions and the dilemma resulting from
instructions that required a representative to violate the constitution or his conscience or his informed judgment. In the end the
proposal was voted down by the overwhelming majority of 41 to
10, and the right to instruct was not added to the United States
Constitution.[41]

39. Jonathan Elliott, ed., *The Debates in the several State Conventions on the
Adoption of the Federal Constitution* (5 v., Philadelphia, 1863-1891) **2**: pp. 328,
335; **3**: p. 659.

40. *Debates and Proceedings in the Congress of the United States 1789-1824*
[Annals of Congress] **1**: p. 744.

41. *Ibid.*, pp. 733-734, 746. The same proposal was rejected in the Senate by
a vote of 14 to 2. L. G. De Pauw *et al.*, eds., *Documentary History of the First
Federal Congress of the United States of America* **1** (Baltimore, 1972): p. 151.

The first Congress under the Constitution thus admitted that the government of the United States, like all governments, was a government of the people and for the people, but that it could not, by means of instructions at least, be a government by the people. At this point the United States was badly in need of a new way to make the people a more effective force in government. Indirect election of the upper branches of government and infrequent elections, while lending stability to government policies, belied the belief that the people had a right to direct their government, even though that belief was continually reiterated, perhaps the more shrilly because of growing doubts.

The founding fathers, uncertain about elections and instructions, placed their hopes for the country's future in giving government a structure that would filter the will of the people and extract a beneficent essence from the raw wishes of the majority. But the structure they devised removed them too far from their avowed premise and did not in fact survive in the way they had planned. The indirect election of the United States Senate by the state legislatures eventually gave way to direct election, and the electoral college that chose the president was almost at once reduced to a collection of straw men who exercised no real choice but did as the people directed. These changes, which reaffirmed and magnified the role of the people in government, came about because a new way was finally worked out, without anyone quite advocating it, to make elections a better index of the will of the people and to give the people, outside government, a continuous influence on it.

That way, of course, was the political party, the unwanted child of popular government. The emergence of the political party has been the subject of a great deal of historical scholarship and a great deal of scholarly puzzlement, for it was not proposed by any political philosopher, and it is difficult to find any political philosopher before the nineteenth century who had a good word to say for it. The honor has often been assigned to Edmund Burke, but the attribution is based on the grudging recognition that Burke accorded to party in a treatise which described the existing government of England in terms so far from reality as to be a travesty.[42] Jefferson and Madison, who built the first national political party in the United States, thought of what they had done more as another revolution — the revolution of 1800 — than as a way of running government. For them as for Lord Bolingbroke a century before,

---

42. "Thoughts on the Cause of the Present Discontents" (1770), *Works* 1: pp. 435-537.

party was a temporary necessity by which the people could over-throw a wicked faction. It was left to the likes of Martin Van Buren, no intellectual giant, to write the apology for parties. And an aura of disrepute still surrounds the word.

The aura is much fainter today than in the eighteenth century, when party and faction were virtually synonymous, and faction was, as it remains, a totally pejorative term. The aura persists because the philosophy of the independent yeoman, or should we say the myth of the independent yeoman, persists, and parties do violence to that philosophy as they always have. Parties express the will of the people as it has always been expressed short of revolution — and sometimes even in revolution — by direction from above. Jefferson's and Madison's republican party did not originate in the grass roots. It originated in Congress, in opposition to Hamilton's financial policies and Washington's and Adams's foreign policies. It organized the people in the same way that the Parliamentary opposition to Walpole had organized them to give instructions to the House of Commons. The Republican party's organization was more widespread and more enduring, and it did not rely on popular deference to an aristocracy as a means to influence the people. But it did give direction. It did not leave the sturdy yeoman alone to think and decide for himself. Insofar as a party succeeds in making the will of the people effective, it does so by commanding their allegiance to an organization that can escape from popular control as easily as government itself can.

Since party has not proved a wholly satisfactory vehicle for popular sovereignty, we have continued to search for more and better ones: The secret ballot (which already prevailed in many colonies before 1776), the direct primary, the initiative, referendum and recall, the Australian ballot, and more recently the public opinion poll, which, like the party, can determine the course of government while remaining outside of government. But the goal continues to elude us.

In sum, the American Revolution marked the culmination, in America at least, of a transformation that took government out of the hands of monarchs claiming to rule by the grace of God and placed it in the hands of the people. But the transformation left unanswered a number of questions that had arisen as soon as the people began to take a hand in government through elected repre-sentatives, whether in England or in England's colonies. How to discover the will of the people? How to get them to express it?

How to know whether there was any will to express? How to make government responsive to it when it was expressed? And what to do when the apparent will of the people ran counter to what their representatives thought good and right for them?

The founding fathers and their fathers before them struggled with these questions, but our devotion to them and to their ideal of popular sovereignty should not seduce us into thinking that their answers or any tried since, including political parties, have achieved the objective. The will of the people is still uncertain, imperfectly realized, and vulnerable. Perhaps the problem is insoluble. Perhaps the questions are unanswerable. But as we look at countries where the quest for better answers has been stifled (and stifled by parties claiming to act in the name of the people) we dare not yet give it up.

EDMUND S. MORGAN
Sterling Professor of History,
Yale University

The Declaration of Independence: Philosophy of Government in a Free Society

I

W HEN IN THE TWO HUNDREDTH ANNIVERSARY of the foundation of the American Republic, an American scholar turns to the great document that proclaimed the birth of our nation and declared the principles to which its Founders committed its people and the governments they were to establish, one's initial and profound instinct is to read the document, and to absorb the beauty of its language and the nobility of its meaning in silent contemplation. Any attempt to present a commentary, an interpretation, an analysis, of the Declaration of Independence, of words and ideas that have shaped one's own people and influenced the course of history elsewhere, seems close to committing an act of blasphemy, of *hubris*. But as with other great works of literature and art, so with the Declaration of Independence: the effort to achieve greater understanding by analyzing its construction and attempting to probe its meaning increases one's awe and appreciation of the work and its creator.

The first sentence of the second paragraph of the Declaration[1] is one of the most remarkable in the entire corpus of political philosophy. It consists of only one hundred and eleven words; in that short space, Thomas Jefferson abstracted from the political tradition of the West, two golden threads, one ancient, venerable, reaching all the way back to the *Iliad* and the Bible; the other, evolving out of the older thread but less than two centuries old in 1776 and leading forth in a new direction, together with the old,

---

1. The text of the Declaration of Independence used is that printed in Julian P. Boyd, editor, *The Papers of Thomas Jefferson* (Princeton University Press, Princeton, New Jersey, 1950-) 1: pp. 429-433.

created a new fabric of which only fleeting glimpses had been caught in ages past.

The old thread was a double-stranded one: it consisted of the ideas that legitimate government rested on the consent of the people, and that its purpose was the welfare of the governed. Both ideas, but especially the latter one, were expressd in the metaphor that described a king, prince, chieftain, or ruler, as a "shepherd of the people." It was a metaphor natural to an age in which man's life was pastoral, or partly so, but it was a metaphor that had a sinister inner meaning within the outward image of peace and tranquillity. The real shepherd of real sheep might indeed guard and protect his charges with care and skill for a limited time, but the welfare of the sheep was not his ultimate end, nor did their wishes override his in the performance of his function. Indeed — why should they? Sheep do not have intelligence equal to that of the shepherd.

The new thread, spun in the seventeenth century from fibers of varying age and origin, wove a new portrait of "the people" by bringing into sharp, clear focus its individual members, and it rendered archaic the metaphor of shepherd and sheep by revising the doctrine of consent from one of formal and usually passive acquiescence to one of potentially continuous control through the right of the people to establish, control, alter, or abolish their governments.

It was this new thread, emerging out of the religious and civil conflicts of the seventeenth century, and growing in strength during the decades of American colonial experience, that gave to the Declaration of Independence its dual characteristics of universal relevance and a vitality so dynamic that its force has not yet been spent, or been withered from the exposure of two centuries of trial and error, of frequent failure and limited success.

What was the philosophy of government distilled in that single sentence, and what the language in which it was expressed, that gave to it a power rarely found in secular literature, and when found, even more rarely serving as the fundamental principles of a people newly united in their corporate capacity as a nation?

I shall not comment on the graceful aspects of Jefferson's felicitous style, believing grace to be a self-evident quality the explication of which would be presumptuous as well as unnecessary. I do wish to suggest that Jefferson achieved a perfect union of thought and word, of content and style, and that in so doing,

he consciously used a combination of generality and precision of
language that rendered the summary statement of this philosophy
of free government both flexible and strict. Without flexibility, the
Declaration of Independence could not have endured throughout
the enormous and unforeseen changes in American society and
the American people since 1776; without strictness, deviations
from the principles of freedom could have been more easily justified
as well as committed, and less readily recognized and amenable
to modern counterparts of the ancient "hue and cry" raised when
a city and its people were discovered to be in danger.

The first two clauses of the great sentence are phrased in language
that is strong, but also broad and even indefinite in meaning:
"We hold these truths to be self-evident, that all men are created
equal." Jefferson knew, as we know, that the truths proclaimed
to be self-evident were not so to all men, were not indeed accepted
as truths by all men living then either in America or abroad. He
was capable of presenting a logical demonstration of the validity
of those truths, but he knew that the ultimate principles upon
which men as individuals, and men as a collective people, base
their lives and conduct are not derived from logic; they are accepted
for other causes which may involve but also transcend the use
of reason. It was better to rest those truths on the unqualified
assertion of self-evidence. The first of the self-evident truths, "that
all men are created equal," was declared with stark simplicity —
unqualified, undefined, unexplained. We may with confidence
conclude that Jefferson's decision to state it thus was deliberate,
because the meaning of man's equality was much debated by his
contemporaries, some of whom attempted to clarify it by stating
that men were equal in rights. But thus to clarify was also to
restrict the meaning, and this Jefferson refused to do. By leaving
the phrase and its meaning indefinite, he left open for his own
generation and for posterity the opportunity to define and re-define
the concept in ways most appropriate for their needs and aspirations.

The language and substance of the next four clauses of the
Declaration, central to its philosophy and crucial to its operative
force, are a careful blend of spaciousness and precision. Of these
four clauses, the first two state that men "are endowed by their
Creator with certain unalienable Rights, that among these are
Life, Liberty, and the pursuit of Happiness." As Jefferson wrote
in later years, he had not attempted to introduce new or original
ideas into the Declaration, and the concept of natural rights was

not new. Again, it is Jefferson's mastery of his native tongue that gave to these lines their lasting resonance. Whoever or whatever man's Creator is, or is perceived to be, the rights of man are inherent in man's nature; they cannot be alienated, cannot be given away or destroyed, without distorting the very nature of man's being. And although through familiarity we tend to think of the rights as a trilogy — life, liberty, and the pursuit of happiness — it is well for us to note that Jefferson prefaced the trilogy with the words, *"among[2] these."* The rights explicitly named are indeed primary, and from the third, the pursuit of happiness, an infinite number of secondary rights could logically be derived. By using the words *among these,* Jefferson made such an exercise in logic unnecessary, and thus paradoxically the very precision of his language provided the means for expanding the list of man's rights that are innate and therefore inalienable.

It is to secure these rights, the Declaration continues, that "Governments are instituted among Men, deriving their just powers from the consent of the governed." The concept that the purpose and function of government were to secure the rights of individuals was not original, though its emergence from two millennia of recorded Western political philosophy scarcely a century and a quarter before 1776 inhibits one from calling it old. The phrase that follows this then familiar concept *is* partly new, and I must respectfully take issue with Thomas Jefferson's denial that the Declaration contained nothing either new or original.[3] These ten words, "deriving their just powers from the consent of the

---

2. Emphasis by C.M.K.

3. In an absolute sense, Jefferson was right, for there were two precedents involving assertions that a government did not have a power or powers not delegated to it by the people. One precedent was specific, narrow, and associated with the evolution of freedom of religion or conscience. The argument was that an individual's soul belonged only to God, that for other human beings to interfere with an individual's soul or conscience was to trespass on God's territory, and that therefore a people's consent to government could not include consent to the exercise of governmental power over the individual conscience because the people could never transfer to a government a power which the people themselves did not and could not possess. The other precedent was more general but shortlived. During the English Civil Wars of the 1640's, the claim was made that the power of Parliament was unlimited and even arbitrary. In opposition to this then extraordinary assertion, some of the Leveller spokesmen argued that Parliament had, or ought to have, only those powers delegated to it by the people. The period of Leveller influence in England was relatively brief, and because of the theory of consent was customarily expressed in general or ambiguous language, Jefferson's unusually precise statement of the theory is of the utmost significance.

governed," cut across centuries of established theory and practice that attributed to government inherent powers. In England, the doctrine of powers inherent in government by the very nature of its existence and functions had long been linked with the crown's prerogative, and more recently extended to the power of Parliament. It was and is a doctrine of indubitable vitality. Only a few years after 1776, and after the Federal Constitution of 1787 created a new government with carefully defined and enumerated powers, the old doctrine was once again brought forth to justify the assumption and exercise of powers *not* assigned to that new government. Since that time, the old doctrine of inherent power has reappeared, frequently — and most recently — with respect to the executive branch. But that doctrine is totally alien to the philosophy of government in a free society enunciated in the Declaration of Independence. It is alien because of the precision of Jefferson's language. He did not use the conventional language, that consent is the basis of legitimate government; that language could easily be interpreted to mean that, when a people give consent to a government, they automatically and of necessity consent also to a reservoir of unknown and undefined powers. Such has been the doctrine set forth in recent years by both elected and appointed officers of our own government. These doctrines are totally contradictory to the Declaration of Independence: *it* states with absolute and unqualified clarity that the "just powers" of a government are those derived from the consent of the governed. The exercise of any other powers, of powers to which the people have not consented, is and should be recognized as, usurpation. So long, that is, as we commit our loyalty to the principles upon which the Republic was founded, and not to any persons who hold temporary office in the government of that Republic, who are here today, but tomorrow, gone.

In the passage that follows this precise definition of the sources of just governmental powers, the Declaration states the right of revolution, though the word *revolution* itself is not used, either here or in any other part of the document. It does not need to be, and because the word has been defined in so many ways during the two centuries of which we now mark the completion, we may again bless the precision of Jefferson's language. The Declaration states that whenever any form of government becomes destructive of the ends for which it was instituted, "it is the Right of the People to alter or abolish it." The combination of the two words is fortunate. *To alter* is a term of indefinite and elastic import: its meaning may range from a small, mild, and moderate change to a major one. *To abolish* is an absolute term, its meaning unqualified and unambiguous. Therefore, the remedies for dysfunctional government allotted to the people are left to the discretion of that people: if a minor alteration will suffice to bring a government back to the performance of its appointed purpose, the people need go no further; but if nothing short of the extreme and ultimate remedy of abolition will suffice, that, too, is unambiguously declared to be the right of the people. Indeed, a few lines later, the Declaration states that it is not only the right but the *duty* of a people "to throw off" governments whose performance has unmistakenly demonstrated a design to establish absolute despotism or tyranny. The ultimate remedy, "to abolish," or "to throw off" a government "long established," is not be undertaken frivolously, "for light and transient causes," nor does the history of mankind .indicate that it will be. But the remedy is there, and its use is declared to be not only a right but a duty. That it should be both, and especially a duty, may at first strike the reader as strange, perhaps new, perhaps an onerous obligation imposed upon mankind. The roots of this concept are old and are to be found in interpretations of the Laws of Nature that antedate by centuries the emergence of the theory of natural rights. In the middle of the thirteenth century, St. Thomas Aquinas declared that the *First Law of Nature* was self-preservation. At the end of the sixteenth century, the Anglican clergyman, Richard Hooker, declared that God had *first* commanded man to preserve himself, and *then* given him laws of nature to govern his conduct. In the middle of the seventeenth century, the English Leveller, Richard Overton, explicitly linked this first law of nature and commandment of God with the newer doctrine of individual rights by defining self-preservation to include not merely bare life, but liberty also. Even the hated and much maligned Thomas Hobbes stated that the right to self-preservation included the means to live well, to live a life that one would not grow weary of.

Thus when Jefferson wrote that it was a duty as well as a right for a people to abolish, to throw off, a government that did not secure to men their natural rights, he expressed no novel or idiosyncratic notion, but a concept deeply rooted in the political tradition of the West, evolving over the centuries, and now embodied in a document that, while stating the principles of a newly emerging nation, yet knew and would know, no national boundaries.

The task of securing their inalienable rights was only begun when a people resorted to the ultimate remedy and abolished or threw off a government destructive of the ends for which it had been created. The people had then "to institute new Government, laying its foundation on such principles and organizing its powers in such form, as to them shall seem most likely to effect their Safety and Happiness."

The responsibility of designing legitimate, just, and effective new governments was thus assigned to the people, and to them also was allotted full and free choice as to the ways and means by which that responsibility should be fulfilled. Theoretically, they might choose monarchy, aristocracy, oligarchy, democracy, any mixture of these traditional forms, or indeed some form altogether new. The long indictment of George III and the British Parliament — or "others," as the Declaration delicately alludes to the latter institution — reflects a conception of what many of the Founding Fathers believed to be the principles and organization of powers conducive to a government consonant with a free society. To some of the constituent elements of such a government, I shall presently turn. But it is important to note that in the central philosophical section of the Declaration, Thomas Jefferson made no attempt to prescribe any particular principles or forms. The people of his own and future generations should be free to discover new principles as well as to act upon old ones, to design new methods of organization as well as to follow what might appear to them to be the tried and true legacies of man's recorded history. Thus the means were left undefined, but to the purpose of securing the inalienable rights of man stated in the first sentence of this paragraph, Jefferson added two more, safety and security. The result is an affirmation of a close connection among liberty, safety, and security. And if, once again, we look at the precise language of the Declaration, we shall find that the words *safety* and *security* are prefaced by the possessive, *their*. It is, then, the collective safety and security of the people that is meant, and these are inextricably linked with the individual rights of life, liberty, and the pursuit of happiness. There is, accordingly, nothing in the Declaration of Independence to suggest that its principal author or those who signed it perceived a conflict, actual or potential, between the liberty of the individual and the security of the people.

II

It is not my purpose, in examining the indictment of George III and the British Parliament, to evaluate or judge the validity of the various counts of which the indictment consists. It is rather that by reading this part of the Declaration so frequently ignored, we may derive a reasonably clear picture of what the Revolutionary generation believed to be the essential constituent and operative elements of good and just government.

The first six counts in the indictment all charge King George the Third with serious abuse or neglect of his legislative power and office. That consideration of the legislative function should lead the long list of allegations was a natural reflection of the fact that for precisely two centuries, the central importance of legislation in modern government had been recognized and accepted.

The first two counts charge the king with misuse of his power to veto colonial legislation and to prohibit the enactment and operation of such legislation by requiring its suspension until his assent had been obtained, an assent sometimes withheld through negligence. Both kinds of action, or lack of action, had inhibited colonial legislatures in their efforts to promote "the public good" and to cope with matters of "immediate and pressing importance." These counts imply with no ambiguity that the job of a government is to govern, of a legislature to legislate. There is here not the slightest hint of anarchy, of the idea that the welfare of society and of its individual members can be achieved without government.

The next four counts all charge the king with obstruction or attempted perversion of the legislative process: He has attempted to deprive a portion of the people of the right of representation — "a right inestimable to them and formidable to tyrants only." He has called legislatures to meet at places other than their usual ones, "uncomfortable, and distant from the depository of their public Records." He has dissolved representative legislatures repeatedly, and refused consent for others to be elected. This last charge is followed by a statement of principle absolute in language and implicitly justifying the assumption of power by the various colonial assemblies elected and operating after the erosion or dissolution of royal authority. When the king has failed to make provision for a legitimate representative legislature, then, "the Legislative powers, incapable of Annihilation, have returned to the People at large for their exercise."

These passages on the legislative function should dispel the notion expressed during Jefferson's own time and repeated frequently in later decades, that the Declaration of Independence was no more than a paraphrase, if not indeed a plagiarism, of John Locke's *Second Treatise of Civil Government*. In that book, Locke had given several instances of legislative misconduct that constituted betrayal of the trust invested in the legislators by the people. One action, or lack of action, that he did not cite was the failure of a legislature to reapportion representative districts in order to provide equitable representation of the people in whatever area of the country they lived. Instead, in the muddle-headed thinking so characteristic of the *Second Treatise,* Locke proposed that a proper exercise of the prerogative power of the executive was itself to effect a redistribution of representative constituencies for the election of members to the legislature. What Locke seemed not to realize was that in granting to the executive — the crown in England — the power to correct malapportionment, he was granting power potentially to reconstitute the legislature completely — a shocking contradiction of Locke's earlier strictures concerning the utter illegitimacy of absolute monarchy.

Thomas Jefferson made no such mistake. Perhaps because of his own sharp mind, reinforced by the debate of the preceding decade over "virtual" versus actual representation, he charged George III with a deliberate attempt to deprive a segment of the population of their right to representation in the colonial legislature. This was an important principle, but most important of all was the statement cited earlier: that when the legislative body is rendered incapable of performing its necessary and legitimate functions, the legislative powers revert to the people for direct exercise by them, or perhaps to be vested by them in some new representative body.

Four subsequent counts in the indictment of George III charge him with actions constituting serious perversions of the rule of law. He has obstructed justice by refusing assent to laws establishing judiciary powers, and has violated the principle of an independent judiciary by making both the tenure and the salary of judges dependent on his will alone. This latter offense was one whose recognition was relatively new. Two thousand years earlier, Aristotle had stated what was even then an ancient maxim — that no man is a good judge in his own cause — but the separation of the judicial from the executive power and function was scarcely a century old in England. It was unknown to Locke's *Second Treatise,* and the union of executive and judicial power was embodied in the venerable term, "The King's Justice." Indeed, one of the causes of the fatal quarrel between Henry II and Thomas Becket had been the attempt of the former to establish a uniform system of justice throughout all England. The troubles of the seventeenth century had led to the recognition that Aristotle's maxim — that no man is a good judge in his own cause — must apply to the chief executive of the government itself, and thus to the rapid emergence of an independent judiciary.

Two other counts cite George III with keeping a standing army within the colonies without their consent, and with an attempt to render the military independent of the civil authority. We are familiar with the constant antagonism and occasional violence between the famous Redcoats and the civilian population in Boston and elsewhere, but that very familiarity may obscure the reason why not only American colonists, but Englishmen in the home country, had so long been opposed to a standing army. Such an army, at the command of the executive or indeed of any man or group within or without the government of the moment, can destroy one of the fundamental principles of government in a free society: that the laws of the society must be, and must be *perceived* to be, so consonant with the general welfare and with the will of the people, that their operation depends largely on the willing obedience of the governed. A standing army provides a means of securing obedience by coercion, and is thus a means of obviating that informal but continuing consent to a government expressed by general and voluntary compliance with the law.

The joint indictment of George III and "others"— i.e., the unmentioned and unmentionable Parliament of Great Britain — is brief and partly repetitive of the accusations directed at the king alone. The two branches of the British government are charged with usurpation of the legislative powers of the colonies, with abridgment of the judicial process and violation of the right to trial by jury. In view of the long debate over taxation without representation, and the frequent occasions upon which Americans had refused to submit to such taxation, it is surprising and slightly amusing to find *this* offense tucked away almost unobtrusively amidst others, and expressed in a mere eight words: "For imposing Taxes on us without our Consent." One may suspect that the brevity and relative inconspicuousness of this central count in the indictment was deliberate. Jefferson and his colleagues in the Continental Congress knew that for the informed part of the audience for whom the Declaration of Independence was intended, no elaboration was necessary. For centuries, Englishmen, and for decades, American colonists, had used the power of the purse to wrest power from monarchs and royal governments, and to increase and secure the liberties of the governed. For most of that other audience, that "candid world" to which the Declaration was submitted, such a power was unknown, and an attempted vitiation of it would probably have been either incomprehensible or seemed a very flimsy reason for breaking away from a system of government then widely reputed to be the best and the finest in the world.

The penultimate count against the king and those "others" charges them with an attempt to alter the fundamental forms of "our Governments." This count, and many of those which precede it, rest on the dual assumption that the legislatures of the colonies had been partly autonomous, and that the colonial governments were and had been based on fundamental constitutions of which the consent of the governed was an integral principle. The abrogation or abridgment of these legitimate and constitutional governments was enough to justify resistance to those parts of the British government which had usurped or misused their powers.

One thing more was needed to complete the statement of causes for the decision to separate from the British government and the British people. For centuries, a general and widely accepted principle in the theory and understanding of politics had been that protection and allegiance were reciprocal, and that when the former failed, the latter lapsed or might be withdrawn. Thus the last allegation against the British monarch conformed to this ancient concept. King George III is charged with having abdicated government in the American colonies, with declaring them "out of his Protection," and indeed with waging war against them. The case for separating from such a government and such a ruler — "a Tyrant . . . unfit to be the ruler of a free people," was complete. The words "free people" were not carelessly chosen, nor were they merely rhetorical.

It is perhaps oxymoronic to speak of a "constitutional revolution," but perhaps one may speak of a legitimate revolution, one based on the consent of the people or of a large proportion thereof. It is of crucial significance that the last paragraph of the Declaration, the formal statement of the decision to separate from

Great Britain and to form a new nation which will assume all the rights and powers acknowledged in international law as pertaining to sovereign states, begins with an affirmation of a principle implicit throughout the Declaration, a principle essential to government in a free society — the consent of the governed as the ultimate authority for the just acts of any government or any group that temporarily assumes the authority to make decisions for the people.

> We, therefore, the Representatives of the United States of America, in General Congress, Assembled, . . . do, in the Name, and by Authority of the Good People of these Colonies, solemnly publish and declare, that these United Colonies are, and of Right ought to be Free and Independent States; . . . and that all political connection between them and the State of Great Britain, is and ought to be totally dissolved. . . . And for the support of this Declaration . . . we mutually pledge to each other our Lives, our Fortunes, and our Sacred Honor.

CECELIA M. KENYON
Charles N. Clark Professor of
Government, Smith College

The Articles of Confederation
and the Creation of a Federal System

PLAYWRIGHTS, even the best of them, suffer from an affliction known in the Broadway idiom as "second act trouble." The one thing that makes this anguish bearable is that it can follow only in the wake of first act success. Assume, then, that a first act has been brought off brilliantly: dramatic conflicts created, the principal characters introduced, the action begun. As the curtain falls on Act I, the tension is high. What is to happen next?

The author is now at the most difficult stage in putting a play together. He knows how he wants his play to end, but he has a long way to go before events can be brought to that conclusion. How is the action to be advanced, the momentum of Act I maintained? This is the moment when inspiration falters. Plays, like great popular movements, fail most often in the second act.

The American Revolution had second act trouble. It opened with dramatic conflict; its first act climax was the Declaration of Independence. In Act III the promise of the Revolution will be fulfilled by ratification of the Constitution of the United States. What lies between is Act II, the Articles of Confederation and the years of early constitutional experience, pre-federal, tentative, and sometimes dismaying, between 1776 and 1787.

I

Act II opens with a familiar line: "We must all hang together or assuredly we shall all hang separately." Sensible patriots had known for a long time that resistance or rebellion against the British Crown was hopeless unless the disparate colonies could be brought into some kind of effective alliance. America's first musical hit, the *Liberty Song* of 1768,[1] had proclaimed the need for unity

---

1. David Ewen, *Songs of America* (Chicago, 1947), pp. 3, 19-21.

of colonial action. Set to a Drury Lane tune and with words by
John Dickinson, of whom we shall be hearing more in a moment,
the refrain rang out from every tavern frequented by the Sons of
Liberty:

> Then join hand in hand, brave Americans all,
> By uniting we stand, by dividing we fall.

Even at the height of revolutionary enthusiasm, there were prudent
members of the Continental Congress who hoped that independence
would not be formally proclaimed until an acceptable plan of
intercolonial association had been worked out and agreed to. So
it is not surprising that when Richard Henry Lee rose in the
Congress on June 7, 1776 to move his resolution that "these united
states are, and of right ought to be, free and independent states,"
he made it part of his motion that "a plan of confederation be
prepared and transmitted to the respective colonies for their consideration and approbation."

In June and early July of 1776, independence and confederation
moved along briskly together. The committee to draft a formal
document of independence was appointed by the Congress on
June 11, the committee to prepare a plan of confederation was
named the following day. Jefferson's draft of the Declaration was
reported to the Congress on June 28; the thirteen-man committee
on confederation presented its plan on July 12. The draft was in
the handwriting of John Dickinson[2] and embodied his ideas as to
a sound pattern of interstate association, although we can infer,
from the unanimous committee recommendation, that Dickinson
had done his best to take account of the views of his committee
colleagues.

John Dickinson was a moderate — and, worse, a lawyer — and
historians have not been as kind to him as to bolder spirits of the
Revolutionary period. He was the committee's natural choice as
its draftsman. Trained at the Middle Temple and one of the first
of the great Philadelphia lawyers, Dickinson had been fighting
the good fight for American liberties, in his own exasperatingly
moderate way, for a long time. He was known throughout the
colonies as the author of *Letters from a Farmer in Pennsylvania,* the
best reasoned statement of the case against the constitutionality
of the Townshend Acts. Congress had entrusted him before with

---

2. Merrill Jensen, *The Articles of Confederation* (Madison, Wis., 1940), p. 128;
Julian P. Boyd, ed., *The Articles of Confederation and Perpetual Union,* Old
South Leaflets *238-239* (Boston, 1960): pp. 5-6.

crucial assignments, as draftsman of the Olive Branch Petition to
George III and as the revisor, to Jefferson's considerable distaste,
of Jefferson's Declaration of the Causes and Necessity of Taking
Up Arms.[3] In an era of remarkably talented public draftsmen,
Dickinson was one of the best. His work on the Articles was
compressed into less than three weeks, because he was unwilling
to sign the Declaration of Independence and left the Congress to
join his militia regiment before July 4. Important changes were
made in the plan of confederation in the course of its progress
through the Congress, but the Dickinson draft was carried over,
stylistically and in most of its detailed provisions, into the Articles
of Confederation as finally adopted[4] and so served, a decade later,
as an important material source of the Constitution of the United
States.

John Dickinson's great reputation and his reluctance to surrender
all hope of ultimate reconciliation with the crown had made him
unpopular in some quarters. "A certain great fortune and piddling
genius," John Adams wrote of Dickinson's Olive Branch Petition,
"has given a silly cast to our whole doings."[5] And shortly after
Dickinson's draft of the Act of Confederation was presented to the
Congress for consideration, Edward Rutledge wrote of it that it had
"the vice of all his productions to a considerable degree; I mean
the vice of refining too much."[6] Rutledge's criticism survives as a
classic misdiagnosis of the practical task of constitution-making.
Dickinson's draft, a manifest working paper designed to serve as
the starting point for discussion in the Congress, was, if anything,
too free-flowing and insufficiently "refined," particularly in its
omission of any clause formally proclaiming the continued sovereignty of the states. Dickinson's failure to take this rhetorical
precaution led to much controversy and delay as the plan of
confederation moved slowly through the Congress and is probably
why subsequent scholars have tended to exaggerate the substantive
differences between the Dickinson draft and the Articles as finally

---

3. Edmund C. Burnett, *The Continental Congress* (New York, 1941), pp.
85-86.
4. The text of the Dickinson draft is set out in Merrill Jensen, *supra* note 2,
pp. 254-262. It is evident from a textual comparison of the Dickinson draft
with the Act of Confederation as ultimately approved by Congress that much of
Dickinson's language was retained. It is to be noted that the Act proceeds, as
Dickinson had, by specific enumeration of the powers that were being delegated
by the states to the central authority.
5. Edmund C. Burnett, *supra* note 3, p. 87.
6. *Idem.,* p. 214.

adopted, even to see the plan of confederation proposed by Dickinson as something qualitatively different from the plan at which the Congress ultimately arrived.[7] Much debate and misunderstanding would have been avoided if Dickinson had included an explicit recital of state sovereignty in his draft. Perhaps we can fault him for failing to foresee the fanciful interpretations that might be given to his text by unfriendly readers in the Congress. But who before had ever been called on to write a constitution for an association of self-consciously independent states?

In November, 1777, the Act of Confederation,[8] as finally agreed to after sixteen months of off-and-on congressional consideration, was sent to the states, accompanied by an urgent plea that they signify their approval within four months, that is, by March 10, 1778. But it was not until three years after the suggested deadline that Maryland, the last hold-out, authorized its delegates to affix their signatures and so complete the process of ratification. The Act of Confederation formally became the first constitution of the United States on March 1, 1781, only four months before Yorktown. Sermons of thanksgiving were preached in the churches when the Articles were promulgated; the appropriate text would have been "How long, O Lord, how long!" Independence and confederation had started out together; it had taken almost five years longer to bring the newly independent states into their first constitutional association. This is always so in matters of govern-

---

7. Thus, for example, the foremost historian of the Articles of Confederation, discerns in the Dickinson draft an attempt by "conservatives" to undermine the political position of the states and create a sovereign Congress. Merrill Jensen, *supra* note 2, pp. 130-137, 161-176. The text of the Dickinson draft does not, in my judgment, support this interpretation. Wary opponents of centralized power, like Dr. Thomas Burke of North Carolina, were, to be sure, alarmed by the Dickinson draft. But their apprehensions, it would seem, related less to what the draft actually provided than to how its ambiguities might conceivably be construed during and after the war to support broad assertions of congressional power over the states. These apprehensions of the congressional "radicals" seem somewhat far-fetched for two reasons: (1) Dickinson's draft provided for a common government of specifically enumerated—and therefore limited—powers; and (2) by Dickinson's draft, as by the Act of Confederation finally approved by Congress in 1777, the common government could act only on and through the states, who would surely not have acquiesced in—and would have been under no constitutional obligation to acquiesce in—assertions by the Congress of powers beyond those delegated to it in the organic instrument of union.

8. Julian P. Boyd is certainly right in his contention that "Act of Confederation" is a more appropriate title than the conventional but cumbersomely plural "Articles of Confederation." Boyd, *supra* note 2, p. 3. Both "Act of Confederation" and "Articles of Confederation" are used in this paper, as best serves the sense of the passage.

ment. A different temper and greater staying power are required to build for the future than to break with the past. Revolt, however principled, is an act of will against an intolerable old order. Constitution-making, the construction of institutions for a new way of government, is a process of reason, compromise, and patience, less exciting than rebellion, divisive in tendency where revolution makes for solidarity, and not a task for the short-winded.

II

The topic assigned to me for this Bicentennial observance is *The Articles of Confederation and the Creation of a Federal System.* A principle of selection is, I think, implied and imposed: the Confederation is to be examined not as a self-contained episode in our political history but as a way-station on the road to American federalism.[9] Accordingly, my emphasis will be on the contribution of the Articles and the experience of the Confederation to the process by which thirteen aggressively independent states, recently colonies, became an effective union, but without losing their separate identities and political significance. This requires, unavoidably, a brief exercise in political taxonomy.[10] Several countries may agree by treaty or in some less formal way to coordinate their separate actions and support each other's interests in one or more matters of shared concern, usually military defense. This is a *league* or alliance. The associating states may go a step farther towards union and subscribe to a constitution whereby some common government comes into existence, and the constituent states are under obligation to act through that new central authority in specified matters, such as customs duties or external relations. That is a *confederation.*

When is the next step reached in the continuum of interstate association? The decisive step is taken when the constituent states entrust the central government with power to deal directly with individual citizens and not simply with and through the state

---

9. In preparing his draft of the Articles of Confederation, Dickinson manifestly drew on such sources as Franklin's 1754 plan of intercolonial union and the Galloway plan of 1774. These and even earlier documentary antecedents of the Dickinson draft are discussed in James H. Hutson, "Tentative Moves Towards Intercolonial Union," pp. 81-94 of the present Bicentennial volume.

10. The analysis here is based on Robert M. MacIver, *The Modern State* (London, 1926), pp. 356-363. The late Professor MacIver was one of the most perceptive of twentieth-century social scientists, and *The Modern State* is a masterpiece in the literature of law-government.

governments. This is the distinctive mark of a true *federation* or federal system. But the power of the central government is not plenary in a federal system; the constituent states retain not only their regional identities but also substantial powers to act on their own independently of the center. To the extent that the states become mere administrative units, charged only with such responsibilities as the central government sees fit to delegate or leave with them, the government is no longer federal but unitary.

A unitary national state, even a genuinely federal government, was out of the question in 1776–1781. The Declaration of the Causes and Necessity of Taking Up Arms had proclaimed that "Our union is perfect." But saying did not make it so. The colonies were scattered along the seaboard. Transportation and communications were so undependable and slow that Boston was more remote from Charleston, even Baltimore from New York, than Paris or New Delhi seem from America today.[11] Colonial rivalries, jealousies, and special interests did not disappear with independence; longstanding intercolonial antagonisms were instead exacerbated in the early attempts to arrive at collective American decisions, and particularly during congressional consideration of the Articles of Confederation. Were the costs of the war and other expenses of the Confederation to be shared by the states in proportion to state populations, as Dickinson had had it, or on some other basis? Was voting in the Congress to be according to population or on the basis of one state, one vote? And no issue was quite as bitterly debated as the question of what provision, if any, the Articles should make concerning the vast western land claims, "to the South Sea," asserted by Virginia, Connecticut and certain other states by virtue of their colonial charters.[12]

There were ideological differences, too, even harder to deal with because they cut across state lines. A good many members of the Continental Congress were determined that no new central government should be raised over the thirteen states. It is not

---

11. "In Europe the powerful local diversities were, for the most part, the institutional detritus of time. In America they were largely the effects of topography, climate, and physical distance. While European politics was primarily the by-product of history, American politics was a by-product of geography." Daniel J. Boorstin, *The Americans: The National Experience* (New York, 1965), pp. 401-402.

12. On the three central issues—representation in Congress, the basis for revenue assessments on the states, and the western land claims, see the masterful analysis in Merrill Jensen, *supra* note 2, pp. 140-160.

that these men were hostile towards all government; most of them favored public intervention in such matters as the relief of debtors and the prevention of profiteering. But it was local government they trusted, and the more local the better. Like the "participatory democracy" theorists of our own day, they idealized small-unit decision-making: the village was best, the county almost as good, the state acceptable. But nation-wide government was to them inherently incompatible with democracy.

These "radicals," as Merrill Jensen characterizes them,[13] found support for their views on the curse of bigness in government in the text of the Declaration of Independence: "whenever any form of government becomes destructive of these ends, it is the right of the people to alter or abolish it." An oppressive or unresponsive county government can be altered or abolished with no particular difficulty. Even a state government is not a citadel powerful enough to withstand an outraged populace bent on the overthrow of arbitrary public authority. But if a distant, nation-wide government, armed with who knows what force, menaces life, liberty, and happiness, of what avail is "the right of the people to alter or abolish it?" The argument seems far-fetched to us, perhaps, but the right of revolution was not a subject for purely theoretical disputation when the Articles of Confederation were before the Continental Congress. A revolution was going on within hearing, and it was against an imperial authority that had asserted precisely the powers over the regional governments that the radicals were determined not to see pass into the hands of an American national state.

So John Dickinson and those who participated in the revision of his draft during the sixteen months the Articles remained unfinished business in the Congress had a tightrope to walk. The constitution they were devising had to provide a sufficient basis for consistent and reasonably unified participation by all the states in the winning of the war and the consolidation of the peace thereafter, but it had to be so drafted as not to arouse the touchy sensibilities of the still newly associated states and the anti-big-government ideologues in the Congress. Neither Dickinson nor those who succeeded him in charge of the bill that became the Act of Confederation tried for a truly federal form of interstate association; there would have been few votes in 1776 and 1777 for a constitution empowering the central authority to tax or otherwise

---

13. Jensen explains his usage of "radical" and "conservative" in *idem.*, p. 10, n. 23.

affect individual citizens directly rather than through the states of their residence. Nineteenth- and twentieth-century scholars who have chided the members of the Continental Congress for the "deficiencies" of the Confederation, for not having created a full-fledged federal system then and there, ignore the political climate of the time.

The Continental Congress, in its inception, was not a national legislature but the council of an alliance for mutual defense. No one then assumed that this mere league would take over tasks of practical government. It was taken for granted that basic public administration during the war and thereafter would be state by state, as it had been in the separate colonies. Congress did not presume even to suggest a uniform pattern of state government; it simply recommended on May 10, 1776, that "the respective assemblies and conventions of the United Colonies . . . adopt such government as shall, in the opinion of the representatives of the people, best conduce to the happiness and safety of their constituents in particular and America in general."[14]

The Declaration of Independence reaffirmed, in effect, the primacy and separateness of the states. In Jefferson's great opening sentence, Americans are "one people," but the Declaration's concluding and operative paragraph asserts not the independence of a people but of "free and independent states." Jefferson's usage in this paragraph is consistent and careful: *"they* [the states] are absolved from all allegiance to the British crown," *"they* have full power to levy war, conclude peace . . . and do all other acts and things which Independent States may of right do." The term "United States of America" appears once in the passage, but it signifies not a political entity but an aggregate of separate sovereignties "united" only in a shared purpose to break off all ties with an imperial power that had oppressed them all. Stylistic purists sometimes annoy us by insisting that "the United States" should be followed by a plural verb form —"the United States are," rather than "the United States is"— but their stuffiness in the matter is a useful reminder of the great fact of our early constitutional history.[15]

---

14. Richard L. Perry, ed., *Sources of Our Liberties* (American Bar Foundation, 1959), p. 316.

15. "The new nation, until the Civil War, was commonly described in the plural. For John Adams in 1774, Massachusetts Bay was 'our country' and the Massachusetts delegation in Congress was 'our embassy.' For Jefferson, too, until much later, 'my country' commonly meant Virginia." Daniel J. Boorstin, *supra* note 11, p. 402.

III

Though remembered now chiefly for its "deficiencies," the Act of Confederation was, in its day, a remarkable step towards national union. It was not, as some would have preferred, just an alliance for the duration of a war; Article XIII stated explicitly that "the union shall be perpetual," a commitment to the future nowhere stated in the Constitution drafted a decade later. And the resounding affirmation in Article II that "each state retains its sovereignty, freedom and independence" obscures the extent to which the Act of Confederation did, in fact, impose restrictions on the autonomy of the state governments, even in their relations with each other. Special compacts were not to be made between two or more states without the consent of the Congress,[16] and each state came under constitutional duty to give full faith and credit to the judgments of courts in other states[17] and to return fugitives from justice who might flee the process of one state and take refuge in another.[18]

The Articles of Confederation — and this has gone almost unnoticed — laid the foundation for what will become national American citizenship. Wholly sovereign states regulate entrance into their territory by visas and immigration procedures and can and commonly do prefer their own citizens over aliens in the granting of work permits, commercial privileges and the like. By Article IV of the Act of Confederation, discriminations by a state against the citizens of another American state are made unconstitutional:

> The free inhabitants of each of these states [unhappy reminder in this phrase of the paradox of slavery in the most passionately libertarian of American generations!] shall be entitled to all privileges and immunities of free citizens in the several states; and the people of each state shall have free ingress and regress to and from any other state, and shall enjoy therein all the privileges of trade and commerce, subject to the same duties, impositions and restrictions as the inhabitants thereof.[19]

---

16. "Article VI. No two or more states shall enter into any treaty, confederation or alliance whatever between them, without the consent of the united states in congress assembled." Article I, section 10 of the Constitution contains an equivalent provision.

17. The full faith and credit clause of article IV of the Act of Confederation was carried over almost word for word in the corresponding provision (Article IV, section 1) of the Constitution.

18. The interstate rendition clause in article IV of the Act of Confederation appears, with insubstantial editorial changes, in article IV, section 2 of the Constitution.

19. Compare the privileges and immunities clauses in the Constitution (article IV, section 2) and in section 1 of the Fourteenth Amendment.

New York, in short, may prefer New Yorkers over Englishmen or Dutchmen or Canadians but not over Marylanders or Virginians.

This assumption by the states of a constitutional duty not to discriminate against the citizens of a sister state in the granting of privileges and opportunities is not to be discounted as a symbol of emerging American nationhood. It was, to be sure, only a duty of equal treatment with a state's own citizens; the Articles of Confederation imposed no other restraints on the power of the state governments over the individuals within their jurisdiction. But we must remember that virtually no such restriction was to be imposed on the state governments by either the Constitution or the Bill of Rights.[20] Constitutional limitations on what a state government may do in dealing with its own citizens will not come into existence in the United States until 1868 when the states, "perhaps without being entirely aware of what they were doing,"[21] ratified the sweepingly phrased Fourteenth Amendment to the Constitution.

We come now to what usually gets all the attention in scholarly analysis of composite governments, the division of functions between the central authority and the regional governments. The drafting of a constitutional document for an association of states is, among other things, an exercise in practical semantics. In the formulation of the Articles of Confederation, as later in the drafting of the Constitution, verbal concessions had to be made to those who were fearful of centralized power and zealous to preserve what they thought of as the inviolable sovereignty of the states. Thus the central authority created by the Act of Confederation was cautiously described in the document itself, never as a "government," usually by the awkward compromise term, "the united states in congress assembled." Dickinson's draft had provided for a central "Council of State" to manage the Confederation's affairs; in the Act as finally adopted this was replaced by "a Committee of the States"

---

20. The Constitution itself imposed only a few restrictions on state action affecting a state's own citizens: bills of attainder, ex post facto laws, and laws impairing the obligation of contracts are all prohibited by article I, section 10. But the guarantees of the Bill of Rights, as drafted and ratified in 1791, ran only against the federal government. This was the constitutional situation until ratification of the Fourteenth Amendment in 1868. The Supreme Court, by expansive interpretation of the due process clause of the Fourteenth Amendment, has held in recent years that most of the liberties specified in the Bill of Rights are incorporated in the due process clause of the Fourteenth Amendment and so guaranteed against infringement by state, as well as federal, action.

21. Henry J. Friendly, *The Constitution*, U.S. Dept. of Justice Bicentennial Lecture Series (1976), 1: p. 12.

empowered to sit only in the recess of Congress. But when we cut through from form to substance, it is evident that the interstate association created by the Articles was a true confederation and not the mere "firm league of friendship" recited in Article III. "The united states in congress assembled" was, within its area of competence, a common government through which the thirteen constituent states were constitutionally bound to act.

The political jurisdiction delegated by the states to the common government, although somewhat more circumscribed than it had been by Dickinson's draft of the Articles, was surprisingly comprehensive. The states were specifically foreclosed from acting, and the central government given exclusive authority to act on behalf of the whole, not only in such business as coinage, interstate postal service, and uniform weights and measures, but also in such great matters as war and peace, diplomatic representation and foreign policy, the settlement of state boundary disputes, external Indian affairs,[22] and the expenditure of funds "for the common defense and general welfare" of the new country. "The united states in congress assembled" was given no authority over interstate and foreign commerce, the states being left free to go their own parochial ways in the regulation and taxing of trade,[23] but in all other substantive respects the division of functions between the state governments and the newly created central government was about the same in the Articles of Confederation as in the Constitution that would be drafted in Philadelphia in 1787.

IV

How, then, are we to account for the "second act trouble," the wavering and indecisive course of American political action that

---

22. "The united states in congress assembled shall also have the sole and exclusive right and power of . . . regulating the trade and managing all affairs with the Indians, not members of any of the states, provided that the legislative right of any state within its own limits be not infringed or violated" (article IX).
23. The only relevant limitation was that states were prohibited from imposing imposts or duties "which may interfere with any stipulations in treaties entered into by the united states in congress assembled, with any king, prince or state, *in pursuance of any treaties already proposed by congress, to the courts of France and Spain* (article VI) [emphasis added]. Dickinson's draft had contained a far more comprehensive prohibition of duties that might interfere with "any stipulations in treaties hereinafter entered into by the united states assembled, with the king or kingdom of Great Britain, or any foreign prince or state." If the state sovereignty zealots had not tampered with Dickinson's draft on this point, the Confederation might not have been embarrassed as it was after 1783 by state disregard of commitments made to Great Britain by the Peace of Paris.

caused many to despair of the future of the union even after the War of Independence had been won? For one thing, the unifying potential of the Act of Confederation had been diminished by the long delay, from 1777 to 1781, in ratification by the states. The Articles served in these intermediate, often disheartening war years as a kind of *de facto* constitution to which reference might be made when claims of national necessity came into collision with stubborn assertions of state prerogative, but they lacked the force and moral sanction of a formally adopted constitutional charter. By the time the Articles had been agreed to by every state, as the rule of unanimity required, they were already largely discredited. American constitution-makers would not run that risk again. The rule of unanimity was rejected by the Constitutional Convention of 1787; ratification by nine states "shall be sufficient for the establishment of this Constitution between the states so ratifying the same."[24]

When the Act of Confederation was endorsed by Congress and sent to the states, no one anticipated that confederation would be kept in political limbo for more than three years. Nor was it clearly perceived that the requirement of unanimous state approval of any subsequent alteration of the instrument's original provisions would, by giving each state a veto, make the Articles unamendable as a practical matter. We can see with the wisdom of hindsight that these consequences were inevitable. But the Articles of Confederation had to be drafted *a priori,* with little relevant experience to go by. In 1776 and 1777, it was not as clear as it became later on that unanimity of the thirteen state governments could not be achieved on practically any proposition at all.

What Dickinson and those who succeeded him in the draftsman's role could not have foreseen was the paralyzing effect on the Confederation government of the provision in Article IX that none of the essential powers delegated to the Congress could be exercised "unless nine states assent to the same." This, on the face of it, seems a not unreasonable provision: the legislative assembly of the new and untried confederation is not to take significant measures unless the action proposed has the support of delegates representing more than two-thirds of the states. But sessions of the Confederation Congress were, by and large, very unevenly attended. It was a rare day when delegates from nine states were on the floor. Measures of great consequence and

---

24. Constitution, article VIII.

urgency often failed in the Congress, or were enacted far too late, not because they were opposed by the representatives of four or more states but because no nine states had their delegates there.[25] The nine-state rule would have been reasonably workable if the states and their delegates had lived up to their responsibilities. But representative government, in the Confederation years, still had a long way to go.

Constitutionalism as a way of government depends on the willingness and determination of the people, particularly of those who hold political power, that the constitutional compact be honored and made to work. The failures of the Confederation — and it had its rebuffs as well as its considerable successes — were not shortcomings of a document, the Act of Confederation, but failures of constitutional obligation. Some of the blame must be assigned to the Congress, too many of whose members were negligent in their attendance, timorous in the assertion of the authority delegated by the Articles, and often more mindful of protocol and petty distinctions than of the needs of the new republic. Greater fault attaches to those political leaders in the states, including many former members of the Continental Congress, who put state interests above the constitutional obligations their states had assumed by ratifying the Act of Confederation.

As a confederation government, "the united states in congress assembled" acted not on individual citizens directly but on and through the state governments. Let us take as our illustration the central and eternal problem of how the costs of government are to be financed. The Articles empowered the Congress to appropriate money for the "common defence or general welfare" of the United States. But the cupboard was bare; how was the money to be raised? The Congress was authorized to issue paper money. This it did until the phrase "not worth a continental" became a scornful idiom. And the Congress had the power to borrow money, which it did until its credit was exhausted everywhere. But the Congress could not lay taxes and collect them from individuals. Replenishment of the treasury from tax revenues could be accomplished only through the agency of the state governments.

The states were under clear constitutional duty to honor the

---

25. For examples, see Edmund C. Burnett, *supra* note 3, pp. 590-593, 638-641, 700-702.

requisitions Congress made on them for funds. Article VIII was explicit and unambiguous on this crucial point:

> All charges of war, and all other expenses that shall be incurred for the common defence or general welfare, and allowed by the united states in congress assembled, shall be defrayed out of a common treasury, which shall be supplied by the several states, in proportion to the value of all land within each state . . . as such land and the buildings and improvements thereon shall be estimated according to such mode as the united states in congress assembled, shall from time to time direct and appoint. The taxes for paying that proportion shall be laid and levied by the authority and direction of the legislatures of the several states within the time agreed on by the united states in congress assembled.

Words could not be plainer: the common treasury "shall" be supplied by the states in proportion; the necessary taxes "shall" be laid by the states within the time fixed by Congress. And, lest there be room for dispute concerning the finality of the Congress's determinations as to how much money was needed and the amount of each state's proportionate share, Article XII was equally clear and explicit:

> Every state shall abide by the determinations of the united states in congress assembled, on all questions which by this confederation are submitted to them.

Can it be said in defense or extenuation of the state leaders responsible for the frequent neglect of urgent congressional requisitions that they had not known what their states were getting into by ratifying the Act of Confederation? The Act itself had given full and painstaking notice. When the state delegates signed their names to the Articles, they wrote them directly under an attestation clause recording that

> we the undersigned delegates . . . do further solemnly plight and engage the faith of our respective constituents, that the articles [of confederation] shall be inviolably observed by the states we respectively represent.

How better could the constitutional obligation have been expressed? Given state fidelity to the solemnly accepted constitutional design, confederation was an entirely workable plan of interstate association.

Yet throughout the Confederation years, Congress was continuously harassed by critical shortages of money. The shabby treatment afforded to the officers and men of the revolutionary armies at the end of the war is but an example, although the most striking one, of the harm done to the stability and reputation of the United States by the persistent unwillingness of state governors and legislators to risk local unpopularity by imposing the taxes necessary to honor the financial requisitions of the Congress. Officers and men, it appeared, were to be discharged without receiving the benefits that had been promised them, even without their long overdue back pay. Washington's letter of October 2, 1782, to the secretary of war, General Benjamin Lincoln, is a moving reminder of how quickly fiery civilian patriots can forget their indebtedness to those who did the fighting:

> When I see such a number of men goaded by a thousand stings of reflexion on the past, and of anticipation on the future, about to be turned into the world, soured by penury and what they call the ingratitude of the public, involved in debts, without one farthing of money to carry them home, after having spent the flower of their days and many of them their patrimonies in establishing the freedom and independence of their country, and suffered everything that human nature is capable of enduring on this side of death . . . I cannot avoid apprehending that a train of evils will follow, of a very serious and distressing nature.[26]

And a train of evils did follow: the Newburgh Addresses of March, 1783, in which the army was exhorted to take forceful action against a weak and impotent Congress and the "obdurate and forgetful states," the sullen sergeants' remonstrance of a few months later, Congress itself virtually besieged by unpaid and mutinous troops and frightened into changing its location from Philadelphia to Princeton.[27]

Our second act had reached its most disquieting moment, the duly constituted legislative authority of the United States menaced by a mob of disaffected soldiers. As one despairing member of the Congress wrote to his far-off governor:

> In this state of things what can Congress do, without the means of paying those debts they constitutionally contracted for the safety of the United States, responsible for every thing, and unable to do any thing, hated by the public creditors, insulted by the soldiery and unsupported by the citizens?[28]

It was a close call for the infant republic. All hope of American

---

26. *Idem.*, p. 552.
27. *Idem.*, pp. 572-580.
28. *Idem.*, p. 580.

federalism might have perished then and there if Washington had been less resolute in his management of the crisis, or if he had not commanded the veneration of his troops in the degree that was the mark of his character.

In the few years of life that remained to it after 1783, the Confederation stumbled from one financial emergency to another. Congressional requisitions for funds were regularly and most earnestly made but met with uneven and grudging responses in the states. One cannot read the history of the Confederation Congress without being reminded of Hotspur's exchange with Owen Glendower:

> *Glendower.* I can call spirits from the vasty deep.
> *Hotspur.* Why, so can I, or so can any man;
> But will they come when you do call for them?[29]

The requisitions directed by the Congress to the states were, to be sure, valid and binding orders under the constitutional scheme of the Articles, but this was small comfort if the requisitions lacked practical efficacy. And constitutional irresponsibility is a contagious political disease; the states that were living up to their constitutional duties, as some were at least most of the time, were becoming restive about the inequality of burden and could not be expected to continue paying their Confederation dues if other states neglected theirs.

What, then, was to be done to put the Confederation's house in order? Inevitably, people concerned about the survival of the precariously situated new union thought first in terms of sanctions that might be brought to bear on a state when the persuasions of the Congress failed. How might a defaulting state be coerced into honoring its financial and other obligations as a member of the Confederation? This was a false clue. The use of national force against a state and its office-holders is a risky and disruptive business, far too drastic for employment except as a last resort and likely, as has happened in our own day, to make defiant state officials heroes in the eyes of their local constituents. The sounder course was to take the decisive step from confederation to federation, that is, to enable the central government to exercise its delegated powers by the enactment of laws addressed to individual citizens and enforceable against them directly by federal officers and in federal tribunals. This decisive step was never a practical

29. King Henry IV, Part I, act III, scene 1.

possibility under the Articles of Confederation. A far more modest
and widely supported proposal that the Congress, as a means of
restoring the credit of the Confederation, be authorized to levy
and collect limited import duties of its own had been pressed for
years but unavailingly.[30] But this lesson of the Confederation was
not lost on the delegates who assembled in Philadelphia in 1787
to frame the second constitution of the United States.[31]

V

There is manifest and striking continuity between the first
American constitution and its far more durable successor. The
Articles of Confederation and American constitutional experience
during the Confederation years were incomparably the most important material sources of the new Constitution. Public men of the
revolutionary generation had a way of embellishing their discourse
with citations to classic works on political philosophy, and they
greatly enjoyed bringing in references to such exotic ventures in
interstate association as the Amphictyonic Council and the Grison
League. When they came to practical judgments, however, they
drew most often on documents they knew by heart and on political
experience in which they themselves had participated. As Max
Farrand wrote of the Constitutional Convention and its committee
on detail:

> The surprising thing, especially to one accustomed to condemn
> the articles of confederation, is to see how large a part of the
> powers vested in congress were taken from the articles of con-
> federation.[32]

Farrand was writing about the crucially important section of
the Constitution in which the delegated powers of Congress are
enumerated, but there are other federalism-related sections in which
the constitutional text borrows the language of the Articles, sometimes word for word. And the members of the Constitutional
Convention were influenced even more by the trial-and-error

---

30. Edmund C. Burnett, *supra* note 3, pp. 479-481, 570-572, 642-644, 661-663.

31. "The great and crucial decision of the Convention that met in Philadelphia
in May, 1789, was the decision that a federal government should be established
with powers to act directly upon individuals and not simply upon the member
states. And this was buttressed by the corollary decision that the 'Constitution,
and the Laws of the United States which shall be made in Pursuance thereof;
and all Treaties made, or which shall be made, under the Authority of the
United States, shall be the Supreme Law of the Land.'" Henry M. Hart, Jr.,
and Herbert Wechsler, *The Federal Courts and the Federal System* (Brooklyn,
1953), pp. 7-8.

32. Max Farrand, *The Framing of the Constitution of the United States* (New
Haven, 1912), p. 140.

experience of the Confederation period. When the design of the Constitution departs most sharply from the plan of the Articles, the probable explanation is that the Constitution's framers made the change to avoid problems of federal-state relations that had caused serious trouble in the Confederation era. "The life of the law," wrote Justice Holmes, "has not been logic: it has been experience."[33] The Constitution of the United States was not drafted *a priori* but on the basis of the known and thoughtfully analyzed experience of the troubled years of the Confederation.

But the Articles of Confederation and the years of interstate association under the plan of the Articles were more than a rehearsal for the Constitutional Convention of 1787. We have seen the seamy side of the Confederation period; let us not discount its triumphs. The War of Independence was brought to a successful conclusion. The exclusive peace-making and diplomatic powers conferred on the central government by the Articles proved adequate and were used forcefully and imaginatively by the Congress's emissaries abroad, Franklin, Jay, and John Adams. The Peace of Paris of 1783 still stands as the greatest diplomatic triumph of American history.[34]

There are other entries on the happy side of the Confederation ledger. First among these is certainly the Ordinance of 1787, by which the problems presented to the new nation by its succession to vast unorganized lands west of the Appalachians were resolved to the great and lasting benefit of the American federal system. The problems had been formidable ones from the earliest days of intercolonial association. In 1776 and 1777, when the Articles of Confederation were going through the congressional wringer, no subject was more bitterly contested than the status of the western lands that Virginia, Connecticut, and five other states asserted were theirs by right of colonial charter grants "to the South Sea."[35] The states without such claims were determined from the outset that the widespread territory that might be won from Great Britain by the united effort of all the colonies should be the common possession of the Confederation. It was Maryland's refusal to ratify the Act of Confederation unless the claimant states agreed to cede their western land claims to the Confederation that delayed the full constitutional effectiveness of the Articles until 1781.

---

33. *The Common Law* (Boston, 1881), p. 1.
34. The definitive study of the Peace of Paris is Richard B. Morris, *The Peacemakers: The Great Powers and American Independence* (New York, 1965).
35. Merrill Jensen, *supra* note 2, pp. 120-124, 198-238.

The claimant states at length yielded, and the western lands became the domain of the Confederation. What was to be their political future? Some seaboard conservatives were fearful of the rough democracy that might spring up on the frontier and wanted to keep the western regions in subordinate, virtually colonial status. The Confederation Congress, in its most far-seeing hour, followed Jefferson's lead[36] and enacted the Northwest Ordinance, by which the vast ceded area was divided into five regions, each of which was to be eligible in time for "admission to a share in the Federal councils on an equal footing with the original states."

The Ordinance of 1787 is a remarkable document in many ways. The inhabitants of the territories are protected in their liberties by a comprehensive bill of rights, and each territory is to have a representative assembly as soon as its population includes five thousand qualified voters. Section VI of the Ordinance, prohibiting slavery in the northwest territory,[37] will be copied almost word for word in the Thirteenth Amendment to the Constitution. The historic significance of the Ordinance for the American federal system is its establishment of the precedent that American federalism is to be continent-wide.[38] It is not empire but federal govern-

---

36. The first ordinance for the government of the western lands, drafted and introduced by Jefferson, was passed by Congress in 1784 but never put into effect. Jefferson's plan, like the Ordinance of 1787, provided for the admission of new states on a basis of full political equality with the older ones. Perry, ed., *supra* note 14, p. 388.

37. "Article VI. There shall be neither slavery nor involuntary servitude in the said territory, otherwise than in the punishment of crime whereof the party shall have been duly convicted." Jefferson's draft of the 1784 ordinance contained a provision that would have abolished slavery in the territory after 1830, but this provision had been stricken from the bill in the course of its passage. Manifestly, Jefferson's 1784 draft was the inspiration of article VI of the Ordinance of 1787.

38. The Constitution (article IV, section 3) is less explicit than the Ordinance of 1787 with respect to the political equality of the new states and simply provides that "new states may be admitted by the Congress into this union." This less than satisfactory formulation came about through a Convention maneuver by Gouverneur Morris, the delegate most fearful of a possible shift of power from the old states to the more numerous new ones. As the draft of the Constitution emerged from the committee on detail, it provided explicitly that the new states were to be admitted "on the same terms with the original states." Morris objected to this clause and successfully proposed the noncommittal substitute that found its way into the Constitution. Max Farrand, ed., *The Records of the Federal Convention of 1787* (4 v., rev. ed., New Haven, 1937) 2: pp. 454-455. It appears from Morris's later correspondence that his undisclosed intent in moving the substitute was to leave Congress with power to govern at least some later-acquired territories "as provinces" with "no voice in our affairs." Max Farrand, *supra* note 32, pp. 144-145. If this was Morris's purpose, his language seems poorly chosen to accomplish it. In any event, the precedent of the Ordinance of 1787 was too strong to be reversed. In later years, and particularly until the Civil

ment that is to take its way westward. It is curious, in a way, that this great act of statesmanship was accomplished in the waning days of the Confederation Congress, even as the delegates to the Constitutional Convention were meeting in Philadelphia to devise the new constitution. But perhaps it is appropriate that the last major enactment of the old constitutional dispensation was its wisest and most enduring achievement.

VI

Psychiatrists of the Freudian persuasion contend that adult character is affected far more by what happens to a person in infancy and early childhood than by anything that may befall him in later years. The poet puts it better: "as the twig is bent, the tree's inclined." So it is, I think, with political societies. The Articles of Confederation served as the constitution of the United States for only a brief time. But these were formative years for the American federal system. Inclinations then imprinted on our political order carry over into the Constitution of 1787 and are discernible even now, after almost two hundred years of ever unfolding constitutional development.

As we read them now, the proceedings of the Confederation Congress seem ancient history, almost a fossil record. Yet that record, however confused and indecisive, yields more evidence than any other on how the American federal system came to take its lasting form. We are right to exalt the Declaration of 1776 and the Constitution of 1787. They are the great events of our early political history. But the Confederation was more than a mere aimless interlude between them. There were hesitations, doubts, and failures of energy in this second act of our historical drama. But the Confederation decade, far better than is commonly known, served to advance the action, and that is what a second act is supposed to do. To edit it out is to miss much of the sense of the play.

HARRY W. JONES
Cardozo Professor of Jurisprudence,
Columbia University

War, the admission of new states was often influenced by considerations of national politics, but there was never a question of keeping a region in permanent colonial status until the nation acquired territories outside the "continental United States." The precedent of the Ordinance of 1787 was most recently reaffirmed by the admission to statehood of Alaska and Hawaii.

Toward "A More Perfect Union": Framing and Implementing the Distinctive Nation-Building Elements of the Constitution

THIS ESSAY is an effort to identify the Constitution's most distinctive contributions to nation-building. I want to ask what was most original, most significant, most lasting about the framework for government that emerged from those remarkable debates during that memorable Philadelphia summer of 1787. I want also to trace some critical steps in the implementation of the key features of that constitutional framework. And I want to note that the debate about the central issues of 1787 continues, and that the arguments of nearly two centuries ago speak in important ways to us today.

In my view, the critical, novel breakthrough at the Constitutional Convention was not the drafting of a written constitution. It was not the emergence of the idea of Union. It was not the establishment of a national government. It was not the specification of congressional powers. It was not the resolution of perplexing problems about the divisibility of sovereignty. It lay not in asserting supremacy of authorized federal action over conflicting state measures. It was not even the Framers' effort to solve the problems of democratic government through republican means. To me, the most distinctive contributions of the Convention lie in the institutions and remedies it sketched for the system we have come to know as federalism.

The Framers were engaged in the never ending search for a proper accommodation between adequate national authority and adequate local autonomy. Their novel theoretical solution was to conceive of a system in which both nation and state could operate directly on the same individuals. But I want especially to emphasize the central features of their practical solution. To me, the critical innovation was the Supremacy Clause in Article VI of the Constitution. It was that Clause that declared the Constitution to be the law of the land, enforceable in courts.[1] There, to me, lies the most creative contribution: the Convention's decision, emanating from surprising sources and not wholly understood in the summer of 1787, to assure the effectiveness of the national government not through resort to military and political confrontations, but rather through invocation of routine judicial processes.

In developing this theme, I shall concentrate on what the Framers did, in a practical, operational way. For purposes of my theme, it is less important why they did it. I believe one can identify the most important institutional and remedial innovations of 1787 without resolving most of the historical controversies about the political and social and economic and philosophical divisions of that day. I recognize that my emphasis on the practical and the operational carries the risk of being viewed as the approach of a stereotypical lawyer — one of those that an Anti-Federalist member of the Massachusetts ratifying convention described as those "lawyers" who "talk so finely, and gloss over matters so smoothly," who try to make "people swallow down the pill," because "they expect to be the managers of this Constitution."[2]

I confess that my emphasis is indeed legalistic. But mine is a conscious stress on what I think to be frequently overlooked yet pervasively important themes. And it is a choice of themes made with some awareness of the focus of other disciplines. I try to be a historian as well as a lawyer. When I was in college, history courses echoed with the teachings of Beard and Parrington and Jensen. While I was in law school, I had a growing sense that more should be said about agreements and less about divisions in the Revolutionary era. I began to fear that my changing views

---

1. The full text of the Supremacy Clause, Article VI, paragraph 2, of the *United States Constitution* "This Constitution, and the Laws of the United States which shall be made in Pursuance thereof; and all Treaties made, or which shall be made, under the Authority of the United States, shall be the supreme Law of the Land; and the Judges in every State shall be bound thereby, any Thing in the Constitution or Laws of any State to the Contrary notwithstanding."

2. Jonathan Elliot, ed., *The Debates in the Several State Conventions on the Adoption of the Federal Constitution as Recommended by the General Convention at Philadelphia, in 1787* (5 v., 2nd ed., Philadelphia, 1876) (hereafter cited as Elliot, *Debates*) 2: p. 102 (quoted in the splendid essay by Cecelia M. Kenyon, "Men of Little Faith: The Anti-Federalists on the Nature of Representative Government," *Wm. & Mary Quart.* 12: (1955): p. 6, n. 4).

stemmed from overexposure to narrow professional training. I
was relieved to find that historians, too, were moving in that
direction, with the consensus scholars of the nineteen fifties and
nineteen sixties revising the revisions of the Progressives and their
followers.[3] More recently still, I have been impressed, and occasionally persuaded, by efforts to revive and modify neo-Progressive
interpretations.[4]

But for the purpose of my theme, I need not take sides in those
historians' disputes. As Gordon S. Wood, one of the best of the
neo-Progressives, has recognized, the ultimate significance of the
Framers' work lies after all in the document they created, whatever
their motives. Even if the battle was one between the elite and
the masses, between the "Worthy" and the "Licentious,"[5] even if
some of the Framers had "partisan and aristocratic purposes,"[6]
they did produce a constitution that has lasted, and they did use
nationalistic as well as democratic language in it. And so I agree
that the Framers' achievement "really transcended their particular
political and social intentions and became more important and
more influential than they themselves anticipated";[7] and I therefore take as my starting point the "whats" rather than the "whys"
of the Convention and the Constitution.

What, then, was the critical breakthrough at the Convention?
As I have indicated, it was not the idea of constitution-making:
written constitutions were an invention of the Old World, not the
New; and it was a practice that had become domesticated long
before 1787. The Revolution spurred an immediate outburst of

3. For a survey of the changing interpretations, see Jack P. Greene, "Introduction—The Reappraisal of the American Revolution in Recent Historical Literature," in: Greene, ed., *The Reinterpretation of the American Revolution:
1763-1789* (New York, 1968), pp. 2-74. Greene's collection of essays is an
excellent sampling of the major contributions of the 1950's and 1960's. For a
more recent review of the literature, see the introduction and bibliography in
Gordon S. Wood, ed., *The Confederation and the Constitution: The Critical
Issues* (Boston, 1973), pp. vii-xv, 181-189. For a succinct and thoughtful survey
of the period, emphasizing consensus rather than divisions, see Edmund S.
Morgan, *The Birth of the Republic: 1763-89* (Chicago, 1956). See also Benjamin F. Wright, *Consensus and Continuity, 1776-1787* (Boston, 1958).
4. See especially Gordon S. Wood, *The Creation of the American Republic:
1776-1787* (Chapel Hill, 1969) (hereafter cited as Wood, *Creation of the American Republic*).
5. *Ibid.,* p. 471.
6. *Ibid.,* p. 615.
7. *Ibid.*

constitution writing in most of the states[8]; and at the national level, the Articles of Confederation, too, were a constitution. Nor can the delegates of 1787 be credited with inventing the idea of Union. An emerging sense of nationhood and efforts at united action antedated the Revolution. Richard Henry Lee's Resolutions of June, 1776, urged not only that political ties with Great Britain be severed, but also that "a plan of confederation be prepared."[9] And the Articles of Confederation, proposed by Congress a decade before the Convention, had "perpetual Union" as their stated goal. Not creating a Union, but strengthening a preexisting one, was the goal of the 1787 Convention. Forming "a *more perfect* Union," not originating a Union, was the prime mission of the Framers, as the words of the Constitution's Preamble confirm.

And so it was with most of the other achievements commonly identified with the work of the Convention. The idea of enumerating delegated, limited national powers had a clear antecedent in the Articles. If the powers of Congress under the Articles had merely been amplified, if the basic structure of government had remained unchanged, one could not credit the Convention with dramatic innovation.[10] There was greater novelty, to be sure, in the notion that sovereignty ultimately derived from the people, that nation and states under the new scheme simply exercised delegated portions of that sovereignty. But solving the problem of theoretically indivisible sovereignty, although of great political and rhetorical significance,[11] would have had little operational consequence without the new Constitution's enforcement machinery.

The essential novelty of the 1787 achievement lies, then, not in those features, but rather in achievements symbolized by the Supremacy Clause. It is easy to overlook the innovative elements of the Supremacy Clause, for the natural inclination is to focus on the notion of supremacy. But that was not a new idea: even

---

8. See, e.g., Hannah Arendt's comment that American independence was "followed by a spontaneous outbreak of constitution-making in all thirteen colonies." Hannah Arendt, *On Revolution* (New York, 1963), p. 139. On the institutionalization of the constitutional convention device in America, see also Robert R. Palmer, *The Age of the Democratic Revolution: A Political History of Europe and America, 1760-1800* (2 v., Princeton, 1959-1964).

9. Charles C. Tansill, ed., *Documents Illustrative of the Formation of the Union of the American States* (Wash., D. C., 1927), p. 21.

10. Compare Article IX of the Articles of Confederation with Article I, Section 8, of the Constitution.

11. See Wood, *Creation of the American Republic*, pp. 530-536.

under the Articles, authorized acts of Congress were theoretically supreme; Article XIII had explicitly admonished every state to "abide" by congressional determinations. The trouble lay in the practice, not the theory. It lay in the absence of an effective national enforcement mechanism, as the congressional experience had repeatedly and frustratingly demonstrated by 1787. The national government could make requests of the states, but could not command. The fatal flaw was the absence of machinery to enforce national measures at the grass roots, against individuals. The critical breakthrough at the Convention, then, was the adoption of a system in which the national government would have that capacity. And the remedy that was truly a novel product of Convention debates rather than a mere elaboration of prior ideas is reflected in the Supremacy Clause. The Constitution and federal laws and treaties were made the supreme law of the land; state judges — and, implicitly, federal judges as well — were "bound" by the supreme federal law, and were commanded to enforce that supreme federal law, "any Thing in the Constitution or Laws of any State to the Contrary notwithstanding." The central phrase in that central clause of the Constitution is "the supreme Law of the Land"; and the most significant word in that phrase is not "supreme" but "Law." The ordinary processes of law, of litigation, of judicial decision-making, were to be the prime devices to enable nation as well as state to act directly upon each individual. Reliance on routine judicial processes, instead of the use of military or political force by nation against state, was the Convention's truly innovative contribution to national autonomy and effectiveness.

The significance of that choice to rely on routine law enforcement processes is not a startling perception for any reader of the Federalist Papers. The central and frequently reiterated themes of Hamilton's early essays are that government under the Articles of Confederation failed because it sought to act against states "as contradistinguished from the INDIVIDUALS of whom they consist," because the theoretically binding congressional acts were "in practice" "mere recommendations, which the States observe or disregard at their option"; that effective government required sanctions, remedies for disobedience of law; that the choice of remedies was between "the COERTION of the magistracy" and "the COERTION of arms";[12] that the Constitution chose to manifest the "majesty of the national authority" "through the medium

---

12. *The Federalist* No. 15 (Cooke ed., Cleveland, 1961), pp. 93, 95 (A. Hamilton).

of the Courts of Justice,"[13] to rely on "the mild and salutary *coertion* of the *magistracy*" rather than "the destructive *coertion* of the *sword*," to rely on *"law"* not *"violence"*;[14] that the decision to "enable the government to employ the ordinary magistracy" in the execution of laws was critical to the extension of national authority "to the individual citizens of the several States"; and that this scheme, again in Hamilton's words, would assure "a regular and peaceable execution of the laws of the Union."[15] It was themes such as those that Madison summarized in Number 39 of *The Federalist*. Madison's description of the new government emphasized, in the terminology of that day, a mixture of "national" and "federal" elements: "national, not federal" in the execution of powers; "federal, not national" in the extent of powers.[16]

If those themes had been as clearly articulated throughout our history as they were in Madison's and Hamilton's essays, it would hardly be worth while to reiterate them here. But those themes are not prominent in most of the historical writing about the period. More important, those themes sound only faintly in the records of the Convention debates themselves.[17] The Convention records encourage preoccupation with such issues as the problem resolved by the Great Compromise: the conflict over representation in the national legislature, the conflict between representation based upon population and representation based upon states. And that preoccupation in turn encourages speculation about the conflicts between large states and small states, and between extreme nationalists and those more concerned about preservation of state autonomy.

But the typical generalizations about divisions at the Convention have very little to do with the evolution of the critical reliance on routine legal proceedings as the central enforcement mechanism. That enforcement scheme, it turns out, was itself a product of perhaps the greatest compromise of all. Ironically, its features were not elaborately debated on the floor of the Convention; its significance was not fully appreciated until after the Convention had adjourned; and, despite its overriding significance to the growth of national power, it stemmed from proposals submitted not by nationalist delegates from large states, but rather by delegates from

13. *Ibid.*, No. 16, p. 102 (A. Hamilton).
14. *Ibid.*, No. 20, p. 129 (A. Hamilton).
15. *Ibid.*, No. 27, pp. 174-175 (A. Hamilton).
16. *Ibid.*, No. 39, p. 257 (J. Madison).
17. See generally Max Farrand, *The Framing of the Constitution of the United States* (New Haven, 1913); Charles Warren, *The Making of the Constitution* (Boston, 1928) (hereafter cited as Warren, *Making the Constitution*).

small states and even by Anti-Federalists. Not James Madison of Virginia or Alexander Hamilton of New York, but William Paterson of New Jersey and Oliver Ellsworth of Connecticut and even George Mason of Virginia and Luther Martin of Maryland deserve most of the credit for the greatest nation-building devices developed at the Convention.

Reliance on routine judicial processes as the central enforcement device, unlike most other features of the Constitution, was not part of the arsenal of remedies that the strongest advocates of institutional reform brought to Philadelphia. Recall the context of the Convention, and the progress of the debates. There was a widely held belief — an important belief even if it rested on shaky factual grounds — that the nation was in crisis, that disunion was imminent. There was widespread recognition too that a stronger national government was necessary. And nationalists such as Madison came to the Convention in search of a "middle ground" between "a due supremacy of the national authority" and some state autonomy.[18] The critical problem of remedies was perceived to be the establishment of adequate coercive authority in the national government.

When the delegates gathered in Philadelphia in May, 1787, most nationalists considered the most obvious coercive weapon to be the use of armed force against recalcitrant states. When the nationalists' Randolph-Madison-Virginia Plan was submitted soon after, the thinking had not moved significantly beyond that point: its solution for the crucial problem of an enforcement mechanism was coercion of states, political as well as military. It provided for a congressional veto of state legislation, and for the use of armed force.[19] Primary reliance instead on the "magistracy,"

18. James Madison to Edmund Randolph, April 8, 1787, *The Papers of James Madison,* ed. Robert A. Rutland and William M. E. Rachal (Chicago, 1975) (hereafter cited as Madison, *Papers*) 9: p. 369.

19. See paragraph 6 of the Virginia Plan, Max Farrand, ed., *The Records of the Federal Convention* (4 v., 2nd ed., New Haven, 1923) (hereafter cited as Farrand, *Records*) 1: p. 21. The Virginia Plan as introduced in late May provided simply for a congressional veto of *unconstitutional* state laws. But other proposals—and Madison's own desires—would have provided for congressional power to veto *all* state laws. See, e.g., Madison to George Washington, April 16, 1787, Madison, *Papers* 9: pp. 382-383, insisting that "a negative *in all cases whatsoever* on the legislative acts of the States . . . appears to me to be absolutely necessary, and to be the least possible encroachment on the State jurisdictions."

In addition to the use of military force and the congressional veto in paragraph 6 of the Virginia Plan, that scheme also provided in paragraph 14, Farrand, *Records* 1: p. 22, that all state officials "ought to be bound by oath to support the articles of Union."

on ordinary judicial processes, was a much later development in the Convention's thinking. It was a development aided by the early crystallization of the notion that effective national government required law enforcement against individuals rather than states. Among the earliest articulators of that emerging consensus was George Mason of Virginia, ultimately an opponent of the Constitution. As he put it at the end of May, "punishment could not in the nature of things be executed on the States collectively, and therefore that such a Govt. was necessary as could directly operate on individuals, and would punish those only whose guilt required it."[20]

By the time William Paterson offered the New Jersey Plan in mid-June, the Convention had already rejected the remedy of military coercion. As Madison apprised Jefferson after the Convention adjourned, the delegates had quickly come to see that primary reliance on military compulsion probably would not work, would require "obnoxious and dangerous" armed force, and would produce "a scene resembling much more a civil war than the administration of regular Government."[21] But Madison's favorite remedy, the congressional veto, was still at center stage. At that point, Paterson's New Jersey Plan revived the notion of military force. But that remedy, so inconsistent with orderly government, was joined with a far more significant provision in Paterson's scheme: that Paterson proposal of mid-June contained the first antecedent of what ultimately became the Supremacy Clause.[22]

---

20. Farrand, *Records* 1: p. 34.

21. Madison to Jefferson, October 24, 1787, *The Writings of James Madison*, ed., Gaillard Hunt (9 v., New York, 1900-1910) (hereafter cited as Madison, *Writings*) 5: p. 19.

22. Farrand, *Records* 1: pp. 242-245.
Paragraph 6 of the Paterson plan provided that "all Acts of the U. States and Congs. made by virtue & in pursuance of the powers hereby & by the articles of confederation vested in them, and all Treaties made & ratified under the authority of the U. States shall be the supreme law of the respective States so far forth as those Acts or Treaties shall relate to the said States or their Citizens, and that the Judiciary of the several States shall be bound thereby in their decisions, any thing in the respective laws of the Individual States to the contrary notwithstanding . . . . " *Ibid.,* p. 245. Note that that antecedent of the Supremacy Clause—and Luther Martin's revival of the provision later in the Convention proceedings—did not include the United States Constitution as being a part of the supreme law of the land. Not until late in the Convention proceedings, on August 23, did the Convention, without discussion, add the Constitution of the United States to the list of legal sources included within "the supreme Law." Farrand, *Records* 2: p. 389.
On the evolution of the Supremacy Clause, see also Henry M. Hart and Herbert Wechsler, *The Federal Courts and the Federal System,* ed., Paul M. Bator, *et al.* (2nd ed., New York, 1973) (hereafter cited as Hart and Wechsler, *Federal Courts*), pp, 10-11, and especially Warren, *Making the Constitution,* pp, 318-322.

National effectiveness through ordinary law enforcement emerged
as the ultimate solution. It emerged only after the New Jersey
Plan itself had been rejected. It reemerged on the Convention
floor in a motion by a delegate from Maryland, Luther Martin —
one of the delegates who refused to sign the finished product, one
of the most vociferous Anti-Federalists in the ratification debates.
And Martin's motion was adopted without dissent — indeed, without discussion.[23] Later, during the ratification controversy, Luther
Martin would claim that his proposal had been hammered into
an objectionable shape on the Convention floor and in the Committees of Detail and of Style.[24] It is true that some significant
changes were made in Martin's language. Martin's motion did not
include the Constitution itself within the categories of supreme
federal law; and it stated that only conflicting state laws, not
conflicting state constitutional provisions, had to yield in the face
of supreme national policies. Yet Martin did not revive the
"supreme law" proposal until mid-July; and he did not revive it
until just after Madison's favorite device, the congressional veto,
had been rejected. Martin's act of reviving the "supreme law"
feature of the discarded Paterson proposal, and especially his
timing, strongly suggest, then, that even he saw some need for a
national coercive authority, and that reliance on normal judicial
processes seemed to him the least abrasive device. Those instincts
were sound.

I suspect that neither Paterson nor Martin — nor, indeed, most
of the delegates — appreciated the significance of what they had
wrought. What they had in fact contributed was the central device
to enable "a complicated and delicate political system" to work
"by peaceful and judicial processes."[25] Those are the words of
Andrew C. McLaughlin, the great constitutional historian of the
early decades of this century, the historian who, above all others,

---

23. Farrand, *Records* 2: pp. 22, 28-29.

24. On Martin's post-Convention objections, see Warren, *Making the Constitution,* pp. 318-322. Martin's discussions of the problem in the period of the
Maryland ratification debates are printed in Farrand, *Records* 3: pp. 281-296.

25. Andrew C. McLaughlin, *The Confederation and the Constitution, 1783-
1789* (New York, 1905), p. 247 (hereafter cited as McLaughlin, *Confederation
and Constitution*).

emphasized the theme that I am trying to revive here. In his view, as in mine, it is of critical operational significance in our governmental scheme that the Constitution is "enforceable like any other law in courts."[26] McLaughlin saw that the Supremacy Clause was "the central clause" of the Constitution, "because without it the whole system would be unwieldy, if not impracticable. Draw out this particular bolt, and the machinery falls to pieces."[27]

The central coercive mechanism adopted at the Convention, then, was a device acceptable to the lowest common denominator among the delegates. To the strongest nationalists, reliance on judicial processes seemed a minimal and probably inadequate scheme. Yet in retrospect it is clear that it was a most effective device, probably the only one that could have worked. The Supremacy Clause of Article VI — introduced by Paterson, revived by Martin — was at the heart of it. Article III of the Constitution, on the judiciary, provided reinforcement. That Article mandated the establishment of a Supreme Court, as Paterson's proposal had contemplated. It did not mandate lower federal courts, as the Virginia Plan had provided: supporters of Paterson's New Jersey Plan argued that Supreme Court review of state court decisions on federal issues would be adequate to assure national supremacy and uniformity, that lower federal courts would be too intrusive. In an important compromise on that issue, creation of lower federal courts was left to the discretion of Congress.[28] And Article III also extended the federal judicial power to questions arising under the Constitution, reemphasizing that constitutional norms would become operative law in ordinary litigation. A "middle way" between excessive consolidation and excessive state autonomy had

---

26. *Ibid.*
McLaughlin's emphasis on the centrality of the Supremacy Clause is developed in *Confederation and Constitution* and is reiterated in his splendid *A Constitutional History of the United States* (New York, 1935). See especially chapter 15 of his 1905 volume and chapter 14 of his 1935 history.

27. McLaughlin, *Confederation and Constitution*, p. 247.

28. See Hart and Wechsler, *Federal Courts*, pp. 11-12. See also *The Federalist* Nos. 80-82 (A. Hamilton), and the reliance on that historical compromise in Justice Joseph Story's opinion for the Court in *Martin v. Hunter's Lessee*, 1 Wheat. 304, 350 (1816). See also the brief discussion in Gerald Gunther, *Cases and Materials on Constitutional Law* (9th ed., New York, 1975) (hereafter cited as Gunther, *Constitutional Law*), pp. 36-37.

been found, though it was not the way Madison would have preferred.[29]

By a narrow vote in the critical states, the Constitution was ratified. In the ratification debates, much more than at the Convention, the fears of excessive national authority surfaced. The defenders of the Constitution slowly came to appreciate the significance of the chosen coercive mechanism, as the Federalist Papers illustrate.[30] Yet the Supremacy Clause and the prospect of Supreme Court review of state court decisions still were not major targets of the Anti-Federalists. The most frequently voiced fears about Supreme Court review went to the risks of jury determinations, if the Court were permitted to review questions of fact.[31] States righters had not yet awakened to the far greater threat from review of questions of federal law.

But the Convention's product provided only a sketch and a framework. Nation-building through legal processes required continuous energy and implementation. A critical first step came in the very first Congress, with the Judiciary Act of 1789.[32] Figures familiar from the Convention debates — figures typically described as moderates or states righters — once again played the leading roles. William Paterson of New Jersey and Oliver Ellsworth of Connecticut, now Federalist members of the Senate, were the chief drafters of the 1789 law. That Act exercised the congressional discretion under Article III to establish "inferior" federal courts.

---

29. Madison, though he clearly spelled out the implications of the Supremacy Clause in *The Federalist,* was not enthusiastic about the primary reliance on judicial remedies. Throughout his life, Madison defended judicial enforcement of constitutional norms and refused to join Jefferson in supporting the Virginia attack on Supreme Court review authority in the years after the War of 1812. Similarly, he defended Supreme Court review during the nullification period. See generally Irving Brant, *James Madison: Commander in Chief 1812-1836* (New York, 1962). See also Irving Brant, *James Madison: Father of the Constitution 1787-1800* (New York, 1950). But after the Convention adjourned, Madison continued to doubt the efficacy of primary reliance on a judicial enforcement remedy and continued to regret the abandonment of his proposal for a congressional veto. See James Madison to Thomas Jefferson, October 24, 1787, Madison, *Writings* 5: pp. 17-35.

30. See, e.g., James Wilson's articulate discussion of the new constitutional scheme at the Pennsylvania ratifying convention, and Oliver Ellsworth's well-known comment at the Connecticut ratifying convention: "Hence we see how necessary for the Union is a coercive principle. No man pretends the contrary: we all see and feel this necessity. The only question is, Shall it be a coercion of law, or a coercion of arms? . . . I am for coercion by law—that coercion which acts only upon delinquent individuals." Elliot, *Debates* 2: p. 197.

31. See Hart and Wechsler, *Federal Courts,* pp. 21-23.

32. 1 Stat. 73.

But those early lower courts were given only a small portion of the potential federal judicial power. Lower federal court jurisdiction did not include general authority over federal questions until well after the Civil War. Under the 1789 structure, state courts, bound by the Supremacy Clause, were ordinarily the initial forums for the decision of federal issues. And that scheme made Section 25 of the 1789 Judiciary Act critical: it provided for Supreme Court review of state court decisions rejecting claims under the federal Constitution, treaties, and laws; and it accordingly became the central implementation of the enforcement method chosen at the Convention.

But constitutional phrases and statutory language could not assure that the critical remedial scheme would work in practice. That was left to the future, especially to the Marshall Court in the decade after the end of the War of 1812.[33] In a sense, the Supreme Court during those years after the Second War for Independence served as a second constitutional convention. The context was remarkably similar to that of 1787. Once again, nationalists bewailed the ineffectiveness of federal law-enforcement machinery. Their concerns were triggered by New England defiance of prewar and wartime measures of the Jefferson and Madison administrations. Once again, talk of disunion and anarchy was in the air, spurred especially by the rumors emanating from the Hartford Convention. And in the final years of that divisive war, the highest court of Virginia joined the states rights challenge and aimed its attack on the nationalistic weapon which the earlier generation of Anti-Federalists had only dimly appreciated: the Supreme Court's review authority over state courts under Section 25 of the 1789 Act. Led by Spencer Roane — political leader, pamphleteer, and the most articulate state judge of his day[34]— the highest Virginia Court found Section 25 unauthorized by the Constitution and refused to obey a Supreme Court mandate.[35]

And so the perennial dispute between excessive centralization and excessive localism erupted once more. In 1787 the battle had been couched in terms of acceptance or rejection of the Constitu-

---

33. The Marshall Court's contributions to the nation-building efforts in that postwar decade will be considered more fully in my forthcoming volume, *The Marshall Court and Nationalism: 1815-1825* (Oliver Wendell Holmes Devise History of the Supreme Court of the United States 3).

34. See Note, "Judge Spencer Roane of Virginia: Champion of States' Rights —Foe of John Marshall," *Harvard Law Rev.* 66 (1953): pp. 1242-1259.

35. *Hunter v. Martin, Devisee of Fairfax*, 4 Munf. 1 (Va., 1815).

tion; at the end of the War of 1812, and for succeeding generations,
the battle was between competing interpretations of a constitution
to which all swore loyalty; but the underlying contentions had
not changed. The Marshall Court, in *Martin v. Hunter's Lessee*
in 1816[36] and once again in *Cohens v. Virginia* in 1821,[37] forcefully rejected Virginia's challenge to Section 25 and to the central
mechanism of federal law enforcement. Again, there was a parallel
to 1787: within the Court, as within the Convention, there was a
remarkably strong nationalistic consensus; outside, in the country
at large, the division was close and deep.

On the critical issue of Supreme Court review authority, the
Court spoke nationalistically and unanimously.[38] It was a Court

---

36. 1 Wheat. 304 (1816).
37. 6 Wheat. 264 (1821).
38. During that postwar decade, the Marshall Court also made its major
contributions to a broad construction of delegated congressional powers under
the Constitution, in such cases as *McCulloch v. Maryland*, 4 Wheat. 316 (1819),
and *Gibbons v. Ogden*, 9 Wheat. 1 (1824). The Marshall Court's pursuit of
that theme is beyond the scope of this paper and will be developed in my forthcoming volume of Supreme Court history, see note 33 above.

It should be noted that the Marshall Court's broad statements were directed
only in part to vindicating the legitimacy of past congressional actions. In a
practical sense, the opinions were also advocacy directed at the legislative and
executive branches, encouraging ever more vigorous national action. Joseph
Story, who had seen state challenges to federal authority at close range during
his New England circuit court duties during the War of 1812, was especially
anxious to use the relative harmony of the postwar years to solidify national
institutions. See note 39 below. And those broad statements from the Marshall
Court were in turn vehement subjects of attack by states righters. Again, Spencer
Roane was the most articulate challenger, especially in pseudonymous newspaper
essays, some of which provoked pseudonymous responses from John Marshall
himself. See generally Gerald Gunther, ed., *John Marshall's Defense of McCulloch v. Maryland* (Stanford, 1969).

It should be noted, however, that the broad construction advocated by John
Marshall was not in his eyes an unlimited one. Roane feared that all-embracive
consolidation was inherent in the principles of *McCulloch v. Maryland*. Marshall,
however, insisted that congressional powers were indeed limited. In view of
the expansion of federal powers in the century and a half since *McCulloch*, it
may well be that Roane's fears had more solid basis than Marshall's confidence
about limitations. See my comment in the Introduction to the McCulloch volume cited above: "The degree of centralization that has taken place [since
McCulloch] may well have come about in the face of Marshall's intent rather
than in accord with his expectations. That centralization may be the inevitable
consequence of economic and social changes. And this development may suggest
the impossibility of articulating general constitutional standards capable of limiting those centralizing forces, particularly through judicial action. But to say
this is very different from saying that Marshall knew he was engaging in a
hopeless task." *Ibid.,* p. 20. Today, limits on congressional exercises of power
stem largely from the political checks on legislators rather than from the efforts
of judges. But the developments since the Marshall Court era suggest that the
fears of consolidation, so seemingly unrealistic to justices such as Story and
Marshall in 1816, retain considerable practical bite.

composed of two Federalists and five Republicans. Yet the seven justices spoke as one. Their unanimity was not the product of some hypnotic spell cast by John Marshall, the Federalist chief justice. Rather, it sprang from genuinely shared convictions. All of the justices, Jeffersonian Republicans as well as Federalists, were committed, unflinching nationalists.[39] Nationalism was expectable from John Marshall and his Virginia colleague, Bushrod Washington, the General's favorite nephew. Both had supported the Constitution at the Virginia ratifying convention in 1788; both had been Federalists in politics shortly before the Jeffersonian victory of 1800. Yet nationalism came equally naturally to the five Republicans. All of them, from William Johnson of South Carolina and Brockholst Livingston of New York and Thomas Todd of Kentucky to Gabriel Duvall of Maryland and Joseph Story of Massachusetts, drew from the quite nationalistic legacy of the Jefferson and Madison Administrations — a nationalism which Jefferson, far more than Madison, was at pains to disavow when he was out of power.

But that spontaneously united Court spoke to an increasingly divided country. *Martin* and *Cohens* did not end the controversy, though the Court remained unswerving. Other states emulated Virginia in challenging the Supreme Court in the ensuing years.[40] That judicial enforcement of the Supremacy Clause, especially through Supreme Court review of state court decisions, was indeed the linchpin of national effectiveness became increasingly evident to those fearful of consolidation. Well before John C. Calhoun publicly proclaimed the doctrines of Nullification, for example, he recognized that elimination of the Supreme Court's review authority would assure the minority veto he sought. A state veto

---

39. Note, e.g., the comment by Justice Joseph Story of Massachusetts, in a memorandum written at the end of the War of 1812: "I hold it to be a maxim, which should never be lost sight of by a great statesman, that the Government of the United States is intrinsically too weak, and the powers of the State Governments too strong; that the danger always is much greater of anarchy in the parts, than of tyranny in the head. And if I were required to point the maxim by reference to the lessons of experience, I should, with the most mortifying and self-humiliating recollections, turn to my native state, as she stood and acted during the late war." William W. Story, ed., *The Life and Letters of Joseph Story* (2 v., Boston, 1815) 1: p. 296 (hereafter cited as Story, *Life and Letters*). Similar, if somewhat less intense, nationalistic responses can be found in the postwar private writings of all of the justices—including all of Story's fellow Republicans, appointed by Presidents Jefferson and Madison.

40. See Charles Warren, "Legislative and Judicial Attacks on the Supreme Court of the United States—A History of the Twenty-Fifth Section of the Judiciary Act," *Amer. Law Rev.* 47 (1913): pp. 1-34; 161-189.

power "would in truth exist," Calhoun wrote in 1827, "were it not
for a provision in a single act of Congress, I mean the 25th Section
of the Judiciary act of 1789; the existence or non-existence of
which provision, would make an entire change in the operation
of our system." If there were no Section 25, he saw, "the practical
consequence would be, that each government would have a negative
on the other, and thus possess the most effectual remedy, that can
be conceived against encroachment." Section 25, Calhoun perceived, was a provision "of the deepest importance, much more
so, than any other in the statute books."[41]

Section 25 and the Supremacy Clause survived the judicial and
legislative onslaughts. Yet even the Marshall Court's considerable
contributions did not end the battle over the underlying issues.
John Marshall and William Johnson and Joseph Story died fearful
that the Union would not survive, despite the unexpected help
from Andrew Jackson in the conflict with South Carolina. A civil
war, a rare resort to arms rather than judicial processes, helped
build the nationalizing forces. Economic and social developments
contributed even more to Joseph Story's central objective, to
"prevent the possibility of a division, by creating great national
interests which shall bind us in an indissoluble chain."[42]

Yet despite the vast proliferation of unifying forces and the
vast increase of national governmental activity that we perceive
as we look back on two hundred years of nation-building, localism
has not died. And we should be glad that that is so. The Union is
no longer in danger. Enforcement of federal law through routine
judicial processes is taken for granted. But the Anti-Federalist
concerns continue to be heard.

And they should be heard. Designing a system that would assure
adequate local autonomy as well as adequate centralization was
an extraordinary challenge in 1787. The solutions of the Framers
and the contributions of the Marshall Court were remarkably
ingenious first steps toward meeting that challenge. Yet the risks
of excesses in either direction persist. It is well, then, that the
Anti-Federalists' skepticism of national power — because of its
distance from the populace, its inefficiency, its tendency toward

41. John C. Calhoun to Littleton W. Tazewell, August 25, 1827, Calhoun
Papers, Library of Congress. See Gunther, *Constitutional Law*, p. 48.
42. Joseph Story to Nathaniel Williams, May 8, 1815, Story, *Life and Letters*
1: p. 254.

tyranny unless carefully controlled — surfaces so frequently in the campaign speeches of this Bicentennial year.

Perhaps, then, I should not speak of the 1787 Convention and of the Marshall Court as the first and second constitutional conventions. More accurately, we are all engaged in a continuing constitutional convention, forever struggling with the problem of efficient governance of a continent with adequate regard to local needs and popular wishes. And rightly so: surely, we must not abandon the debate about the central problems that confronted the Framers.

GERALD GUNTHER
William Nelson Cromwell
Professor of Law, Stanford
University School of Law

Creative Adaptations to the Future

THERE ARE NOW GREAT TRAGEDIES in the world. There are also disasters that have not yet occurred and may never happen, yet that contribute to contemporary gloom because they exist vividly in our collective imagination. For example, global nuclear warfare, the melting of the polar ice cap by the heat from industrial activities, the coming of a new ice age resulting from cosmic forces which cannot be controlled, the manipulation of man's nature through genetic engineering and behavior control, are among the threats that make us apprehensive about the future — even though they exist so far only in our minds.

Even more pervasive is the fear of the social and environmental disasters that will inevitably occur *if* world population, technological development and environmental pollution continue to increase at the present rates. The consequences of such continued growth are indeed frightening. The earth will soon be overpopulated and its resources depleted. Pollutants will dim our vision, rot our lungs, and ruin the environment. The need for strict supervision over all aspects of social and technological structures will threaten civil liberties. The gap between rich and poor nations will widen and will drive the hungry, angry people of the world to acts of desperation, including the use of nuclear weapons for blackmail.

Thus, it is quite reasonable to believe that industrial civilization will eventually collapse *if* the future is to be a magnified version of the present; but it is just as reasonable to believe that industrialized countries can continue to prosper *if* they change their course. The prospects for our type of civilization depend less on what is going on now than on future trends that will be determined, not by natural forces, but by human choices. The most impressive manifestation of freedom is precisely the ability of human beings to act in the service of situations that have not yet occurred.

The easiest way to imagine the future is admittedly to extrapolate from major existing trends, but this is probably futile because

162

present trends are not likely to continue much longer, at least in the countries of Western civilization. Even now, changes are occurring not only in the rates of quantitative growth, but also in the qualitative aspects of human life and of technologic and economic activities.

In nature, any excessive growth of a living system usually brings into play counterforces that check its further growth; the outcome of this automatic self-correcting process is a state of approximate ecological equilibrium. In human affairs, the blind homeostatic mechanisms of nature are supplemented by human interventions. Human beings are rarely passive witnesses of events; they respond to them through activities governed in large part by their imaginings of the future. Their interventions may not be wise, but they inevitably alter the course of events and make mockery of any attempt to predict the future from extrapolation of existing trends.

History is the record not only of quantitative growth, but also and more interestingly of qualitative changes brought about by social evolution. The logical future always yields to the willed future. Wherever human beings are concerned, trend is not destiny.

Anticipations of the future have always influenced human history, but it is only during our times that they have been based on a large body of scientific knowledge. All modern societies are engaged in attempts to develop rational methods for anticipating the probable long-range consequences of social and technological innovations. The future is no longer only imagined; more and more it can be an educated guess of what will be the outcome of certain courses of action.

Throughout history, disasters have taken humankind by surprise. Famines, epidemics, economic depressions, environmental catastrophes appeared capriciously — as acts of God. In contrast, it is now possible, if not to predict, at least to anticipate the occurrence and course of certain events. For example, the 1917–1919 epidemic of Spanish influenza killed more than 20 million people without anyone being able at the time to understand its origin and nature, or to influence its course. While new strains of the influenza virus still emerge at frequent intervals, it is now usually possible to detect them early in their spread and to minimize their pathological effects. A similar contrast exists between the epidemics of bubonic plague which decimated Europe on several occasions during historical times, and the recent outbreaks of this disease on the American continent. These new outbreaks of the plague were detected early and remained localized because they could be rapidly brought under control. Influenza and plague are no longer whims of fate; to a large extent, their origin is understood, their future course is predictable, and their effects are controllable.

Admittedly, few are the situations in which diagnostic and preventive measures can be as effective as in the case of influenza and plague. Nevertheless, anticipations of the future are rapidly becoming important in many other aspects of life. Famines still occur, but not quite as unexpectedly as before, and the fact that they can be anticipated makes it possible to deal with them more effectively than in the past. The early signs of business depressions are detected through economic indicators, and corrective measures — clumsy as they may be — can be taken to soften their social impact. Scientific methods are being developed to recognize the premonitory signs of earthquakes and of volcanic eruptions — even of a new ice age or of a melting of the polar ice cap. One of the really new aspects of modern societies is thus the development of techniques to anticipate the future, and to act accordingly.

The penetration of the future into social consciousness accounts in large part for the popular interest in "future shock." This arresting phrase denotes the disturbances that will occur when people experience the effects of certain social and technological innovations at some unspecified time in the future. However, the very anticipation of these future disturbances makes it probable that they will not occur, at least in their predicted form — precisely because they have been predicted. The very possibility to anticipate the future consequences of many trends and innovations provides a chance for adaptive responses even before these consequences have become manifest.

Modern societies thus undergo changes adaptive not only to the contemporary events they *experience* but also to the future consequences of situations and trends they *imagine*. The first expressions of such adaptive responses to the future are naturally measures designed to prevent or minimize the potentially deleterious effects of existing forces. Since these measures are taken in advance of the effects, they correspond to a preventive phase of adaptation. Other adaptations to the future have a more creative character and are indeed the chief mechanisms by which human beings invent and create the world in which they will live. A few examples will suffice to illustrate how such preventive and creative adaptations to the future are now taking place, especially in the parts of the world where education and information generate awareness of the long-range possible consequences of existing trends.

Environmental degradation became a widely recognized public issue only two decades ago. Concern for the quality of the environment reached its emotional peak on Earth Day in 1970, and it achieved international recognition through the Conference on the Human Environment held in Stockholm under the sponsorship of the United Nations in 1972.

The manifestations on Earth Day and the discussions at the Stockholm Conference were focused on the damage done to natural ecosystems by human interventions, especially by the pollutants of industrial and domestic origin. As a result of the programs instituted to deal with pollution problems, there are many local situations in which environmental quality is now better than it was twenty years ago. Air pollution has somewhat decreased in a few of the largest American and European cities. Several streams and lakes that were so grossly polluted as to be qualified as "dead" have been returned to a level of purity compatible with a desirable aquatic life. Forests that had been devastated are being allowed to recover and furthermore reforestation is going on in several parts of the world, for example, in continental China and in Algeria. Regions that had become deserts have been made to reacquire a diversified flora and fauna. While environmental degradation is still an enormous problem over much of the world, industrial societies are learning to deal with it by working with nature.

An interesting aspect of environmental control is that in many cases preventive steps have been taken long before the situation had become desperate. The air of cities had not become really poisonous before measures were taken to decrease air pollution. Lakes and rivers were not completely dead before measures were taken to decrease water pollution. The preventive measures were therefore a response, not to actual emergencies, but rather to the anticipations of future emergencies.

Adaptive responses to the future commonly go beyond the management of crises. For example, the right to a good environment is coming to be regarded as one of the fundamental inalienable rights — like the right to freedom, to education, and to health care. Furthermore, the phrase "good environment" is no longer taken to mean only freedom from noxious influences; it implies also surroundings which provide social, emotional, and esthetic satisfactions. During the first half of the twentieth century, city

planners had been primarily concerned with problems of public
health and of urban design for greater mobility and efficiency in
the various aspects of economic and domestic life. Urbanologists
are now beginning to emphasize, in addition, factors which contribute in other ways to the quality of life — for example the role
of so-called "city centers" in the furtherance of social and cultural
activities. The search for "spirit of place" goes beyond correcting
the gross ills of urban agglomerations; it is a creative response
directed at certain positive values that only the city can provide.

One of the reasons for worrying about the future is that, while
the world population continues to increase, the earth's resources
are limited and will eventually be depleted. Evidence for the acute
awareness of this danger among scientists, economists, and public
servants can be found in the February 20, 1976, issue of *Science,*
which is entirely devoted to the problem of materials, both the
renewable and non-renewable resources. The general public also
is aware of the resource problem, as revealed by a recent Harris
poll in which ninety per cent of the persons interviewed agreed
that we "will have to find ways to cut back on the amount of things
we consume and waste." It is clear that awareness of the "resource"
problem does not depend on a precise quantitative knowledge of
supplies and demand.

Real shortages of materials or energy have not yet occurred
except when caused by temporary economic dislocations. Yet,
much work has already been done to prevent shortages, or to
provide substitutes if they do occur. Except for the period of the
oil embargo by the Arab states, for example, there has not been
any significant shortage of fossil fuels, though their cost has
increased. Moreover, the world reserves of petroleum will not
be exhausted for several decades and coal is probably abundant
enough to meet human needs for a few centuries. Yet steps have
already been taken to deal with possible energy shortages during
the twenty-first century; humankind has begun to adapt itself to
the Resource Future Shock.

Numerous examples could be given here to illustrate the wide
range of preventive adaptation measures — by conservation, re-
cycling, substitution, and development of new sources — that have
been taken or are being contemplated to deal with shortages of
materials and energy that probably will not happen because of
these very measures.

Along with this preventive approach to shortages, there is

emerging a creative approach based on a better understanding of the relation of human life to the earth's ecosystems. It is now realized that humankind cannot continue forever to mine the earth's materials and to burn fossil fuels, since natural supplies will inevitably be depleted at some time in the future. Industrialized societies can therefore survive only if they develop a self-sustaining economy, somewhat analogous to that of nature, to replace the purely exploitative economy that they have practiced since the Industrial Revolution.

The problem of material resources could be solved in theory if a renewable source of energy were available, since this would permit extraction of the needed materials from even very low-grade ores and to produce substitutes almost at will by synthetic chemistry. In theory also, renewable sources of energy might be provided by one or another of several technologies such as nuclear fission (in the breeder reactors), nuclear fusion, collection of solar energy from sunlight, either by physico-chemical means or by photosynthesis. However, while there may be no theoretical limits to the *production* of energy by these techniques, there are ecological limits to the safe *use* of energy. Both the production and consumption of energy always bring about the release of heat which in turn often has undesirable ecological effects. Even in the case of solar energy, local concentrations of heat are likely to cause disturbances in the overall ecological economy of the earth. Thus, the range of creative adaptations to the future is limited by the constraints associated with the earth's ecosystems — let alone the constraints associated with human nature.

A century ago, John Stuart Mill had recognized that there were inescapable limits to economic and technologic growth, and had affirmed that humankind would eventually be compelled to develop a form of civilization based on what he called a "stationary state." This concept has recently been given a more quantitative form, by the extrapolations summarized in the famous book *Limits to Growth,* in which it is stated that the present exponential rates of growth will inevitably result in the destruction of industrial societies.

The phrases "stationary state" and "limits to growth" have static connotations and have led many persons to assume that humankind is about to enter a period of stagnation leading to decadence. In reality, however, these phrases only mean that industrial societies cannot continue indefinitely to use more and more of the resources they have been using, just to produce faster and faster, more and more of the goods they have been producing in obscene abundance during the past few decades. There are obvious limits to such purely quantitative growth. On the other hand, it is possible to envisage instead of a stationary state a "steady state," namely one in which quantitative growth will taper off, but qualitative changes can continue or even increase in the technological and cultural systems. Here could be mentioned examples illustrating that in a properly managed self-sustaining economy materials retain their value throughout the system by being recycled instead of being discarded.

Even more important in the long run will be certain changes in life style and in environmental management that are likely to influence the very structure of society. For the first time since the Industrial Revolution, technological and economic growth at any price — merely for growth's sake — is no longer socially acceptable and has come indeed to be considered immoral. Enterprising people who had dedicated themselves to the pursuit of quantitative growth in the past will probably redirect their energy to more interesting causes such as the development of social conditions and environmental surroundings favorable to health, to human relationships, to enjoyable ways of life. There is evidence even now that prosperous people are beginning to move in the direction of a less consumptive society as they have already moved in the direction of smaller families. Many members of the upper and middle class are becoming weary of the economic rat race and of industrial expansion; there is among them a trend toward the cultivation of simpler pleasures and of life styles that require less expenditures of resources than did the grand manners of preceding generations. Just as this bellwether group led the movement toward fewer children, so it may eventually transmit its less voracious material values to the rest of the population.

There are no visible limits to the kind of growth associated with qualitative changes in the ways of life and in environmental management. Social evolution is endlessly inventive of new attitudes, new resources, and new techniques that enable humankind to reach the new goals imagined by the new mentality.

Inventing possible futures and planning for them is not of course a prerogative of our times, but there is a change in the *kinds* of future that are being invented, because they inevitably reflect the knowledge, illusions, hopes, and fears of present-day society.

Until a very few decades ago, it was generally taken for granted in the Western world that all innovations, especially those based on scientific knowledge, would eventually benefit human life. This view was forcefully expressed by Condorcet, Franklin, and other philosophers of the Enlightenment; it motivated the technological euphoria of the Industrial Revolution. When the city of Chicago held a World's Fair in 1933 to celebrate its one hundredth anniversary, the general theme of the exhibits was the crucial importance of the contributions that scientific technology had made to the prosperity and welfare of humankind during the "Century of Progress." One of the subtitles of the guidebook to the Fair proclaimed "Science discovers, industry applies, man conforms," and the text continued, "Individuals, groups, entire races fall into step with . . . science and industry." There could not be a more explicit statement of the then prevailing belief that the achievements of scientific technology are the true criteria of progress. Inventing the future meant at that time imagining technologic utopias.

Though scientific technology is even more successful in the 1970's than it was in 1933, no one would now dare state that humankind must "conform" to its dictates, or "fall into step" with science and industry. Almost everyone would affirm instead that technology must conform to human nature and be kept within ecological constraints. As a consequence of this change in attitude, the interest in social and technological innovations is now counterbalanced by an equally strong concern with the long-range effects of these innovations. The new law requiring a statement of environmental impact for each important social venture is the legal expression of this concern. Increasingly in the future, things that could be done may not be done, simply because they are not desirable from the human or ecological point of view.

Whereas the widespread concern for long-range consequences is somewhat reassuring, there are of course many other aspects of the modern world that justify a deep sense of alarm for the future. Deforestation, erosion, and other forms of environmental degradation are lowering and perhaps destroying capabilities for food production, especially in the tropical and semi-tropical parts of the world. Deserts are on the march, and several developing countries are "losing ground" in the literal sense of the words.

Awareness of long-range consequences does not necessarily imply that an adequate effort will be made, early enough, to avoid the dangers inherent in technologic growth. Industrial societies may elect to pursue certain innovations as far as possible, to the point of absurdity as they have repeatedly done in the past. The social feedback may not always be rapid enough to prevent crucial processes from overshooting and generating environmental or social catastrophes.

Catastrophic declines following overshoot have indeed occurred in the past and probably account for the demise of several ancient civilizations, for example in the Middle East, in Cambodia, and in Central and South America, but this does not mean that present civilizations are condemned to a similar fate. Even if overshoot takes place, irreversible damage can probably be prevented by taking advantage of scientific knowledge concerning the phenomenal resiliency of natural and social systems. The so-called balance of nature is not as delicately poised and easily upset as commonly stated. Natural systems are interlaced with checks and balances which endow them with great stability and with the ability to recover from even drastic ecological disturbances. To a certain extent this is true even for some man-made ecosystems. The toughness of nature is documented by the recovery of wild and cultivated landscapes following the ecological disturbances caused by floods, volcanic eruptions, and modern warfare. Social systems, also, can rapidly recover from major disturbances as shown by what happened in Germany, Japan, and other nations where the economic and social structure was destroyed by war, yet was reconstituted within a very few decades. As Gibbon wrote in *The Decline and Fall of the Roman Empire,*

> The more . . . necessary arts can be performed without superior talents or national subordination. . . . Private genius and public industry may be extirpated; but these hardy plants survive the tempest, and strike an everlasting root into the most unfavorable soil.

Individual civilizations are mortal, but the fundamental attributes of natural systems and of human beings can survive countless ordeals.

As already mentioned, the new assets of our own civilization are a greater ability to anticipate the dangers inherent in almost any form of excessive growth, and to change established trends on the basis of these anticipations.

It is worthy of note in passing that choices concerning the future are less likely to emerge from official directives than from social awareness of the long-range consequences of social and technological trends. Education and information are creating in modern societies a new form of the old town meeting and of participatory democracy which, even though still unstructured and clumsy, nevertheless has already proved fairly effective. The rejection of potentially dangerous trends, by grassroot movements, makes it unlikely that Aldous Huxley's *Brave New World* and George Orwell's *1984* will occur as predicted, any more than will the distressing anti-human technologic utopias and future shock that have contributed so much to the gloom of our times.

The most pervasive cause of gloom in the countries of Western civilization, however, may not be crowding, shortages, pollutants, the fear of nuclear warfare or of Big Brother. It may be rather the humiliating awareness that the operations of modern societies escape human control because their size gives them a complexity beyond human understanding. Social systems cannot be really understood even by those expected to run them; in fact they cannot be *run* rationally and can only be operated by empirical faith.

Meddling with one part of a complex social structure involves a very great risk of setting off destructive reverberations in some other, often remote part. Experience shows indeed that attempts to introduce helpful social changes commonly make matters worse rather than better, even if the intervention is based on common sense and good will. In order safely to adjust a single component of a system, it is necessary first to understand in detail the inter-relationships of all its other components — but even with the help of the largest computer this is beyond possibility for a complex social system. The discouraging conclusion therefore seems to be that the only safe course is to let things take care of themselves, because almost any kind of intervention is likely to cause trouble.

The awareness of the practical impossibility of understanding complex social and technological systems is now sufficient to generate adaptive responses. One approach to the management of complex societies is not to pretend to understand the inter-relationship of their parts, but paradoxically to increase still further social diversity by multiplying the courses of action — in the hope that the successful ones will emerge through empirical selection. An opposite approach is to simplify the social systems, or rather to create, along with the existing ones, others which are simple enough to be understood. Here again, there is some evidence that such a process of adaptation to the future has begun. A multiplicity of programs for "alternative technologies" and "alternative social structures," much simpler than the prevailing ones, are emerging at an accelerated rate in all industrialized societies. Small enterprises based on the use of local resources in energy and materials may come to complement the global industrial civilization, and generate a new social and technological regionalism more readily apprehended by the human mind. The countercultures which started a generation ago as destructive anti-establishment protests are now being replaced by creative experimental movements through which Western civilization is adapting itself to a new social and technological future.

To the extent that our societies can develop a prospective view of the future, they can overcome the myth of inevitability. Animals are essentially prisoners of biological evolution, but human beings are blessed with the freedom and inventiveness of social evolution. When engaged on a dangerous course, they can retrace their steps and start in a new direction toward another kind of future world they imagine. They can thus continuously adapt to what they visualize and want to achieve, in an endless evolutionary process of creation. For them, trend is not destiny.

POSTSCRIPTUM

After my presentation, Professor Ernst Mayr expressed doubts concerning the extent to which modern societies will succeed in avoiding ecological disasters. He pointed out in particular that tropical forests are rapidly being destroyed and that much of the attendant environmental degradation will prove irreversible.

I am, of course, in full agreement with Professor Mayr's remarks, and share his concern. In fact, I had mentioned the destruction of tropical forests and the dangers of ecologic overshoots in parts of my written text that I did not have time to present orally. I know that history is replete with ecological disasters, that deserts are on the march in several parts of the globe, and that we are literally "losing ground." If I did not elaborate on these well-known facts, it was only because I had elected to focus my lecture on the creative rather than on the destructive aspects of human interventions into nature. More specifically I wanted to emphasize that modern societies have begun to anticipate the problems of the future, and to adapt to expected difficulties by developing preventive measures.

Professor Mayr's remarks provide an excellent illustration of my thesis. In the past, natural ecosystems have been transformed or devastated without awareness of long-range consequences. As is well known, the origin of many deserts is in such human interventions. Ecological mismanagement is of course still prevalent today but there are now many far-seeing, learned, and concerned scholars to sound the alarm, as Professor Mayr has done.

I differ from Professor Mayr only on one point. He spoke as if he believed that human beings will not be able or willing to change their behavior. I have more faith than he has in their common sense and in their willingness to heed warnings when they are expressed with the kind of clarity and sincerity that shone through his words.

RENÉ J. DUBOS
Scientist, Professor Emeritus,
Rockefeller University

Can Democratic Government Survive?

THE QUESTION ASSIGNED ME rather strongly implies that the prospects for democratic government lie somewhere in the range between gloomy and bleak. The truthful answer is that of course democratic government can survive, but it need not, and there are trends that threaten the continuity of its processes. They are only trends, however, and Adam Smith reminds us that there is a lot of ruin in a great nation. For that reason, I stress at the outset that this is not a forecast, delivered with glum satisfaction, of the coming of the totalitarian night. It is an attempt, necessarily in summary form, to name the danger so it may be avoided. The worry is hardly a new one, though it seems more widespread today.

Sir Henry Maine made the point that, looking back, we are amazed at the blindness of the privileged classes in France to the approach of the Revolution that was to overwhelm them.[1] Yet Maine finds "the blindness of the French nobility and clergy eminently pardonable. The Monarchy . . . appeared to have roots deeper in the past than any existing European institution."[2] In his own place and time, men looked upon popular government and the democratic principle as destined to last forever, and Maine asked whether the confidence of the French upper classes just before the Revolution "conveys a caution to other generations than theirs."[3]

We are no longer so sanguine about the prospects for democratic government as were Maine's contemporaries. The democratic principle is in rhetorical ascendancy everywhere and yet in actuality, as a matter of practice rather than declamation, it is in retreat around the world. I shall not discuss the possibility that it may perish first in Europe and later in the United States under the combined forces of the external pressure of communist regimes

---

1. Sir Henry Sumner Maine, *Popular Government* (London, 1886), p. 1.
2. *Idem.* at p. 2.
3. *Idem.* at p. 5.

and the growth within democracies of political parties sympathetic to such governments. The internal health of democracy is related to that external threat, however, for the trends to be discussed cause a loss of self-confidence and will, a condition sometimes referred to as a failure of nerve, which places democracies at a grave disadvantage internationally. Unlike the sudden cataclysm that overtook the French monarchy, ours appears to be a slow crisis that gives ample warning of the unhappy condition toward which matters tend.

My thesis is, first, that we live in a climate of opinion and feeling whose dominant characteristics are increasingly egalitarianism, insecurity, guilt, and a consequent resort to law; and, second, that though equality of condition will never be achieved, we are likely, in seeking it through law, to risk the survival of democratic institutions or, more likely, to render them irrelevant.

Equality has always been a primary American value enshrined, somewhat ambiguously, in the Declaration of Independence, by a man who knew a sense of guilt because of his own inconsistencies on the subject. What is new, arising within the last decade or so, is a strong shift from the assumption that the ideal is one of equality of opportunity coupled with some mitigation of inequalities of outcome through devices such as the progressive income tax, to an assumption that the only truly moral society would be one in which outcomes were completely equal. It is not clear what caused that shift but it is tolerably clear that it is occurring.

I do not maintain that complete equality of condition is an articulated political goal, though one hears it put that plainly in the academic community, which is often unfortunately, a weather-vane. But it is the tendency of our political rhetoric and our moral assumptions. More equality is constantly demanded and no stopping place for the progression is suggested.

The Supreme Court is an excellent barometer of changes in the political and moral atmosphere, not because it follows the election returns, but because men reading the words of the Constitution unconsciously pour into them the animating conceptions of their age. Until fairly recently the predominant clause of the Fourteenth Amendment was the due process clause with its emphasis on liberty. In 1927, Mr. Justice Holmes felt able to brush aside an appeal to the equal protection clause in a non-racial context as "the usual last resort of constitutional arguments."[4] Since then the equal

---

4. *Buck v. Bell,* 274 U.S. 200, 208 (1927).

protection clause has become paramount and sweeps wider in the name of equality than substantive due process ever did in the name of liberty. That is more than a constitutional lawyer's footnote. It is an indication of a moral and political gale blowing through our time.

It would be possible to fill up the remainder of this paper simply cataloging the number of programs and agencies that have been put in place or greatly expanded since 1960 whose objective is greater equality. Welfare, unemployment compensation, food stamps, housing subsidies, educational subsidies, medical services, legal services, the list goes on. Enormous bureaucracies, of which Health, Education, and Welfare (HEW) and Housing and Urban Development (HUD) are representative, have sprung up in the name of equality. But the effort is not merely to transfer wealth to the poor. That trend is troublesome only because regulation of the poor and others comes with the money. More worrisome is the desire to level or control persons and institutions perceived as having wealth or power or prestige.

A strong egalitarian philosophy implies other things, among them: extensive regulation of individuals by law (because equality of condition does not come about naturally) and a depreciation of the value of democratic processes. If equality is the ultimate and most profound political good, there is really very little to vote about. Only a society with a profusion of competing values, all regarded as legitimate, needs to vote. In such a society, there being no way of saying that one outcome is *a priori* better than another, it is the legitimacy of the process that validates the result; not, as in a thoroughly egalitarian society, the morality of the result that validates the process. There is thus a built-in tension between the ideal of equality of condition and the ideal of democracy.[5] That tension is not merely philosophic, which is how it has just been stated, but exists as well at the level of practical governance.

A modern society whose predominant value is equality of condition necessarily displays three related symptoms: widespread feelings of personal insecurity; a deep-seated sense of guilt; and, in consequence of the first two, the spread of an oppressive and excessive legalism throughout the social body.

---

5. It may be worth stressing, to avoid confusion, that this is not the same as the familiar point that equality and liberty are conflicting values. That is a related problem but not the one addressed here.

At a time when we have achieved greater personal security for the individual than ever before in recorded history, we have become increasingly anxious. Security has become a religion and we demand it not only from government but from schools and employers, we demand it not only from major catastrophe but from minor inconvenience; not only, to take health plans as an example, from the financial disaster of major surgery and prolonged hospitalization but from having to pay for a medical checkup — and we demand it as of right. So it is in all our relationships. We have even thrown constitutional protection around the imposition of minor disciplinary measures by school authorities. Why we have become so fearful, our psyches so easily bruised, I do not know. But David Riesman's picture of university students some twenty years ago seems a passingly accurate description of our society now.

Riesman had students read about Indian cultures, including the Pueblo and Kwakiutl, and asked which most closely resembled the culture of the United States. The Pueblo was presented as a peaceable, cooperative, relatively unemotional society, in which no one wishes to be thought a great man and everyone wishes to be thought a good fellow. Kwakiutl society, on the other hand, was pictured as intensely rivalrous, marked by conspicuous consumption, competition for status, and power drive. The great majority of the students questioned saw American society as essentially Kwakiutl. Riesman points out that this self-image is wide of the mark, that Americans tend to be a mild and cooperative people and bear a good many resemblances to the characteristics ascribed to the Pueblo.[6]

It is not clear why we perceive our relatively safe and cooperative society as dangerous and ruthless, but it is clear that many do and so continually seek additional protection and security, much of it through government.

It is also clear that a society whose morality is egalitarian but whose structure is necessarily hierarchical, a society that feels there are unjustifiable inequalities throughout its social, political, and economic order, is a society that feels guilty. We do.

Daniel Moynihan notes, "We are hopelessly a culture of conscience, and usually of bad conscience. . . ."[7] James Dickey

---

6. David Riesman, *The Lonely Crowd* (abr. ed., New Haven, 1961), pp. 225-235.

7. Daniel P. Moynihan, "How Much Does Freedom Matter?" *The Atlantic* **236**, 1 (1975): pp. 19, 25.

remarks: "The main emotion of our time is guilt."[8] Bad social conscience is taught to the young as dogma. Randall Jarrell wrote of a fictional but not untypical New England college that it could have carved on an administration building: *Ye shall know the truth, and the truth shall make you feel guilty.*[9] In certain academic circles, with which I was once familiar, a sense of guilt became as essential to good standing as proper manners used to be.

A society whose members feel insecure and guilty seeks security and expiation in trying to legislate equality. Our legislatures, our bureaucracies, and our courts are attempting to guarantee every right, major or minor or merely symbolic, people think they ought ideally to possess. I am not concerned that we shall achieve equality of condition. We shall not. A moment ago I said that we were necessarily a hierarchial society. By that I meant simply that any big, complex society must depend upon differential rewards of some kind to operate effectively. There is, as has been remarked, a "natural tyranny of the bell-shaped curve" in the distribution of the world's goods. Because of the inefficiency it imposes, the effort to achieve equality may, as in England, result in everybody having less, but what there is will be distributed unequally.

The problem is that the enormous profusion of regulations is incompatible with democratic processes. Democratic government is limited government for the simple reason that there are economies of scale in governmental institutions, as in all others. Since we can hardly have a dozen congresses and presidents simultaneously at work, the only available alternative is government by semi-independent and increasingly independent bureaucracies.

As government spreads, bureaucracies get beyond the power of the elected representatives to control. Government is too big, too complicated, there are too many decisions continually to be made. The staffs of both the presidency and Congress have been so enlarged in the effort to cope with the workload that both institutions have become bureaucratized. The general proportions of the problem may be seen in the fact that in a ten-year period federal litigation in the Supreme Court increased two and one-half times and that was primarily due to the growth of regulation.

---

8. Bill Moyers' Journal, "A Conversation with James Dickey," Jan. 25, 1976.
9. Randall Jarrell, *Pictures from an Institution* (Knopf, 1954), p. 221.

The result is a serious institutional overload for all branches of government.

Democratic processes become increasingly irrelevant. They simply are not the processes by which we are ruled. And there is increasing acceptance of this condition, in part because egalitarians do not care greatly about process. Alexander Bickel noted that, for example, they prefer an activist Supreme Court as a means of displacing democratic choice by moral principle.[10] To take a current illustration, there is now before the States, and close to ratification, the Equal Rights Amendment which provides that it shall be primarily the function of the judiciary to define and enforce equality between the sexes.[11] The amendment, we are assured, does not mean that no distinctions whatever may be made between men and women, that women must, for instance, be conscripted for combat duty. Yet it is proposed, and nobody opposes this aspect, that the Supreme Court rather than Congress or the state legislatures make the necessary detailed and sensitive political choices to write a code for the nation. In that sense, the amendment represents less a revolution in sexual equality than it does a revolution in constitutional methods of government.

This development was presaged by our readiness to be governed by agencies. The Federal Communications Commission, established to regulate radio broadcasting, itself undertook to regulate television and is now controlling the development of the entire new technology of cable. It was the FCC, with the approval of the courts, and not Congress, that legislated the controversial fairness doctrine.[12] I say these things not to be critical of the agency or of Congress but simply to cite one of the better known instances of important policy choice, the basics of government, left to non-

---

10. Alexander M. Bickel, *The Morality of Consent* (New Haven and London, 1975), p. 8.

11. The amendment is to be self-executing (i.e., enforceable by courts at the suit of an aggrieved party without any additional clarification by Congress) and Section 1 states simply: "Equality of rights under the law shall not be denied or abridged by the United States or by any State on account of sex." Section 2 states: "The Congress shall have the power to enforce, by appropriate legislation, the provisions of this article." The power to enforce cannot detract from the rights given, though unspecified, by the first section. Hence it would be for the judiciary rather than the legislature to determine in the myriad instances in which the question will arise when men and women must be treated identically and when they may be treated differently.

12. See *Red Lion Broadcasting Co. v. Federal Communications Commission*, 395 U.S. 367, 375-386 (1969).

democratic processes. It is true that Congress can alter the decisions made by bureaucracies but that is by no means a complete answer. So much law is made non-democratically, by bureaucracies, that no legislature can focus on more than a small fraction of the choices made. Moreover, the bureaucracies develop rather small but intense constituencies which often have more political influence than an electorate aggrieved by the total amount of regulation but rarely unified in opposition to any one.

The prospect, then, is the increasing irrelevance of democratic government. What replaces it is bureaucratic and judicial government, which may be benign and well intentioned, and may respond somewhat to popular desires, though not always, but cannot by definition be democratic.

Tocqueville, it must be said, forecast all of this well over a century ago. Men in democracies are well aware of the danger of anarchy inherent in a condition of equality, but are less alert, and so more vulnerable, to a form of depotism, which he said

> covers the surface of society with a network of small complicated rules, minute and uniform, through which the most original minds and the most energetic characters cannot penetrate. . . . The will of man is not shattered, but softened, bent,, and guided. . . .[13]

This "servitude of the regular, quiet, and gentle kind,"[14] he saw was not at all incompatible with the sovereignty of the people; it is just that sovereignty, the ability to elect representatives from time to time, became less and less important.[15]

The effect of such servitude upon the character of the people, Tocqueville saw, could be disastrous.[16] I wonder whether it is far-fetched to think there may be a connection between the rise of egalitarian bureaucracies, the proliferation of "small, complicated rules," our sense of guilt, and the symptoms of enervation and loss of self-confidence that seem to afflict all western democracies, in domestic matters as well as international. That there is a decline in self-confidence seems plain. It takes confidence in your values to punish for crime, and yet punishment rates in the United States and all of the western world decline even as crime rates soar. It takes assurance to enforce community standards of

---

13. Alexis de Tocqueville, *Democracy In America* (2 v., New York, 1954) **2**: p. 337.

14. *Ibid.*

15. *Idem.* at pp. 336-339.

16. *Ibid.*

behavior and, though most of us do not like it, pornography in its ugliest forms has become what a national magazine calls a plague.

If there is a connection, and I think one likely, then something very ominous and perhaps irreversible is happening to us as a people and as a community. It is disturbing in many respects but in none more so than in relation to the prospects for democratic government. A people without energy and self-confidence runs a greater risk of tyranny.

Tocqueville thought he saw a protection against this but it is now proving illusory. Aristocratic countries, he said, abound in powerful individuals who cannot be easily oppressed and "such persons restrain a government within general habits of moderation and reserve."[17] Democracies contain no such persons but their role, Tocqueville thought, may be played by great private corporations and associations, each of which "is a powerful and enlightened member of the community, which cannot be disposed of at pleasure or oppressed without remonstrance, and which, by defending its own rights against the encroachments of the government, saves the common liberties of the country."[18]

He did not foresee that in an age of egalitarian passion these great institutions might play the role of aristocrats not by succeeding to their power but by sharing their fate. Egalitarians necessarily dislike any center of power other than government. The great private institutions that were supposed to intermediate between the individual and the power of the state are becoming instead the conduits by which government regulation controls the individual. In the process the strength of these institutions is sapped. They do not remonstrate with government so much as seek a truce with it, a truce that never holds for long.

The great business corporations have long since ceased to seek more than an accommodation and now other institutions are being drawn into the web of regulation. Private universities are becoming unhappily aware of the regulation they accepted when they accepted federal money. The question arises whether any private university or any other institution can live apart from the federal government.

The trend seems faster. That is true, in part, because centers of resistance have steadily weakened under the pressure, and, in part, because government has devised, as Robert Nisbet points out,

---

17. *Idem.* at p. 342.
18. *Ibid.*

new, softer, and less resistible modes of coercion.[19] Its motives are benign and, indeed, the institutions ask for subsidies or contracts to which conditions will be attached. Regulation also begets regulation. An unregulated area causes difficulty for regulation in a neighboring regulated area and regulation expands to control it. Competition from trucks made it difficult to regulate railroads — which were being regulated on the theory that they had no competition — and so the ICC gained control over the trucking industry.

Moreover, the world proves more resistant to public policy than regulators expect. People can be regulated but the expected results do not appear and the response is a demand for more complete control of them and of the social process. Martin Mayer states the progression of regulation in the field of racial equality: "nondiscrimination became equal opportunity became affirmative action became goals became quotas became 'equality of outcomes.' "[20] Nondiscrimination, as an ideal, was an objection to government interference in free social processes, but the results were not the expected millennium, and hence the movement, by stages, to equality of outcomes, which, as an ideal, is government objection to free social processes. The same progression may be traced in a variety of fields of regulation.

The gradual displacement of democratic government by bureaucratic government does not necessarily suggest that the relatively mild and well-intentioned, though insistent, reign of the bureaucracies will be stable. If it is true that bureaucratic egalitarianism suffocates the spirit, weakens the morale and self-confidence of the community, while it saps the strength of intermediate institutions, then it leaves society as an aggregation of individual particles ranged against the state. That kind of society — anxious, insecure, irritated, bored, the people an undifferentiated mass — may perhaps more easily be swept by mass movements joined to populist rhetoric and transcendental principles. Such movements create excitement and a sense of purpose; they promise the restoration of the lost but longed-for sense of community. In a word, a society so reduced is more vulnerable to totalitarianism.

If I have extrapolated rather liberally from observed trends, I claim that my topic gives me license, indeed requires it of me. It is quite likely that I am wrong, that forces I do not foresee will

---

19. Robert Nisbet, *Twilight of Authority* (New York, 1975), pp, 223-229.
20. Martin Mayer, *Today and Tomorrow in America* (New York, 1976), p. 4.

alter our direction, but we have moved far enough in that direction that it is at least legitimate to be concerned.

The concepts that drive us toward more governmental regulation of formerly private economic and social processes seem, on the evidence so far, more persuasive politically than the concepts that oppose them. The moral superiority of equality and the effectiveness of legal regulation are powerful ideas because they are simple ideas. Our constitutional system, the institutions of capitalism, the desirability of hierarchy, and the limits of law's effectiveness, on the other hand, require a complex understanding.

In any discussion of these trends a mention of the role played in our polity by the intellectual classes is mandatory. The breadth and intensity of the recent attack upon intellectuals by intellectuals is little short of astounding, and, in my view, we cannot have too much of it. The case has been made, perhaps most effectively by Joseph Schumpeter,[21] that the intellectual classes, given their typical desire to politicize all of society's processes, pose the greatest danger to the future of democratic government. They could not accomplish that alone but their increased size and prestige makes them almost irresistible when allied, as they frequently are, with the powerful forces of populism.

The intellectual classes I refer to, by the way, are not composed of persons who are necessarily intellectually distinguished or even competent. They belong to the class less because of their abilities than because they have been to universities and regard themselves, whether accurately or not, as possessing a superior understanding and, often, because they work with ideas, as do academics, journalists, lawyers, and so on. The earmark of the breed is anti-bourgeois sentiment, probably, it has been suggested, because a business civilization confers money, prestige, and power upon the bourgeoisie that intellectuals desire. The demand for equality of condition — not between intellectuals and the bourgeoisie, that would be too crass, but rather, altruistically, throughout the society — is perceived, though not necessarily accurately, as a means of shifting power from private institutions to the state, and hence from the bourgeoisie to the intellectuals.

It is necessary that intellectuals attack in the name of equality. A century ago, as Irving Kristol has said, the intellectual alienated

---

21. Joseph A. Schumpeter, *Capitalism, Socialism, and Democracy* (2nd ed., New York, 1947).

from bourgeois culture was more likely to move right than left but the attenuation of aristocratic traditions means that the only permissible anti-bourgeois arguments must today be framed in "democratic" or egalitarian terms.[22]

It is impossible in short compass to give an adequate impression of the amount of intellectual energy, in both teaching and writing, that is devoted to attempts to prove free economic and social processes so defective that legal intervention is required. Much of the literature is itself so deficient, so palpably illogical and at variance with observable fact, that one must conclude it is the rationalization of prejudice rather than the explanation of positions arrived at by a process of intellectuation. The weight of this intellectual product upon legislative opinion in the middle and upper middle classes is enormous. The effect of it upon the disseminators of popular information and upon policy-makers in government is profound. That is why the alliance or, perhaps more accurately, the congruence of intellectual opinion with populist politics has such a profound impact upon the direction of our society.

Perversely enough, the spread of secondary and higher education, along with the extension of the suffrage, has reinforced these trends. The complexity of institutions and relationships in our society was never well understood and the freedom and power of those institutions and relationships rested in no small measure on an unreasoned, awed acceptance of them. The spread of education, particularly university education, has served to decrease that awe without increasing, in the same proportions, the reality of understanding. We are left unhappily in between. Respect founded in ignorance is lost but is not fully replaced in respect founded upon sophistication.

Up to this point I have spoken, rather summarily, entirely about trends and causes that seem to me threatening to democracy. Rather than close on a note of unrelieved pessimism, leaving behind an incorrect impression that I deplore any mitigation of inequality as well as all education beyond the vocational, I would like, though even more summarily, to suggest that there are countertrends and alternatives.

Rather recently there has occurred a shift in opinion about the omniscience and omnicompetence of government. It is popular

---

22. Irving Kristol, "About Equality," *Commentary* **54**, 5 (1972): pp. 41, 44.

to lay that shift to Watergate and Vietnam, but I think much of the change may be laid to the fact that people are having their first intensive experience with government regulation in matters that affect them intimately and immediately, in their schools, on the job, and in their families. Detailed bureaucratic government may be benevolent in intention but it is often perceived by its beneficiaries as officious intermeddling.[23]

The criticism of intellectuals by intellectuals, for which I have expressed a taste, represents a crumbling of the rather monolithic aspect of received intellectual opinion that was characteristic in the 1960's. The intellectual community shows signs that it may, just possibly, begin to behave somewhat more as a community defined by intellectual rigor rather than moral fervor. The campus turbulence of the 1960's made it plain that egalitarian ideals can be weapons against as well as for the intellectual class's hierarchy, and the government's recent interest in having a say in university faculty hiring and other policies seems to have suggested that the state may not be a threat to the bourgeoisie alone.

We may be ready to be more thoughtful about what government can and cannot accomplish while remaining democratic. There are ways to mitigate inequalities and to accomplish many goals of regulation through market mechanisms or automatic devices that do not require minute bureaucratic control of social processes. There is, for example, no good reason why redistribution of income should take the form of specific programs in agriculture, housing, education, health, and so forth, which always involve an elaborate attempt to control both the recipients of the largesse and the industry in question. If redistribution of income is the real purpose, and not the desire to regulate the free sector, devices like the negative income tax are available. Elected officials can control it as they cannot control the innumerable decisions inherent in regulation of details.

---

23. It should be said, however, that the same persons who object to the cost of government and the ubiquity of bureaucratic regulation also frequently insist that government deal with still more problems. Much of the public demands of government the very programs whose implementation irritates them. We may, therefore, be creating conditions in which public policy is bound to be perceived as consistently failing. Institutions are thought to be incompetent because they have been assigned tasks in which competence is not possible. The failure to understand that our demands are the source of our dissatisfactions thus generates a public mood that is not favorable to the survival of democratic government.

Similarly, bureaucratic government would be diminished and made subject to democratic decision-making if problems such as those relating to the environment were handled through market or automatic mechanisms. We have been trying to handle water and air pollution by legislating new technologies into existence from Washington. Results might be better and democratic procedures more effective if government auctioned off regional pollution vouchers that were freely transferable. The market would then assign the rights to tolerable levels of pollution to uses where they were most needed. An alternative would be to impose taxes according to degrees of pollutant emission. Government would have to decide only the sources of pollution and the degree considered tolerable. It would not have to require or impose and then supervise enormously complex plans and technological responses.

Greater sophistication about modes of social control would do much to preserve the capacity of democratic institutions to govern. But the truth remains, and must not be blinked, that there are many things an egalitarian impulse leads to which cannot be accomplished by methods other than direct and detailed manipulation of people and institutions. I have tried to suggest that we must finally choose between doing those things and preserving democracy in substance as well as in form. Adam Smith did say that there is a lot of ruin in a great nation but he did not say the supply was inexhaustible.

ROBERT H. BORK
Solicitor General of the United States

The Rebirth of a Nation

SOME OF OUR FELLOW CITIZENS, including some informed observers of the American scene, think of these times, the two hundredth anniversary of the founding of the Republic, as the shoddiest, the saddest, the least hopeful period in our history, the least auspicious of occasions for celebration. In this hallowed place of our independence, in this Society, founded and distinguished by the great men who claimed and won that independence for us, we might do well to look at the facts behind that unhappy, unwelcome assertion.

Unfortunately, a lot of the facts are undeniable. Here, as we enter upon the third century of the Republic's history, we are only too familiar with the dishonesty that has characterized the conduct of our public affairs, and with the unabashed bribery and corruption, the utter disregard of the basic decencies of the market place, that have entered into the transactions of private business, in our country. We have come through an unhappy, a grim decade. In it we have fought and lost a war — though we preferred to say say it was not a war — which divided and confused this country as no conflict has done since the War between the States over a hundred years ago. We are even now barely emerging from a profound economic depression, though some public financiers and economists prefer to say it is only a recession. We can derive little comfort from that subtlety of terminology.

The brutal fact is that all told it has been and for many it is still a bad time.

Well, we have managed depressions before, when we had leaders with the courage to tell us the facts about them. I do not know whether we have learned how to deal with the ethical consequences of evasions of reality that may be more insidious than the economic depression itself.

For example, the use of a decline in economic activity as a screen behind which to cause the weak and vulnerable to be more

187

dependent than ever. I refer to the representation by honorable men of the involuntary idleness of millions of Americans not as the human waste and reproach and curse that it is, but as a convenient cure for inflation. Or, again, the specious argument that the way to provide our people with enough energy to keep our productivity at capacity is to cut back on the very energy that is America's life blood, instead of providing more of it. Called — miscalled —"conserving," this is the road to the de-energizing of a country built upon human and physical energy.

Such pernicious evasions of the truth as these, if we swallow them, may do us more damage than the events that monopolize the headlines.

This is an age, some observers would say, in which colorless mediocrity and timidity appear to be preferred to eminence and courage; in which men of ability and ideals shun rather than seek public office; in which stagnation and retreat and resignation are publicly espoused as serious alternatives for ideas of growth and dynamism; in which the essential human values of mankind, established and fought for over so many long years, in this country as in others, are now being disparaged and discarded. It is a time, certainly, when low expectations rather than high hopes, hesitancy, fear of the future rather than faith in it, characterize the utterances of both those in high office and those who report on public affairs, through the printed word and the overwhelming power of the electronic media.

The proposition, in fact, is that America has reached a new and dismal low in morality, in dedication to the truth, in the pursuit of ordinary honesty, as well as in enterprise and adventure. In short, that the Republic, instead of entering its third century with high hopes, with the creativeness and energy and forwardness that has been so much in its character in the past, has now reached the end of the road, and is drying up; and that there is no body of thought, no inspiration, no leadership, no ideas, nothing, that can avert a sad, painful awakening from what was only a great dream, the American Republic.

I do not accept that proposition for one moment.

The concept of the founder of this Society and his comrades is *not* a dream whose epoch has passed. It can be made real. Which of us now is prepared to tell the younger generation, our sons and daughters, and our grandchildren, that their lives can be any less exciting and productive than ours have been? Not I.

For they would violently disagree with me, and they would be right to disagree.

I see this difficult and troubled time, a time of soul-searching, not all of it unhealthy, as a new beginning, another of those times of rebirth that marked the American past, times which generated in their day a resurgence of spirit and achievements in human progress which most of the people of the world have looked at with admiration, and, indeed, envy.

This is not the beginning of the end, merely the preparation for a fresh advance. We have so many exciting new things to learn, and such enormous resources of human energy and ingenuity and imagination with which to apply them — apply them not merely for the betterment of our own society, but also for the betterment of others.

My sense that this is a time for affirmation and optimism about the future rests upon some deeply felt and time-tested convictions. One is that, whatever our recent experience, there is inherent in, and natural to, the American character, a regard for what is true and right, in methods as well as in purposes, and an instinctive repudiation of what is wrong. This instinct is enduring, the recent aberrations we have witnessed are not.

My second conviction is that human creativity, *the prime mover* in the improvement of all human prospects — whether in an individual or a nation — is the product not of ease and satisfaction, but of conflict and trial, and of turmoil and testing.

History offers the very birth of the Republic as an example of the power of those convictions. A sense of what was right and what was wrong, of what was true and what was false, of what was fair and unfair, had a great deal to do with that creative act. The birth of the Republic did not occur in an atmosphere of calm; quite the contrary, it was not an act of pure intellect. It was rather the product of conflicting ideas and of the conflict of strong, determined, and highly educated, intelligent, creative, and combative personalities.

So I would like to suggest to this gathering of scholars, men and women of ideas, people who deal, at least to some extent, in abstractions and theories, with considerations, in short, of the intellect, that it is just such conflicts in the recent past that may produce the creativity of thought and action from which will issue the Rebirth of this nation.

Thought *and* Action. How divorced and separate those two

concepts have become over the years! My own life has been a matter of acts, of doing, or trying to do, some concrete and specific things, making some grand, you might say grandiose, plans for effecting physcial change, and for seeing to it that the changes took place. I have not been unaware during those years of doing, of creating physical and psychic change in this country and in far distant places of the moral and philosophical *meaning* of such changes.

Today I am honored to be in the presence of men and women whose prime responsibility is different from the one that was and is mine, who are concerned with thought, abstractions, theories, a scholarly knowledge of the past, a comprehension of private and public ethics, men and women with a profound understanding of what behavior is becoming and what behavior is unbecoming. For myself, as a manager of concrete events, I do not believe such theoretical and scholarly considerations have nothing to do with my managerial function; indeed, I believe what the manager manages *to do* is worthless without those intangible philosophical considerations that are your special concern.

In the presence of this remarkable gathering, representative of the intellectual resources of this country, and of other countries too, I pose a question which has come into my mind often enough.

Simply stated, my question is this: what do the inner life and outward manifestations of the man of action have to do with the contemplations of the theoretician, the intellectual, the scholar, the philosopher?

Many of our so-called men of action would reply: precious little. As a group, I am afraid that those of us with responsibilities in business, in government, in administration, and in engineering and technology, tend, consciously or unconsciously, to downgrade the occupations of the theoreticians and intellectuals, the men of thought. There are those among us who think of poetry and drama, of literature and scholarship, of concern with the remote past, of philosophy, as being of a second order of capability, not really relevant to the on-going daily mundane affairs for which we, as a group, are responsible. I will not represent my kind as utter philistines, for we certainly are not. Indeed, you will be as aware as I am of the enormous contributions which particular men of affairs, men absorbed in the business world, have made to the arts and to the enjoyment of the arts by others. Still, though we enjoy music and poetry and art, it is for most of us as occasional pleasurable relaxations from the realities of the world with which we deal, not as subjects of major substance.

I cannot, even in this distinguished company, absolve scholars and philosophers from blame for the divorce between thought and action. Such a gap between action and thought did not exist with the scholarly but pragmatic activists — Franklin among them — of the early days of the birth of the nation. There has grown up, however, in recent years a superior aloofness among scholars and philosophers, an aversion for the rough and sweaty arena of human endeavor, perhaps even a sort of intellectual enjoyment in watching the poor fellows who have the job of trying to get things done make a mess of whatever it is they are trying to do. And too often when scholars and intellectuals analyze the shortcomings of the man of action, they use the erudite jargon of their expertise, terms that few outside the select circle can understand.

This division is damaging to all of us. One lesson in particular emerges from the recent apparent decline in private and public standards of behavior. It is this: in order to be effective as actors, properly to discharge their responsibilities in the public arena of government, and the quasi-public arena of the management and conduct of private corporate affairs, our men of action need to draw upon the *full* intellectual resources of the nation, the full comprehension of philosophy, literature, history, poetry, and art. For what is the result if they don't, and the dichotomy persists? We get action, but for action's sake; and action without moral purpose and direction, derived from our total philosophical and artistic heritage, is inevitably sterile. It can even be dangerous to our institutions, as we have seen, and to the health and sanity of individual life.

My affirmation of the vigor, the excitement, and creativity of America's future rests upon the availability to the country of two major resources. There are the physical resources, of course, and these I believe to be practically without limit, and, as I further believe, still largely undeveloped. And second, there are the intellectual, spiritual, artistic, and philosophical resources.

Both are needed to sustain the kind of future we want to see. What we make of the future will not depend simply upon our physical assets nor upon our managerial capacities for government and production, but upon the essential interplay between the processes of action and the processes of thought: upon a partnership — more than a partnership, an *identity* — between the men who deal essentially with things and the men who deal principally with ideas and emotions and human values.

That division of thought and action I referred to is not a necessary nor even a traditional one in this country, for as we all know thinking and doing were much the same thing to the founders of the Republic. Those men were as resolute in deed as they were bold in ideas. The interdependence and interaction of these two qualities of American life can produce the rebirth of the nation to which I look forward, which I myself believe is already on the way.

What I foresee is something that has not often been achieved, but is surely not unachievable: namely, the men of ideas and scholarship, who make humanism their vocation and contribution to society, becoming more and more involved in the pragmatic and practical application of the ideas, philosophy, and theories which they develop. And as a fruitful corollary to that proposition, the men and women of action, with a new respect for and understanding of the place of theories, abstractions, and humanism in the great scheme of things, themselves becoming practitioners and originators of philosophy and ideas.

Is that impossible? I do not think so. Certainly there are some impediments in the way of accomplishing the interrelation and interdependence of thought and action which have to be removed, some attitudes of mind which have to be changed.

An example of such an impediment which ought to be removed promptly: the increasing perversion of the humane discipline of economics to a mathematical and quantitative technique. I despair when I note the subjection of considerations of the human heart and imagination and compassion to the heartless, unimaginative quantification of the computer, and the misuse of the computer, a valuable tool — properly employed — for purposes for which it is not adapted and which it cannot serve. Hence the exposition some few years ago of the facile and misleading so-called "limits of growth" philosophy. How thin, how superficial and even technically sloppy that doctrine was! How basically wrong it was bound to be, conceived as it was without understanding of the human spirit, without the guidance of men of hope and historical perspective or philosophy, without, apparently, any recognition of the past and progress of the human race and of the endless horizons of the human will and ambition.

Well, the sophomoric mentalities who conducted that headline-seeking exercise in sterility and negativism have now admitted —

here in meeting assembled a few days ago in Philadelphia — of all places — their lack of understanding of the dynamism of the human spirit and the true use of mathematics. All the same their prediction of catastrophe, and similar sophisticated nonsense, has contributed not a little to widespread loss of faith in the future, and loss of momentum that we call depression.

All this too will pass. The time of our rebirth will come, and come more readily, once we recognize, those of us who are responsible for getting things done in business and in government, that the specific and concrete things we try to do have to be built on a foundation of ideas, of thought, of principles.

This will be a period in which the private individual and his non-governmental institutions will become even more important than the kind of political institutions the nation acquired in its beginnings. We shall no longer think of power in a democratic and technical society as synonymous with government and government action. Indeed, *the authority of ideas and imagination and of scholarly understanding* will come to have more influence on human events than the power of political institutions.

I speak of the greater authority of ideas as if this were something new. Perhaps it is merely that changes in the modes of communication are now making it more apparent. I wonder whether it has not always been true, that we in this country, and other peoples too, may not have overstated the importance of political power and governmental functions, and understated the authority that resides outside of government, the authority that emanates from the ideas and emotions of private people.

In fact, is not that kind of authority beginning to reassert itself already? Contrast the apathy — the not wholly unjustifiable apathy, I must confess — of the voters in our elections, with the positive eagerness of countless non-elected individual citizens to play their parts in shaping the present and future courses of their communities and their country.

I entertain the feeling that there is a real though quiet revolution going on around us, in which the private individual, in spontaneous association with other private individuals, is asserting more control and direction over his life than at any other comparable time in the Republic's history. The heightened stature of the individual, the increasingly effective influence of his *extra*-governmental organizations and associations, in matters close to his daily life, these constitute the most heartening promise for the American future.

There are those who believe that the very complexity of our society, the size of the public institutions and private corporations which *appear* to dominate it, the impact of technology and the machine, are bound to diminish the stature of the individual man and reduce the importance of his voice and his role in society.

I see little evidence that this is actually happening. I believe the trend is otherwise. In many ways the individual has become more consequential and self-assertive than ever. His favor and assent have always, of course, been the central objective of men who seek to possess political power, and today they woo him more ardently than ever. Some seek to persuade, others to manipulate him, but none dare ignore him.

The individual and his volunteer friends may ignore them. For as I see it the citizen somehow seems to feel that it is no longer necessarily in politics or in government that he can most usefully bring his ideas and energies to bear upon his own problems, upon his family's well-being, and upon the state of his country. He strives for his ends in his own ways, in his own communities, in his own private organizations and associations, quite outside the country's regular political and institutional apparatus. And often he strives for them amazingly successfully. For example, the contemporary environmental protection movement, now so powerful, and rightly so, was the child and creation of private citizens, not of public servants or political office-holders. Such examples of the affirmative, creative power of the individual in his own and the country's affairs and its future are certain to multiply.

The future, we all know, cannot be expected to repeat the patterns of the past. Many of the old slogans and formulae no longer fit: Square Deal, New Deal, New Frontier, so many others, useful enough, no doubt, in their day, even inspiring to their own generation — but now faded, out-of-date, not revivable, largely irrelevant to our present imperatives.

For one thing, such slogans were the concoctions of a centralized culture, in which a few, a very few, great centers of government, of finance and business activity, of the arts, and, yes, of public-relations wizardry and image building, managed to dominate the rest of America. I believe all that is on its way out. We are today, and we shall become increasingly so in the future, a diversified and decentralized society. A society enlivened and dispersed over hundreds and thousands of cities and towns, of centers of influence. There is where individual Americans will want to do their thinking for themselves and arrive at the solutions appropriate to their own communities.

This will not be turning our backs upon the great, the abiding truths of our history. It will merely be a reaffirmation of them. The recent past, a period of conflict and turmoil, has surely brought home to us some sense of how to organize a better future. What will it rest upon? I have tried to suggest the essential elements — as I myself see them — in a reborn America: the remarriage of ideas and abstractions with action; the persistence of individuality; the diversity, the enormously valuable diversity, of the sources of energy and ideas in this country; the authority of ideas and imagination and culture.

Abstractions! But we have been learning, all of us, that concrete specifics alone do not count. The ways we do things, our standards of behavior, our private and public conduct of ourselves, cannot be wholly separate from the things we do, the life of action. The third century of the Republic should stand for more than machinery, technical advancement, or refurbished political institutions. There is another goal common to all of us, which we can seek together, managers, administrators, people of affairs, scientists, scholars, whatever we are — a moral purpose of our striving.

Here we join, men of action and men of mind. And if we can come a little closer to finding that purpose than we have been before, this country may have cause to rejoice in the third century of its journey.

> DAVID E. LILIENTHAL
> Chairman and Chief Executive Officer, Development and Resources Corporation; Formerly Chairman of the Tennessee Valley Authority and the U. S. Atomic Energy Commission

George Washington:
The Evidence of the Portraits

W ASHINGTON WAS THE CENTRAL FIGURE of the event whose bicentennial we are celebrating: commander in chief of the army during the war for independence; chairman of the convention that drew up our form of government; first president of the republic, setting precedents that have shaped our history. He was also a member of the American Philosophical Society, elected in January, 1780. The circumstances of his election are worth noting. The Society was rebuilding its membership after the disruption of its activities by the British occupation of Philadelphia. Twenty-two new members were elected on January 16, 1780. The names read like a who's who of the American cause at that moment. "His Excellency George Washington, Esq., General and Commander in Chief of the Armies of the United States of North America" heads the list, which included, among others, Jefferson, Adams, Jay, Hamilton, the two Laurens, father and son, and the French minister.

The war for independence was then a stalemate, British forces holding New York City, Washington's army camped in the hills of New Jersey around Morristown. The winter of 1779–1780 was a terrible one for the army. The snow lay four to six feet deep in northern Jersey and all the hardships of Valley Forge were re-enacted at Morristown. The soldiers were ill clad, cold, hungry, their pay months in arrears. Washington's great problem was to hold his army together, when he wrote to acknowledge his election on February 15; but before his letter was read to the Society, disaster had been added to stalemate. On May 16 a British land and naval force commanded by Sir Henry Clinton captured Charleston, South Carolina, and, together with the city, took prisoner the entire Continental Army of the South, including the Virginia and Carolina regiments sent as reinforcements from the northern army. There were rumors of a French expeditionary force on its way to North America, but news of Rochambeau's landing in Rhode Island did not come until the end of July.

The atmosphere in Philadelphia must have been discouraging when a meeting of the Society was held on June 15. General Reed, the president of Pennsylvania (as the office was then called) and patron of the Society, was in the chair; the French minister, all the officers of the Society and an unusually large number of members were present. They heard Timothy Matlack give a paper on the growth of trees; then the secretary read Washington's brief letter of acceptance, ending:

> The arts and sciences essential to the prosperity of the State, and to the ornament and happiness of human life, have a primary claim to the encouragement of every lover of his country and of mankind.[1]

At another time Washington might have been elected as a Virginia planter noted for efforts to better American agriculture and to promote internal improvements. In 1780 it seems fair to say, his election was an affirmation by the Society, at a difficult moment of the war, of confidence in the general and loyalty to the American cause.

At news of Washington's death, a special meeting of the Society was called on December 27, 1799. The minutes read:

> The American Philosophical Society, taking into consideration the loss of their fellow member George Washington, a citizen distinguished by his virtues & by his eminent services to his country, Resolved, That as a mark of their high respect & veneration for his character, it be recommended to the members to wear a black crepe around the left arm, as mourning, for 30 days.

> Agreed, That a portrait of George Washington be procured to be hung in the Society's Hall.

Three years and some months later, on April 1, 1803, a portrait by Gilbert Stuart was shown to the Society. A committee of three members, Mr. W. Hamilton, Mr. Latrobe, and Dr. Jacobs, was appointed to consider the price and the likeness. On May 20, having weighed the matter carefully, they made their report:

> That the Portrait is equal if not superior to other copies of the bust of Mr. Stuart's whole length portrait of General Washington,

---

1. Jared Sparks, *The Writings of George Washington* (12 v., Boston, 1834-1838) 6: p. 466.

made by himself, which your committee have seen. The picture possesses the strong likeness and spirit of the original; and it having been painted about 6 years ago the present state of the coloring proves that more than usual attention has been paid to the goodness and durability of the colours which have been used.

The commendation of your committee can add nothing to the acknowledged merit of Mr. Stuart's performance nor is it necessary to remark on the peculiarities in the drawing in this individual portrait, for they are those which the original possesses.

The price of the portrait as it includes the frame, is below that of other portraits of the same kind, by the amount of the value of the frame which may be about 16 dollars.

Upon the whole, as it is now impossible to obtain an original portrait of this illustrious Member of the American Philosophical Society, your Committee are of the opinion, that it is not probable that a wish of the Society to possess his likeness will ever be better fulfilled than by the acquisition of that now offered.

On the basis of this carefully worded opinion, the Society purchased the portrait, which has ever since looked down with impassive gravity upon our meetings. It is the only one of Stuart's many replicas of the "Athenaeum" portrait belonging to an organization that purchased it from the artist himself.[2]

What does our portrait tell us of our fellow member? Stuart's "Athenaeum" likeness may be so dulled by familiarity that it has lost all meaning for us. Washington was, however, painted and modeled from life by many other artists; American-born, English, French, Italian, Swiss, Danish, Swedish observers studied his features and left a record of the man. Stuart's likeness is one piece of evidence among a crowd of witnesses to the appearance, the character, the growth and change of a personality central in our history.

---

2. [Anna Wells Rutledge and Charles Coleman Sellers], *A Catalogue of Portraits and Other Works of Art in the Possession of the American Philosophical Society,* Memoirs Amer. Philos. Soc. **54** (Philadelphia, 1961): p. 99. In the standard reference works it appears as follows:
Mantle Fielding, *Gilbert Stuart's Portraits of Washington* (Philadelphia, 1923), pp. 153-154, No. 34.
Lawrence Park, *Gilbert Stuart, An Illustrated Descriptive List of his Works Compiled by Lawrence Park. With an Account of his Life by John Hill Morgan and an Appreciation by Royal Cortissoz* (4 v., New York, 1926) **2**: pp. 864-865, No. 35.
John Hill Morgan and Mantle Fielding, *The Life Portraits of Washington and their Replicas* (Philadelphia, 1931), pp. 274-275, No. 35.
Gustavus A. Eisen, *Portraits of Washington* (3 v., New York, 1932) **1**: p. 154.

One must start by accepting the fact that there are striking differences in the reports of these artists, not only in interpretation of his character but in descriptions of his appearance. A well-trained Italian sculptor, Guiseppe Ceracchi (1751–1802), visited the United States twice, in 1791–1792 and again in 1793–1794, seeking from Congress a commission to erect a heroic equestrian monument to Washington. He made studies of his subject from life, from which he later made a number of marble busts, now to be seen in the National Portrait Gallery, Washington; the Metropolitan Museum of Art, New York; and the Gibbes Memorial Gallery, Charleston. Ceracchi was an enthusiastic republican who saw Washington as the re-creation of ancient Roman virtues. His busts show us a figure in Roman armor or classical costume, most often with a mass of curly hair (although a bust in the Metropolitan Museum has close-cropped hair), and enormous breadth of shoulders.

Christian Gullager (1759–1826), a Danish artist, a product of the Royal Academy of Copenhagen, migrated to New England in the 1780's. While the general was attending a church service at Boston in 1789, Gullager made a drawing, then followed him to Newburyport where he was given a sitting of two and a half hours. A portrait by Gullager that tradition calls *Washington* gives him a prognathous jaw, like one of the later Hapsburgs, and an expression only to be described as a leer.

A Swedish artist, Adolph Wertmuller (1751–1811), who enjoyed a considerable success in Paris during the 1780's, migrated to Philadelphia in 1794 and shortly after painted Washington from life. His likeness shows a man with an oval shaped head and a bright-eyed, eager-to-please expression.

The first American-born artist to paint Washington was Charles Willson Peale (1741–1827). A miniature now at Mount Vernon was painted from two sittings in May, 1776, as a memento for Mrs. Washington of the husband who was setting off for the war. Peale likewise shows us a man with an oval face, a small tight mouth, and a determined expression.

Twenty years later Stuart shows us a square face, a broad mouth, a heavy jaw and chin, and a singularly impassive expression. This — the dominant image — was painted after the lower portion of his face had been distorted by ill-fitting false teeth. Mrs. Washington is said to have disliked this portrait, while the artist and the general approved of it; and the American people have accepted it as the one and only Washington.

What are we to believe?

Only one portrait exists of Washington before the Revolution. Painted by Charles Willson Peale at Mount Vernon in May, 1772, it shows the Virginia colonel at age forty. He wears the uniform of the Virginia regiment which he had commanded during the French and Indian War. In the landscape background Indians camp beside a waterfall; in the distance rise the forest-covered mountains where he had won his reputation as a soldier. Here is a tough frontier fighter, marching orders in his pocket, a rifle slung over his shoulders, a sword (still preserved at Mount Vernon) at his side. The face (fig. 1) is a soldier's face, marked by resolution and sense of duty, strong and good-humored. One would expect this man to treat the men of his command with firm but fair discipline. In the mouth there is a hint of the quality of reserve, of which Aaron Bancroft, who had fought at Lexington and Bunker Hill and wrote an early life of Washington, said, "No art or address could draw from him an opinion which he thought prudent to conceal."[3] The alert spring of the body suggests physical strength. Peale told an anecdote of this, an incident of his visit to Mount Vernon. One afternoon the artist and some other young men were in their shirtsleeves enjoying the sport of pitching the bar, when Washington happened by. He picked up the bar and, without even taking off his coat, threw it beyond their farthest mark. "When you beat my pitch, young gentlemen," he said pleasantly, "I'll try again."[4]

Seven years later, in the early months of 1779, Peale painted a second portrait (fig. 2). Washington was now the commander in chief of the Armies of the United States. His forces had cleared the enemy from New England, Pennsylvania, and New Jersey; France had declared itself an ally. When the general came to Philadelphia to consult with the Congress about the war, the Supreme Executive Council, the governing body of the state of

3. Aaron Bancroft, *An Essay on the Life of George Washington, Commander in Chief of the American Army, through the Revolutionary War: and the First President of the United States* (Worcester, Mass., 1807), p. 527.

4. Peale's son Rembrandt recalled this story in his reminiscences of Washington, *The Crayon* 2 (1856): p. 388. It is logically related to Peale's stay at Mount Vernon in 1772 by Charles Coleman Sellers in *Charles Willson Peale, Volume I, Early Life (1741-1790)*, Memoirs Amer. Philos. Society 23, 1 (Philadelphia, 1947): p. 109. George Washington Parke Custis's *Recollections* also place it in 1772.

Pennsylvania, asked him to pose for a portrait to be hung in the State House. Peale chose to paint Washington as the victor of the battles of Trenton and Princeton. A relaxed and confident figure, he leans against one of his cannons. Captured Hessian battle flags are at his feet; a British flag fallen to the ground is at the left; and in the distance a file of red-coated prisoners marches under guard past Nassau Hall.

This portrait is a celebration of victory. Many replicas by the artist and by his family attest to its popularity. To our eyes, accustomed to Gilbert Stuart's full-length portrait, the elongated figure appears strange. The head seems too small in relation to the body, the narrow shoulders and the great length of the arms and legs are surprising. Yet there is abundant evidence for the truth of Peale's image. The tailor's measurements given in Washington's orders to his agent in London before the war; the uniform worn when he said farewell to his officers in 1783 (in the Museum of History and Technology, Washington) agree that he was a tall man, 6 feet 2 inches in his prime, but slender rather than heavily built, of equal breadth from shoulder to hip. His strength was in his "long, large, and sinewy limbs," wrote George Washington Parke Custis.

> His frame showed an extraordinary development of bone and muscle; his joints were large, as were his feet; and could a cast have been preserved of his hand, to be exhibited in those degenerate days, it would be said to have belonged to the being of a fabulous age. During Lafayette's visit to Mount Vernon in 1825, he said to the writer, "I never saw so large a hand on any human being, as the General's. It was in this portico, in 1784 that you were introduced to me by the general. You were a very little gentleman, with a feather in your hat, and holding fast to *one finger* of the good general's remarkable hand, which was all that you could do, my dear sir, at that time."[5]

Peale had another opportunity to draw the general from life four years later, when Washington passed through Philadelphia in December, 1783, on his way home to Mount Vernon. The artist then had orders for full-length portraits from the College of New Jersey, and from the state of Maryland.

The Continental Congress had been at Princeton from August to November of 1783. On September 24, both the Congress and

---

5. George Washington Parke Custis, *Recollections and Private Memoirs of Washington* (New York, 1860), p. 484.

the commanding general had attended the college commencement, at which Dr. Ashbel Green delivered an address in praise of Washington. At the close of the exercises the trustees of the college voted to request the general to sit for a portrait by Peale, to hang in the college hall in the place of the portrait of King George III "which was torn away by a ball from the American artillery during the battle of Princeton."[6] Peale chose to represent Washington again at Princeton, but now during the battle, waving his sword in a gesture of command, while beside him an aide supports the body of the dying General Mercer. It was a natural choice: not only had Nassau Hall been the closing scene of the fighting but Peale had seen Washington in action there. When Mercer's advance was overrun by the British, the regiment of Pennsylvania militia in which the artist was serving as an officer found itself in the front line of battle. Washington himself, galloping up, took command, formed the militia's line and, taking position in their front, steadied them to stand against the charge of the British dragoons.

From the same life study, Peale painted for Maryland in 1784 an allegory of the victory of Yorktown. Washington stands accompanied by Lafayette, as symbol of the French alliance, and by Colonel Tench Tilghman, symbol of Maryland's role in the war. In the distance are a French soldier, carrying the Bourbon fleur-de-lis battle flag, and an American, with the newly adopted American flag of stars and stripes. Between them walks a dejected British prisoner carrying his colors cased. It was an appropriate picture for the Maryland State House, to hang in the room where Washington had returned to Congress the commission as commander in chief given to him eight years before. But neither battle nor allegory was Peale's forte. These full-length portraits of 1784 are records of Washington's appearance at the close of the war, but they do not suggest the immense moral authority that made possible his greatest service as a soldier in 1783.

The reason for the Continental Congress's presence at Princeton instead of Philadelphia in 1783 had been fear of Pennsylvania troops who, unpaid and hungry, were on the verge of mutiny. Washington stated that he was told of the Continental army "that a large part of them have no other prospect before them but a Gaol, if they are turned loose without a liquidation of Accts. and

---

6. Donald D. Egbert, *Princeton Portraits* (Princeton, 1947), p. 322; Charles Coleman Sellers, "Portraits and Miniatures by Charles Willson Peale," *Trans. Amer. Philos. Soc.* **42**, 1 (1952): pp. 235-236.; No. 933.

an assurance of that justice to which they are so worthily entitled."[7] When given a furlough to go home (in effect demobilized) they could not even be given a little money for the journey. Many of the unpaid and bitter Continental officers were near the breaking point. The Continental Congress, under the Articles of Confederation, had no power to compel the states to pay their allotted share of the army's support. After the signing of the preliminary articles of peace on January 20, 1783, when peace was obviously near, the army feared that, at the peace, the Congress would dissolve and its debts would be forgotten. Some penniless officers could then face debtor's prison. A group of hotheads in the army and in Congress talked of a military takeover, making Washington a dictator who would force the states to pay the army's claims. This was a pattern that has recurred throughout history: the successful leader of a revolt makes himself the new chieftain, or king, or emperor, and the army rules the state. It did not happen here because Washington, by a moving appeal to his officers at Newburgh, New York in March, 1783, put an end to it. By stepping aside so firmly, he gave our republic its chance.

The portrait that, in my opinion, best suggests the personal authority that he had developed during the war is an engraving (fig. 3), executed by Peale in August, 1780. It is a very rare print of which only six impressions are known to exist. It shows a grave face emanating an air of unconscious power. Better than any other made during the war, this likeness suggests, to my mind, the qualities in Washington that one finds in the Newburgh address, and in the Farewell Orders to Armies of the United States issued at Rocky Hill on November 2, 1783 — words so firm, so manly, so magnanimous in their conception of the soldier's duty as a citizen, that no one, aware of the circumstances of that year, can read them without emotion.

The blue flag with its circle of thirteen stars above Washington's head in this print was the flag carried by the army through the war, until superseded in 1783 by the stars and stripes. The blue ribbon across the breast, the insignia of the commander-in-chief since 1775, and an attractive feature of the portrait of 1779, has now disappeared. An order issued by Washington on June 18, 1780, had substituted silver stars on the epaulettes for the ribbon. Peale, a soldier himself, was exact and careful in these details of military

---

7. Washington to Alexander Hamilton, March 12, 1783. *The Writings of George Washington* (39 v., Washington, D. C., 1938) **26**: p. 217.

insignia and dress. This is another reason for my belief that he was exact and careful in his representation of Washington's person. Peale, both artist and scientist, aimed at truth, and, I am convinced, he gives us a correct image of Washington's general appearance during his years in the army, but he missed one quality. All contemporary descriptions speak of the dignity and grace of Washington's carriage. He was a big man, of great physical strength, graceful in his movements: he loved the formal dances of the time and was a good dancer. "All that was dignified and graceful" was George Washington Parke Custis's phrase. "Easy, erect, and noble" was Jefferson's description of him.

This noble and imposing posture is shown by Joseph Wright, in a portrait painted in 1783–1784. Wright was the son of the famous American sculptress, Patience Wright. After her husband's death she supported herself and her children by making and exhibiting wax portraits, first in Bordentown, then in New York, and finally after 1772 in London where her wax portrait heads had great success. The son was trained as a painter under Benjamin West but his outspoken American sympathies eventually made London too hot for him. He went to Paris to join the circle of Franklin, who sent him, in 1783, to America with a commission to paint General and Mrs. Washington. Wright found the general at Rocky Hill near Princeton and there painted a small sketch (pronounced "very like" by his contemporary, the painter, William Dunlap) from which he painted a number of portraits. Washington evidently thought well of the likeness. When the Count de Solms wrote to beg a portrait for his Gallery of Military Heroes at Königstein, Prussia, Washington sent him one by Wright, saying it was thought "a better likeness of me than any other painter has done: his forte seems to be in giving the distinguishing characteristics with more boldness than delicacy."[8] Samuel Powel, mayor of Philadelphia, owned another, signed 1784, now in the Historical Society of Pennsylvania (fig. 4); Jefferson owned a third. Wright's portrait clearly illustrates Jefferson's "easy, erect and noble" description of Washington's carriage.

Also in the year 1784 the Legislature of Virginia voted to procure "a statue of General Washington, to be of the finest marble and the best workmanship" and requested Governor Benjamin Harrison to arrange the matter. The governor promptly wrote to

8. Washington to the Comte de Solms, January 3, 1784. *The Writings of George Washington* (39 v., Washington, D. C., 1938) **27**: p. 291.

Thomas Jefferson, newly arrived in Paris as American minister to France, referring the choice of a sculptor to him; and to Peale in Philadelphia ordering a replica of his portrait to be sent to Paris for the likeness. Governor Harrison assumed that a marble statue must be made in Europe. "The intention of the Assembly is that the statue should be the work of a most masterly hand. I shall therefore leave it to you to find out the best in any of the European States" (Harrison to Thomas Jefferson, July 20, 1784).[9] This was both an affectionate and courageous act of the Assembly. Virginia was then the largest and most populous state, but its treasury was as exhausted as any other's. The Assembly directed the treasurer to pay for the statue "out of the first money that shall arise under the law for recruiting this state's quota of men to serve in the Continental army"; but the treasurer informed the governor, "There is no money in the Treasury at present arising from this law, and very uncertain when any may come in."[10] Fortunately for us, the parties concerned went forward on faith.

Houdon, then aged forty-four, was one of the great portrait artists of the century. He had exhibited at the Salon since 1769. His portrait style derived its extraordinary vividness partly from his study of the ruthless realism of Roman portrait busts; but this was tempered by the elegance of his time, and by the sophisticated perception of life prevailing among French artists and intellectuals of the Enlightenment. He had had great success with such complex personalities as Voltaire, Franklin, Buffon, and Diderot. An artist of such caliber was unwilling to work from a likeness painted by another man: he left France on the vessel bringing Franklin home, presented himself at Mount Vernon in October, 1785, and spent fifteen days studying his subject from life. He took back to Paris a life mask and a portrait bust in plaster, from which he made the statue for Virginia as well as a number of busts.

The life mask (fig. 5), after adventurous wanderings about the world, came to rest finally in the Pierpont Morgan Library, New York. This was Washington's face at age fifty-three. When one lies down on one's back to permit the making of a life mask, the

---

9. The correspondence, preserved in the Governor's MS Letter Book and the State Papers of Virginia, has been published by Charles Henry Hart and Edward Biddle. *Memoirs of the Life and Works of Jean Antoine Houdon* (Philadelphia, 1911), pp. 182-198; by Julian P. Boyd, *The Papers of Thomas Jefferson* (19 v., Princeton, N. J., 1950) 7: p. 378; and most recently by H. H. Arnason, *The Sculptures of Houdon* (New York, 1975), pp. 72-74.

10. Hart and Biddle, p. 183.

soft parts of the face fall into different positions from those when one stands erect: Washington's face is broadened and softened, yet shows the same regular oval that one sees in Peale's portraits. The bone structure, the breadth of the upper portion of the nose, the massive strength of the forehead and eye sockets are remarkable. Gilbert Stuart, when painting his portrait of 1796, remarked to an Irish gentleman that he found the structure of Washington's head different from any features he had ever observed. Stuart said this indicated the strongest and most ungovernable passions, that if he had been born in the forest he would have been the fiercest of savages. Houdon, on the contrary, emphasized the gravity and mildness of the face. In this he agrees with other French observers among the officers, diplomats, and travelers who met Washington during the Revolution and described his face and manner in their memoirs.

Peter Stephen Duponceau, who came to America as aide and interpreter to von Steuben, said of his first sight of Washington at Valley Forge, "I could not keep my eyes from that imposing countenance; grave, yet not severe; affable without familiarity. Its predominant expression was calm dignity."[11]

Washington had none of the hauteur to which a portraitist was accustomed in Europeans of similar rank. There is a story that Houdon waited several days, observing his subject, without choosing the expression he wished to represent. Then a horse dealer came from Alexandria to show Washington a handsome pair of horses. Washington politely invited all the guests in the house, Houdon among them, to inspect the pair. When asked the price, the dealer named a figure so outrageous that Washington, indignant, ordered the man off the place. That was the moment for which Houdon had been waiting. He gave the bust, which he modeled in clay and presented to Washington (fig. 6), the lifted chin, the look of authority, of that moment. *Non e vero, e ben trovato.*[12]

Houdon took to Paris a mold of Washington's face, measurements of his dimensions, and a bust presumably in plaster. From these he executed over a period of years a number of busts in marble, each differing slightly in expression and costume, and the full-length statue in marble, which is in the rotunda of the Virginia

11. Peter Stephen Duponceau, "The Autobiography of Peter Stephen Duponceau," *Penna. Mag. History and Biography* 63: (1939): pp. 189-227.

12. The anecdote is in Elizabeth Bryant Johnston, *Original Portraits of Washington* (Boston, 1882), p. 157.

Capitol at Richmond (fig. 7). It is one of the noblest and most satisfying of the portraits of Washington. He stands at ease, tall and calm, his head somewhat lifted, dressed in his regimentals, not in the classical dress Houdon would have preferred. His right hand rests on a cane, the left on the *fasces* and a plowshare, symbols of the modern Cincinnatus, who left his plow to lead his people in war but after saving the state returned again to his fields. A sword and cloak hang upon the fasces. Although the costume is of the eighteenth century, Houdon gave the statue a quality of classical dignity and repose, different from the sparkling informality of his portrayal of French intellectuals. This, too, tells us something about the impression made by Washington's personality upon his world, which saw him as a wise, noble, authoritative figure from another mold than the common. Houdon gives us the man of whom a lively observer, the Comte de Ségur, presented to Washington by Rochambeau at West Point, said:

> His presence almost foretold his history: simplicity, grandeur, dignity, calm, kindness, firmness were stamped upon his face and upon his countenance as well as upon his character. His figure was noble and tall; the expression of his face was pleasant and kind; his smile was gentle, his manners simple without being familiar.[13]

The next important portrait comes two years later. Watching the increasing weakness and confusion of the Confederation, the jealousies and quarrels among the states, the effect of the unpaid foreign debts, Washington was gravely disturbed. When open disorders broke out in western Massachusetts, he burst out in a letter to Benjamin Lincoln (November 7, 1786), "Are we to have the goodly fabrick we were nine years raising, pulled over our heads?"[14]

Largely on his initiative, a convention of the states was called to meet at Philadelphia in May, 1787. Peale, hopeful that a new mezzotint likeness of Washington might solve his own acute financial problems, wrote asking permission to make a new and up-to-date portrait from which he could make a print; and the general, always kind to old soldiers, granted his request. The result is the portrait of 1787, in the Pennsylvania Academy of the Fine Arts, of the man who, at age fifty-five, presided over the delegates

---

13. Comte de Ségur, *Memoirs, souvenirs et anecdotes par M. le Comte de Ségur* (Paris, 1859), quoted in Gilbert Chinard, *George Washington as the French Knew Him* (Princeton, 1940), p. 28.

14. *The Writings of George Washington* **29**: p. 59.

meeting through the hot summer of 1787 to discuss how they might arrive at "a more perfect union." As we know, they devised a novel form of double government, leaving the states as they were before, but superimposing upon them a new national government. Out of their deliberations came what a recent Canadian student has called,

> an audacious and radical achievement, carried out so deliberately and independently: the establishment of a republic in a world of monarchies; the establishment of a federal system of government in a world of unitary states; the construction of governments, central and local, under plainly written constitutions, in a world ruled by fiat and custom; above all, the successful "reduction to practice" of the principle of government by consent of the governed. . . .[15]

It was the common opinion of the delegates, that only one man could make the experiment succeed: Washington must head and organize this government. The role and powers of the executive in the new Constitution were predicated in the general trust in his integrity, modesty, and selflessness.

This is the face of their presiding officer (fig. 8). It is the same oval face, with deep eye sockets, heavy bone structure of brow and nose, and rather small mouth and eyes shown in all Peale's portraits. More important it shows the same mild, calm, steady personality described in written accounts. A typical example is Barbé-Marbois, who first meeting Washington in 1779 as secretary to the Chevalier de la Luzerne, France's first envoy, described their reception:

> He received us with the noble, modest and gentlemanly urbanity and with that graciousness which seems to be the basis of his character. . . . He carries himself freely and with a sort of military grace. He is masculine looking, without his features being less gentle on that account.[16]

It is a very different face Gilbert Stuart shows us seven years later. In 1789, George Washington Parke Custis tells us, the general lost his teeth. A marked change occurs in the appearance of his face in Stuart's portraits and others painted after that date; but an even more marked change is apparent in the characterization. Stuart painted his first portrait at Philadelphia in 1795, in a studio at the southeast corner of Fifth and Chestnut Streets just across the way from Philosophical Hall. It was shortly after taken

15. William H. Nelson, "The Revolutionary Character of the American Revolution," *Amer. Hist. Rev.* **70** (1965): pp. 998-1014.
16. Chinard, *op. cit.*, note 13, pp. 74-75.

to London, where it came into the possession of a fellow member of our Society, Samuel Vaughan, from whom it acquired its name, the "Vaughan" portrait. Never so popular as the second "Athenaeum" portrait, it exists in far fewer replicas; yet it has always been considered the more correct likeness of the two. It is known that Stuart had great trouble with it and was dissatisfied with the result. Stuart was a fluent and brilliant talker who excelled in putting a sitter at his ease; yet he was overawed by Washington. The sad result is that the open, candid, gentle face of 1787 is gone: the dominant impression here is of a great and remote dignity. A great gentleman he was, certainly, but he was more than that.

In the following year, 1796, in a studio at Germantown, Stuart tried again.[17] The result is the "Athenaeum" portrait (fig. 9), so-called because it was purchased from the artist's widow by a group of gentlemen for the Boston Athenaeum. This shows the left side of Washington's head. The likeness is so popular and well known, the source of innumerable replicas by Stuart and copies by others, as well as countless reproductions, that comment is unnecessary, with this disclaimer: Washington was then sixty-four years old, growing deaf, in failing health. He was also extremely unhappy that the violent political passions aroused by the war between Great Britain and revolutionary France seemed about to tear apart the fragile unity of the new federal republic. He was himself subject to a storm of violent, scurrilous abuse by those who hated him for his policy of neutrality and for attempting to reach a settlement of our differences with Great Britain. This was the man over whom Stuart's art drew a veil of serene dignity and calm. The "Athenaeum" head is idealized into the perfect image of the Elder Statesman, the Father of his Country, and was accepted as such by those who wished to remember him so. It is a remarkable symbolic portrait, but not a truthful one.

We have another simple, factual portrayal of Washington's face at this same moment. It so happened that in the 1790's Charles Willson Peale was absorbed in natural science and in the creation of the first natural history museum in America. Wishing to turn the practice of portrait painting over to his gifted son and favorite pupil, Rembrandt, he thought a portrait of Washington the best start for the son's career. Washington consented to sit, and to lend confidence to the boy (just seventeen) the father also painted a

---

17. The studio was a little two-story barn back of a house at 5140 Main Street, Germantown, which Stuart had rented from Samuel Bringhurst.

portrait (now in the New-York Historical Society). In a lecture on "Washington and his Portraits" that he frequently gave in later life, Rembrandt Peale said:

> It was in the autumn of 1795 that, at my father's request, Washington consented to sit to me—and the hour appointed was 7 o'clock in the morning . . . I enjoyed the rare advantage of studying the desired countenance whilst in conversation with my father. He could not sit the next day, Mrs. Washington informing me that he was engaged to sit to Mr. Stuart. . . .[18]

With the candor of youth, young Rembrandt Peale simply painted what he saw — the old, worn, sad face of a man suffering under a storm of vituperative abuse, that we prefer to forget ever happened (fig. 10).

From the "Athenaeum" portrait came the full-length standing "Lansdowne" portrait (1796) (fig. 11) commissioned by Senator William Bingham, the least satisfactory of Stuart's portraits of Washington.[19] When Washington entered the home of Mr. Bingham at this time, he seemed to one observer still a most impressive, even majestic figure; but Stuart did not paint from life. The pose was borrowed from an engraving after a seventeenth-century French portrait of Bossuet, by Rigaud. G. W. P. Custis records the family tradition that a Philadelphia lawyer and poet, Stuart's landlord, and a much smaller man than Washington, posed for the body. An important detail, the outstretched hand, was painted from a plaster cast of Stuart's own hand, made for the purpose by C. W. Peale. The result is an awkward, graceless image resembling neither Washington's carriage nor his posture. It is my opinion that this stiff, unreal image — so pompous and so omnipresent — more than any other single thing has made Washington unreal in the minds of his countrymen.

The portraits of Washington as president fall into two general categories — Stuart's well-painted ideal images, and portraits by the Peales and other artists showing an old man in failing health.

There is one great exception. John Trumbull returned to America in the autumn of 1788, having spent seven years, studying and

---

18. Rembrandt Peale, MS lecture, "Washington and His Portraits." Haverford College Library.

19. Stuart made two versions of this, one of which was a gift from Mr. Bingham to the Earl of Shelburne, afterwards Lord Lansdowne; the other hung in Mr. Bingham's country home, "Lansdowne," on the west bank of the Schuylkill, the grounds of which are now included in Fairmount Park. The Bingham version is in the Pennsylvania Academy of the Fine Arts, Philadelphia.

painting, in London and Paris. He brought with him two completed studies, *The Battle of Bunker's Hill* and the *Death of General Montgomery in the Attack on Quebec,* for his series of paintings celebrating the great events of the war for independence, and three unfinished battle scenes in which Washington was to appear. He found Washington in New York City, the temporary capital, absorbed in the problems of organizing the new federal government. Trumbull was cordially received. Unlike the other artists who wished to paint the president, he was the son of an old friend, the war governor of Connecticut, and had himself been an aide-de-camp to the general during the war. On January 23, Washington noted in his diary: "went with Mrs. Washington in the forenoon to see the Paintings of Mr. Jn.° Trumbull." They were evidently favorably impressed, for in the months following the general recorded fourteen sittings given to Trumbull between February 10 and July 13. On March 1 he noted: "Exercised on horseback this forenoon, attended by Mr. John Trumbull, who wanted to see me mounted."[20] This was significant, for Jefferson speaks of the general as "the best horseman of his age, and the most graceful figure that could be seen on horseback."[21] Trumbull's three brilliant battle pictures, *The Capture of the Hessians at Trenton, The Death of General Mercer at Princeton,* and *The Surrender of Cornwallis at Yorktown,* are our only evidence for this aspect of the man.

At the conclusion of this series of sittings, in July, 1790, Trumbull painted a small cabinet-sized portrait (30 × 20 inches) of the general as a gift for Mrs. Washington (fig. 12). It hung in the New Room at Mount Vernon during her lifetime and is the only picture mentioned in her will. It was left to her granddaughter, Elizabeth Parke Law, who married in 1817 Lloyd Nicholas Rogers, of "Druid Hill," Baltimore. From Mrs. Rogers it descended in the family until it was sold in the 1960's, to Henry Francis du Pont for the Winterthur Museum.[22]

This portrait, showing Washington in the fifty-eighth year of his age and the first of his presidency, is one of the least known of the important documents, having been shown publicly only once, in 1889, in an exhibition commemorating his first inauguration.

20. *The Diaries of George Washington, 1748-1799,* ed. John C. Fitzpatrick (4 v., Boston, 1925) 4: pp. 71 ff.
21. *The Writings of Thomas Jefferson,* ed. Albert Ellery Bergh (18 v., Washington, 1907) 14: pp. 46-52.
22. E. P. Richardson, "A Penetrating Characterization of Washington by John Trumbull," *Winterthur Portfolio* 3 (1967): pp. 1-23.

It is one that I wish to emphasize. George Washington Parke Custis, who knew the family pictures well, said of it:

> The figure of Washington, as delineated by Col. Trumbull, is the most perfect extant. So is the costume, the uniform of the staff in the war for independence, being the ancient *Whig colors,* blue and buff—a very splendid performance throughout, and the objection of the face as being too florid, not a correct one. He was both fair and florid.[23]

The general stands beside a white horse, fully caparisoned, resting his right arm on the saddle. Custis says that the horse and man posed for the portrait. "Easy, erect, and noble"—Jefferson's phrase, comes to life. In the background Trumbull commemorated one of the war's happy events, the reunion of the French and American armies at Verplanck's Point on the Hudson, the year after Yorktown. After Cornwallis's surrender the American army had marched north to resume its watch over the British forces in New York, but the French remained to winter in Virginia. They did not meet again until September, 1782.

What was Verplanck's Point? After Howe's army occupied New York city in 1776, the first crossing of the Hudson River in American hands was King's Ferry, between Verplanck's and Stony Point, just below the Highlands. Much hard fighting took place over control of that strategic link between New England and the remaining colonies, but for most of the war the Americans held it and used it. In his *Memoirs* Rochambeau describes the reunion of the armies there:

> The junction with Washington's army took place at King's Ferry on the Hudson River. The general, wishing to show his respect for France and his gratitude for its generous acts, had us pass between two ranks of his troops, clothed, equipped, and armed for the first time since the revolution, partly in materials and arms brought from France, partly from English stores taken with the army of Cornwallis and which the French army had generously given over to the American army. General Washington had his drums beat the French march during this entire review, and the two armies rejoined each other with the liveliest signs of mutual pleasure.[24]

It is thus both a portrait of Washington in the first year of his presidency and a celebration of victory in the war for independence.

---

23. Custis, *op. cit.,* pp. 519-520.
24. *Memoirs militaires, historiques et publiques de Rochambeau, ancien Marechal de France, et Grand Officier de la Legion d'Honneur* (2 v., Paris, 1809) 1: p. 309.

As a portrait, it reveals in a penetrating way three traits hardly seen so clearly by other painters: his instinctive air of authority, born of years of command; his self-control, masking a passionate temper; and most of all, his melancholy (fig. 13).

One cannot read his diary and letters without being struck by his melancholy, although he was not given to self-revelation. He had left Mount Vernon with sadness to preside over a new experiment in human government. As he journeyed to his inauguration, while crowds cheered and pretty girls presented flowers, he was greatly troubled by what he saw ahead. He was only too aware of the difficulties and hazards to be met in the task of uniting thirteen jealous and quarreling states. He had lived through too much, and seen too much of the instability of men and human affairs to be an optimist. Years later Thomas Jefferson would write to Dr. Walter Jones his estimate of Washington as he had observed him during this first administration:[25]

> He has often declared to me that he considered our new constitution as an experiment in the practicability of republican government, and with what dose of liberty man could be entrusted for his own good; that he was determined the experiment should have a fair trial, and would give the last drop of his blood to support it. And these declarations he repeated to me the oftener, and the more pointedly, because he knew my suspicions of Col. Hamilton's views. . . . I do believe that General Washington had not a firm confidence in the durability of our government. He was naturally mistrustful of men, inclined to gloomy apprehensions. . . .

Trumbull caught that veil of melancholy in the face of the man who, from a sense of duty, had left his beloved Mount Vernon, to undertake the task of giving his country a firmer and better union. Washington had no reason to know what a success he would make of it, or that we should now be celebrating it, but he was determined to give his life for it, if that had to be.

EDGAR P. RICHARDSON
Art Historian; Former Director,
Detroit Institute of Arts

---

25. *The Writings of Thomas Jefferson* 9: pp. 449-450.

FIG. 1. Charles Willson Peale, *George Washington in the Uniform of a Virginia Colonial Colonel,* 1772. Washington and Lee University, Lexington, Virginia.

FIG. 2. Charles Willson Peale, *George Washington at Princeton,* 1779. Pennsylvania Academy of the Fine Arts, Philadelphia.

215

FIG. 3. Charles Willson Peale, *George Washington*, Mezzotint, 1780. Metropolitan Museum of Art, New York; bequest of Charles Allen Munn, 1924.

FIG. 4. Joseph Wright, *George Washington,* 1784. Historical Society of Pennsylvania, Philadelphia; gift of Mrs. Walter K. Earle, in memory of Marion Eppley, 1972.

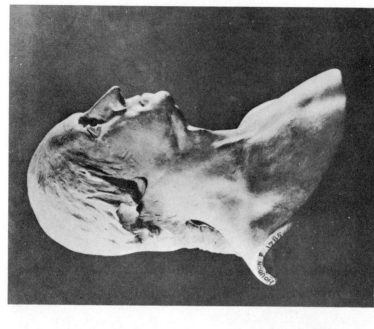

FIG. 6. Jean Antoine Houdon, *George Washington*, terra cotta, 1785. The Mount Vernon Ladies Association, Mount Vernon, Virginia.

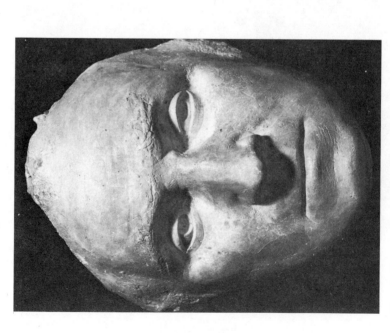

FIG. 5. Jean Antoine Houdon, *Life Mask of Washington*, 1785. Pierpont Morgan Library, New York.

218

Fig. 7. Jean Antoine Houdon, *George Washington,* marble, signed 1788. Capitol, Richmond, Virginia. Photo. by H. H. Arnason.

FIG. 8. Charles Willson Peale, *George Washington*, 1787. Pennsylvania Academy of the Fine Arts, Philadelphia.

FIG. 9. Gilbert Stuart, *George Washington (The Athenaeum Portrait)* (detail), 1796. Museum of Fine Arts, Boston; on deposit from the Boston Athenaeum.

221

FIG. 10. Rembrandt Peale, *George Washington*, autumn of 1795. Historical Society of Pennsylvania, Philadelphia.

FIG. 11. Gilbert Stuart, *George Washington* (*The Lansdowne Portrait*), 1796. Pennsylvania Academy of the Fine Arts, Philadelphia, bequest of William Bingham, 1811.

Fig. 12. John Trumbull, *Washington at Verplanck's Point*, 1790. Henry Francis duPont Winterthur Museum, Winterthur, Delaware.

FIG. 13. John Trumbull, *Washington at Verplanck's Point* (detail), Henry Francis duPont Winterthur Museum, Winterthur, Delaware.

225

Index